DEFAMATION:
LIBEL and SLANDER

Readings from
COMMUNICATIONS AND THE LAW

Edited by
The Honorable Theodore R. Kupferman

1. Defamation: Libel and Slander
ISBN 0-88736-507-8   CIP 1990

2. Privacy and Publicity
ISBN 0-88736-508-6   CIP 1990

3. Censorship, Secrecy, Access and Obscenity
ISBN 0-88736-509-4   CIP 1990

4. Advertising and Commercial Speech
ISBN 0-88736-510-8   CIP 1990

DEFAMATION: LIBEL AND SLANDER

Readings From *Communications and the Law, 1*

Edited by
The Honorable Theodore R. Kupferman

Meckler
Westport • London

Citations to the original appearance of articles collected in this volume
appear at the back of this book.

Library of Congress Cataloging-in-Publication Data

Defamation : libel and slander / edited by Theodore R. Kupferman.
      p. cm. -- (Readings from Communications and the law ; 1)
   ISBN 0-88736-507-8 (alk. paper) : $
   1. Libel and slander -- United States. I. Kupferman, Theodore R.
II. Series.
KF 1266. A75D44   1990
346.7303 ' 4 -- dc20
[347. 30634]   89-31992
                                       CIP

British Library Cataloguing in Publication Data

Defamation : libel and slander : readings from
  Communications and the law.
  1. United States. Defamation. Law
  I. Kupferman, Theordore R. II. Communications and the law
  347. 3063 ' . 4

  ISBN 0-88736-507-8

Meckler Corporation, 11 Ferry Lane West, Westport, CT 06880.
Meckler Ltd., Grosvenor Gardens House, Grosvenor Gardens,
  London SW1W 0BS, U.K.

Printed on acid free paper.
Printed and bound in the United States of America.

CONTENTS

PREFACE

When *Communications and the Law* commenced publication in the winter of 1979 as a quarterly review, as Editor-in-Chief I stated:

> We will endeavor through articles, guest editorials, symposia, reviews, and commentaries, to analyze those aspects which affect the law in the area of communications. This will involve a broad range of issues from censorship to new technological uses. Every phase of the law involving communications, from a picket's shout to publicist's release, in business or entertainment or government, will be grist for our literary mill. We will not only cover communications law, we will consider the means by which the law is communicated.
>
> This is our first issue. We will publish on a quarterly basis and endeavor to be timely as well as knowledgeable and provocative. To the extent possible, we will present a balanced point of view, and, of course, you will help us to do so.

Our first article, included in our volume on "Censorship, Secrecy, Access, and Obscenity," was by James C. Goodale, then Executive Vice President of the New York Times and now a partner in the well-known law firm of Debevoise & Plimpton.

We have fulfilled the promise of the first issue and continue to cover all germane areas. Not surprisingly, this has meant that a great many subjects have been covered, some of which were of only passing interest to every reader.

It occured to the publisher that there might be a specific need for a compilation of those articles covering a more narrow defined topic like this one on Defamation and so we present, with some update, those outstanding articles in this field.

Our first two articles discuss *Herbert v Lando*, 441 U.S. 153, from different perspectives. After much substantial litigation, the complaint was dismissed, 781 F.2d 298, but precedent remains.

Judge Goldfluss has since left the Bench to devote more time to his writings and is the author of two well-selling works of fiction, *The Judgment* and *The Power*.

Donna Lee Dickerson discussed, in 1981, "Neutral Reportage," which has now become a routine defense for communicators.

The other articles gathered together in this volume are all self-explanatory and complement one another.

HOWARD E. GOLDFLUSS

Herbert v. Lando:

No Cause For Alarm

Mr. Goldfluss is Acting Justice, New York
State Supreme Court, and Associate
Professor of Criminology, Fordham
University.

A public figure, in order to recover for damages incurred from a defamatory publication, must prove the falsity of the damaging material. He has the additional burden of proving malice—that it was published with the knowledge that it was false, or in reckless disregard of whether it was false or not. So spoke the Supreme Court in *New York Times Company* v. *Sullivan*.[1]

Three years after *Sullivan,* the Court further defined this burden by stating, in *St. Amant* v. *Thompson,*[2] that the plaintiff must introduce evidence "that the defendant in fact entertained serious doubts as to the truth of his publication"; and defined it again in *Gertz* v. *Robert Welch, Inc.*[3] by stating that the defendant has a "subjective awareness of probable falsity."

Whatever the language, the meaning is that inquiry must be made into the defendant's subjective state of mind. Nevertheless, the Second

1. 376 U.S. 254 (1964).
2. 390 U.S. 727 (1967).
3. 418 U.S. 323, 335 N. 6 (1974).

Circuit Court of Appeals in New York, in *Herbert* v. *Lando*,[4] held that an allegedly defamed public figure may *not* compel a media defendant to answer questions bearing on his state of mind. The court based its reasoning on the ground that to do so would intrude on the heart of the editorial process—it would be a direct violation of the First Amendment. This decision has since been reversed by the Supreme Court.[5] Before analyzing the reversal, and the basis for it, a review of the facts of the *Herbert* case, and its status prior to the action by the Supreme Court, is necessary.

Anthony Herbert is a retired army officer who served for an extended period of time in Vietnam. In 1969 and 1970, he received widespread media attention when he charged that atrocities occurred in Vietnam, and that his superior officers covered up reports of these atrocities. Three years later, in February 1973, the Columbia Broadcasting System telecast a segment on its "Sixty Minutes" program, produced by respondent Barry Lando and narrated by Mike Wallace. According to Herbert's complaint, later filed in district court, the program falsely and maliciously portrayed him as a liar—that he was making these war crime charges solely because he was relieved from command. He sought substantial damages for injury to his reputation and for the diminished value of his book, published a short time before the alleged defamation. In his action, Herbert was faced with the burden of showing actual malice, as previously defined. He chose to follow a method suggested in *Gertz* v. *Robert Welch*, that is, to demonstrate that there were obvious reasons to doubt the veracity of the informant or the accuracy of his reports. Toward this end, he sought an order to compel answers to a variety of questions in a pretrial deposition. Response was refused by the defendants on the ground that the First Amendment protected them in the form of absolute privilege against inquiry into the state of mind of those who report, publish, or participate in the editorial process. The specific inquiries to which they objected were as follows:

1. Lando's conclusions during his research and investigation regarding people or leads to be pursued, or not pursued, in connection with the "Sixty Minutes" segment.

2. Lando's conclusions about facts imparted by interviewees and his state of mind with respect to the veracity of persons interviewed.

3. The basis for Lando's testimony that he did reach a conclusion concerning the veracity of persons interviewed.

4. Conversations between Lando and Wallace about matter to be included or excluded from the broadcast publication.

---

4. 568 F.2d 974, Rvsd.
5. Herbert v. Lando, 99 S.Ct. ___, ___ U.S. ___, No. 77-1105, 47 L.W. 4401.

5. Lando's intentions as manifested by his decision to include or exclude certain material.

The district court ruled that since *New York Times* v. *Sullivan* made the defendant's state of mind of "central importance" to the issue of malice, the said inquiries were relevant and entirely appropriate. Herbert was obliged to discover whether Lando had any reason to doubt the veracity of certain of his sources or (of equal significance) to prefer the veracity of one source over another. Rejecting the claim of constitutional privilege, the district court found nothing in the First Amendment requiring that the weight of the plaintiff's burden of proof be increased by creating barriers to discovery.

The Court of Appeals, by a divided panel, reversed and held that the First Amendment privilege not to answer was absolute, basing its findings on Fourteenth Amendment grounds as well.

Herbert was then placed in the classic "catch 22" position—you're damned if you do and you're damned if you don't. In effect, the appellate court decision meant that the defendants had the absolute privilege to resist inquiry into the very matter that the plaintiff was obliged to prove with "convincing clarity." Hercules could not have borne such a burden. Indeed, after the Court of Appeals decision, a district judge correctly analyzed the status of an allegedly libeled plaintiff by observing "in light of *Herbert* . . . practical litigants may well conclude that any remedy for libel against a journalist by a public figure is illusory."[6]

In voting for reversal, Circuit Judge Oakes took the position that the very inquiry into the editorial process is, in and of itself, a prior restraint. He reasoned that, even if the discovery operates *after* publication, it in effect serves as a prior restraint to subsequent publications. In reference to the chilling effect this has on the reporting and editorial process, he expressed that "it is one thing to tell the press its end product is subject to the actual malice standard and that a plaintiff is entitled to prove actual malice; it is quite another to say that the editorial process which produced the end product in question is itself discoverable. Such an inquiry chills not simply the material published but the relationship among editors."[7]

In dealing with this contention, the Supreme Court did not discount the relationship between consultation and discussions on the one hand and sound decisions on the other—necessitating confidentiality in the decision-making process. The Court also pointed out that, in the case of libel, the press has an obvious interest in refraining from publishing false

---

6. Reliance Ins. Co. v. Barron's, 442 F. Supp. 1341 (Brieant, J.). It is significant that the judge made this lament while apparently applying the law then in existence in upholding his earlier grant of summary judgment to a libel defendant.
7. *See* note 4, *supra,* at 993 (Meskill, J., dissenting).

information, and that it was not unreasonable to invoke proceedings useful toward that end. The media has all the more reason to resort to prepublication precautions in its awareness that liability attaches to knowing or reckless error. Inquiry by the alleged defamed plaintiff is not, in and of itself, chilling; indeed, as Judge White pointed out, there is "[no] sound reason to believe that editorial exchanges and the editorial process are so subject to distortion and to such recurring misunderstanding that they should be immune from examination in order to avoid erroneous judgments in defamation suits."[8]

The Supreme Court reaffirmed First Amendment protection for the editorial process, and stated clearly that casual inquiry to satisfy curiosity or serve some general end, such as the public interest, would not survive First Amendment protection. In the *Herbert* case, where there was a *specific* claim of injury arising from a publication that was alleged to have been knowing or recklessly false, no such "casual inquiry" existed. Besides, *New York Times* v. *Sullivan* had specifically removed First Amendment protection from defamatory falsehood published with actual malice—with knowledge or reckless disregard for the truth. How may an allegedly damaged plaintiff discover this without being able to determine the journalist's "subjective awareness of probable falsity," or, in simpler language, *his state of mind?* Justice White termed it an anomalous situation to base liability on a journalist's subjective attitude and, at the same time, bar from disclosure the most direct evidence of that attitude. It is safe to assume that the framers of the First Amendment did not intend to defeat logic by utilizing its protection in such a manner.

Chief Judge Kaufman, in the Court of Appeals opinion to reverse, emphasized the tri-parte nature of press functions. He said that the press acquires information, processes that information, and disseminates it, and that the free flow of information would be impeded if the chain were broken. He reasoned, therefore, that full protection must be given to all three stages. The question that arises from this determination is whether the premise that absolute privilege exists for any of the links of the chain is accurate. Seemingly there is indication to the contrary. Judge Kaufman acknowledged that the press's right to gather information is subject to limitations similar to those imposed on the general public when he referred to *Saxbe* v. *Washington Post* in a footnote;[9] the opinion in this case was that reporters do not have an access right to prison inmates for interviews apart from rights of the public generally. Moreover, *Times* v. *Sullivan* set forth that the privilege protecting the press's right to disseminate information is qualified. Even the rule against prior restraint is

8. Herbert v. Lando, 47 L.W. 4401 at 4406.
9. 568 F.2d 977. N-11, *in re* to Saxbe v. Washington Post, 417 U.S. 843 (1974).

not *technically* absolute; theoretically, the party who seeks such restraint may, under certain circumstances, overcome the "heavy presumption" against the restraint's validity.[10]

Additionally, in *Herbert*, the Supreme Court concludes that no line of demarcation is perceptible in determining the "outer boundaries of the editorial privilege now urged."[11] The opinion of the Court of Appeals did not state, and the respondent did not explain, where the editorial process begins and ends. And interestingly, respondent Lando was willing to testify as to what he "knew" and what he had "learned" from his inter- views, as opposed to what he "believed." This caused Justice White to question the lack of clarity as to why the suggested editorial privilege would not cover knowledge, as well as belief, about the truth of published reports. The oral argument on this point underlined the apparent incon- sistency when it was suggested that the privilege would extend to questions in "why" form, but not as to "who," "what," "where," or "when."[12] Yet, Lando's deposition indicated that questions soliciting "why" answers relating to the editorial process were answered. One could draw the conclusion that the respondent sought to have the privilege invoked selectively to his choice.

In relation to public policy, a raison d'etre for the First Amendment privilege was referred to by the Court. The Court realistically took cognizance of the fact that, while spreading false information carries no First Amendment credentials, some error is inevitable. In such cases liability must be limited to instances where some degree of culpability is present, over and above mere error, in order to eliminate a Sword of Damocles poised over the head of a free press—inevitably leading to un- due self-censorship and the suppression of truthful material. But some liability must exist, not only to compensate for injury to others, but, of equal importance, to deter publication of irresponsible information threatening such injury. Proof in such cases cannot be limited to direct evidence only—the "malice" requirement makes limitation untenable. Indirect evidence must also be allowable because if such proof results in liability for damages, thereby discouraging the publication of erroneous information, then a salutory purpose would be served—a "chilling effect" on media irresponsibility.

Justice Powell, in the *Herbert* case, refused to extend the Court's ruling in *Times* v. *Sullivan* to create an evidentiary privilege. He set forth clearly that the Court's prior decisions, in *Miami Herald Publishing Company* v. *Tornillo*[13] and *Columbia Broadcasting System Inc.* v.

10. *See* Organization For a Better Austin v. Keefe, 402 U.S. 415 (1971).
11. 47 L.W. 4405.
12. Trial of Oral Argument at 32-34.
13. 418 U.S. 241 (1974).

Democratic National Committee,[14] did not support the theory that the prepublication editorial process enjoys a special status under the First Amendment. These cases reiterated the fundamental principle that coerced publications of particular views, *as much as their suppression* violates freedom of speech. For example, in the *Miami Herald* case, the Court struck down, as undue interference with the editorial process, a Florida statute granting a candidate the right to equal space in reply to criticism of his record by a newspaper. The Court found that the editorial process is the basis for expression, and to regulate the process is to regulate expression. Thus, the protection of the editorial process becomes a matter of First Amendment concern.

The Court, in *Herbert,* distinguished between the above proposition and the situation with which they were confronted. In the *Herbert* case, there were no governmental regulations involved. Therefore, if First Amendment values were involved, the Court would have to depend on the determination of whether Herbert's intent to use discovery was a means to intimidate the press. The Court dwelled upon this comparison of merit in First Amendment frame of reference: What was Herbert seeking? Was he seeking a means to inhibit the editorial process or impair communication so that editorial process was affected? Or was he seeking to sustain a burden imposed upon him by the *Sullivan* decision in the only manner that he could?

The public has a bilateral interest in "accurate and effective reporting by the news media"; this interest focuses upon an uninhibited editorial process, as well as upon a truthful presentation of the facts. There is no alternative to self-regulation of the press, but this principle does not mean, nor was it ever intended to mean, that self-regulation grants privilege which amounts to immunity from deliberate cases of malicious and false reporting. This very end is accomplished if the plaintiff is barred from using the vehicle to prove this malice or falsity. Prior to the court's finding in *Herbert,* the assertion of privilege was rejected by Judge Levet in a roughly similar case, *Buckley* v. *Vidal,*[15] in the Southern District of New York. William Buckley, in a libel action against Gore Vidal, moved to compel the production of documents pursuant to Rule 34 of the Federal Rules of Civil Procedure. He sought discovery of manuscripts written by Vidal, together with all notes, memoranda, papers from people employed by Vidal to investigate Buckley, and materials that served as a basis for derogatory remarks by Vidal. While this evidence could be termed—in the context of the meaning later alleged in *Herbert* v. *Lando*—a part of the "editorial process," Vidal resisted discovery on broad First Amendment grounds only. The

14. 412 U.S. 94 (1973).
15. Buckley v. Vidal, 50 F.R.D. 211 (S.D.N.Y. 1970).

trial judge, although cognizant of plaintiff's burden, rejected Vidal's position because he reasoned that such burden could possibly be sustained. In *Buckley,* the court held that the only test was whether the course of action passed constitutional muster. Once passing that test, the plaintiff must be allowed reasonable opportunity for discovery.

Judge Haight, in district court, cited the *Buckley* case with approval when finding for *Herbert.*[16] The Court of Appeals summarily rejected it: "To the extent that (Buckley) is inconsistent with this opinion, the Court obviously now declines to follow it."[17] Apparently, the Supreme Court had no hesitancy in following it. Reason dictates that full discovery be available to the plaintiff, because libel cases have held that the defendant's inability to establish a basis for his defamatory charges has been a *crucial* factor in determining recklessness as to truth or falsity. In *Varnish* v. *Best Medium Publishing Company,*[18] the Court relied on the defendant's admission that he had no basis for his defendant's assertion in upholding a libel verdict. In *Goldwater* v. *Ginzburg,*[19] the defendant's failure to establish a basis for his statements was pivotal; in *Davis* v. *Schuchat,*[20] the district judge relied on evidence that the defendant had "no possible foundation" for his statements in upholding a libel verdict.

Let us examine the negative impact of a different view. Assuming direct evidence of the state of mind of the defendant is unobtainable because of First Amendment privilege, the plaintiff would then be constrained to rely on evidence regarding use of the material itself. In *Herbert* v. *Lando,* Judge Oakes proposed that the "obvious starting point" for proving actual malice would be the establishment of an inconsistency between a television program's content and contrary facts.[21] That is, of course, true as far as it goes. But the falsity of the statement is not the sole issue we deal with in applying *Sullivan* standards. The plaintiff can in no way establish malice by mere assertion and proof of inconsistency alone. If so limited, the jury would only have an inference to rely on, namely, that if there was a disparity between the truth and what was published, the defendant did not believe what he printed. One could readily foresee confusion in the jury room as to why the plaintiff did not question the defendant on the very point the jury was obliged to decide.

There has been much made of the "privilege" concept on purely legal grounds, but one should examine the practical effect of its implementation. It may very well be that the controversy causing national headlines which proclaim the imminent demise of freedom of the press is

16. 73 F.R.D. 387 (S.D.N.Y. 1971).
17. 568 F.2d at 995, N. 38 (Oakes, J.).
18. 405 F.2d 608 (2d Cir. 1988), *cert. denied,* 394 U.S. 987 (1969).
19. 414 F.2d 324.
20. 510 F.2d 731 (D.C. Cir. 1978).
21. *Id.* at 992.

a "sound and fury signifying nothing." Although the *Herbert* decision now requires that the defendant in a libel action testify to the operation of his mind, it does not necessarily, or even logically, follow that the defendant is likely to admit that he harbored serious doubts as to the truth of the statements he caused to be published. It is reasonable to expect that a question directed to the defendant on that issue would be met with a denial, or a self-serving declaration, which could in no way be construed as an admission.

Even if the Supreme Court had upheld Lando's position on privilege, it could be a strategic mistake to invoke the privilege. Counsel for the defendant would have to ponder the effect of a refusal to answer questions before a jury on First Amendment grounds, on the very issue that the jury must decide. American juries have an underlying sense of fairness and, although not versed in the law, they could react to such declination by drawing an adverse inference. Of course, the trial judge will instruct the jury not to draw any adverse inference from the assertion by the witness of a constitutional right, but I have always had doubts as to the degree of acceptability by the jury to such an admonition.

The Supreme Court, in *Herbert,* indicated through its decision that somewhere along the line the true intent and meaning of the First Amendment has been bypassed in a morass of technical and strained interpretation. The original intent of the First Amendment was to foster self-government ideals in a democratic form. It sought to bar the state from imposing an authoritative version of truth on its citizens, and to bar it further from interfering with the communicative process through which its citizens exercise their rights. It protects those who would expose state abuses. It does not mean absolute privilege—a potentially dangerous concept—as amply demonstrated in *United States* v. *Nixon.*[22] Even a privilege rooted in the Constitution must give way in proper circumstances. The President has an absolute executive privilege against disclosure of materials subpoenaed for a judicial proceeding; yet, the circumstances of the Watergate cover-up situation caused the Supreme Court to hold that even a constitutionally-based immunity must yield to a demonstrated and specific need for evidence. In taking this course, the Court demonstrated in *Nixon,* and in *Herbert,* that barriers to the acquisition of evidence should seldom be supported by judicial process. Whatever their origins, these barriers are in derogation of the truth-seeking process and, toward the fulfillment of that end, there are no sacred cows.

22. 418 U.S. 683 (1974).

ANDRE E. BRIOD

Herbert v. Lando:

Threat to the Press, Or

Boomerang for Public Officials?

Mr. Briod founded Briod & Wallhauser, Inc., a Newark-based public relations and public affairs firm in 1966. He was formerly a general news reporter and writer for the *Newark News,* and is a graduate of Haverford College (Pa.) and Seton Hall Law School (N.J.).

I. INTRODUCTION

No issue in recent years has so abruptly stirred the passions of the press as the decision of the Supreme Court that journalists, when they are being sued for libel by public officials or public figures, may be asked about their state of mind at the time they prepared the news accounts which provoked the libel actions.

That was the holding of the Court in *Herbert* v. *Lando*[1], a 6–3 decision announced on 18 April 1979.[2]

1. 441 U.S. 153, 99 S. Ct. 1635, 60 L. Ed. 2d 115 (1979).
2. The majority opinion, written by Justice White, was concurred in by Chief Justice Burger and Justices Blackmun, Powell, Rehnquist, and Stevens. Justice Powell also wrote a concurring opinion, while separate dissents were written by Justices Brennan, Stewart, and Marshall. *See* this study, pp. 69-73. *See also* Goldtluss, *Herbert v. Lando: No Cause For Alarm,* COMM. AND THE LAW, 1, no. 3 (Summer, 1979): 61–68.

Rage was the editorial norm for the many who editorialized on the subject. "Outrage" was a word used frequently to express their widely felt indignation when the decision was announced.

So vehement, so uncompromising was the expression of the press' anger at what journalists generally seemed to regard as license to invade the most sacrosanct sanctum of the reporter—his or her mind—that the Supreme Court apparently was moved to dispatch one of its own into the field on a public relations effort in defense of its opinion.

The Supreme Court, as any reader of *The Brethren*[3] knows, does not favor the public with much detail on the inner processes by which it arrives at decisions, whether those formal decisions which reach the record or the informal ones which encourage members to step up their public speaking activities. The general view of the press, however, was that the Court's members felt the need to try to blunt the hostile feelings which had erupted among newsmen concerned with the implications of *Herbert v. Lando*.

Whether that speculation is accurate, what is fact is that one of the Court's key members, Justice William J. Brennan, Jr., publicly chastised the press for what he said was a needless and ill-considered overreaction to *Herbert v. Lando*.[4] What is significant, however, is that the justice who undertook the mission in defense of the opinion was the very author of the senior dissenting opinion in the case.

As if for emphasis, Justice Brennan chose the dedication of the Samuel I. Newhouse Law Center at the Rutgers University Campus in Newark as the platform from which to take the press to task. The center was being dedicated to the memory of a man who certainly ranked as one of the nation's press lords.

Justice Brennan, in his remarks, took note not only of some of the major papers and television outlets that had been most uncompromising in their criticism, but also zeroed in on what he said were "unfortunate" inaccuracies in the characterization of that decision by at least two newspapers and probable misunderstandings on the part of others.[5]

Justice Brennan's statement in defense of the Court, and in criticism of the press, included these two assertions:

> The question raised by *Herbert* is whether the press' ability to perform the communicative functions required by our democratic society would be significantly impaired if an editorial privilege were not created.[6]

3. B. Woodward & S. Armstrong, The Brethren (1979).
4. Address by Justice Brennan at dedication of Newhouse Law Center, Rutgers University, Newark, N.J., Oct. 17, 1979
5. *Id.* at 9.
6. *Id.* at 10.

> In my view reporters will not cease to publish because they are later asked about their state-of-mind.[7]

It is precisely those questions with which this study seeks to deal. Its aim is to determine whether there is yet any clear sign that the press, at the working level, has in fact been affected in its performance of its "communicative functions" or can validly anticipate that it will be affected. It seeks also to determine whether Justice Brennan is privy to what goes on in the real world of the press when he says that reporters will not stop publishing in the face of state-of-mind inquiry.

His prediction that the press would not "cease to publish" presumably was a rhetorical expression of an opinion that material which would otherwise have been published will not be excluded from print because of fears over the meaning of *Herbert* v. *Lando.*

It possibly would please the justice to know that in the short time since the decision, the experience of the press in the field, as drawn from a study detailed in this paper, would appear to support that view. It might be a source of distress to him, if not to some of those justices who were in the majority, that many in the news media expect to be affected in the future. Moreover, an overwhelming majority of the sixty-seven newsmen and women interviewed in depth in this study still do not like *Herbert* v. *Lando,* even most of those who do not expect to be affected.

On the other hand, the writers of those editorials that were the most shrill in predicting dire consequences for a free press might be at least dismayed to learn that many of their colleagues out in the field are not so sure that their vehement editorial reaction was justified.

It should be noted that those strenuous protests have since abated, apparently having been diluted by growing press concerns about the closing of certain trial-related proceedings[8] or the threat of newsroom searches where a search warrant has been served.[9]

This paper does not presume to offer any conclusions on whether the basic holding of *Herbert* v. *Lando* is right or wrong, good or bad. Better, more qualified minds will, no doubt, continue to grapple with that issue. Rather, this study takes note of the arguments raised in the vehement press protests and seeks to answer in a general way the questions posed by Justice Brennan. More specifically, this article attempts to explore the following:

- Whether the fears of the press that it would suffer substantial impact on its freedom to function as intended under the Constitution have been realized in

---

7. *Id.*
8. 443 U.S. _____, 99 S. Ct. 2898 (1979); *see also* N.Y. Times, *Rising Number of Court Cases Closed to Press,* Oct. 13, 1979, § A, at 10.
9. Zurcher v. Stanford Daily News, 46 U.S. 547, 98 S. Ct. 1970, 56 L. Ed. 525 (1978).

any significant degree during the brief period since the Supreme Court made its ruling in *Herbert* v. *Lando.*

- Whether the press, at the working level, believes that the threat of state-of-mind inquiry will have real or practical effects on its future activities.
- To determine whether, in practical terms, *Herbert* v. *Lando* poses hazards or problems for journalists seeking to do their jobs conscientiously.
- To find out if attitudes toward *Herbert* v. *Lando,* whether negative or positive, correlate in some general way with groups within the community of journalists, such as those who are younger or older, editors or reporters on the beat, men or women, those who adhere to the ideal of objective journalism as a paramount standard or those who place primary emphasis on investigative or interpretive reporting.

This study does not contain definitive answers to all of the questions; it attempts to offer insights. These insights, if they are such, are based on the responses of a sampling of sixty-seven newsmen and newswomen representing forty different news organizations in five states and the District of Columbia. Twelve are women. There are twenty-four who fall in a group labeled as "generally younger."[10] Nineteen, by general definition, rank as editors,[11] while four are publishers.

While eschewing a claim that this study offers definitive answers down the line to all questions, it seems that it does lead to one overall conclusion which can very well be stated at the outset. It is this: The Supreme Court, by its holding in *Herbert* v. *Lando,* has provided libel plaintiffs with an additional weapon which, upon analysis, will probably turn out to be useless. Most journalists recognize this, but they are still extremely hostile to the idea that they might be subject in the future to state-of-mind inquiry in a courtroom. This hostility is founded more on principle than on immediate practical concerns. Nevertheless, the deci-

---

10. "Generally younger" was an arbitrary designation by the writer, with the dividing line falling at age forty-two. It was the view of the writer that those under forty-two learned their journalism in a somewhat different climate than those over that age. This subjective judgment may be debatable, but it is not central to the findings of the study.
11. The designation "editors" did not include another eight editors of weekly newspapers who, by any definition, certainly qualify. For purposes of this study, however, the opinions of weekly newspaper editors were recorded separately.

sion provoked an initial burst of editorial outrage, and while that anger has cooled somewhat, the fundamental opposition has not.

To state it another way, the Supreme Court appears to have handed public officials or public figures who are libel plaintiffs a feather duster with which to go out and fight the press. The press has responded to this dubious threat with a barrage from its heaviest cannon. The barrage has abated, but the troops in the press corps are still at fixed bayonets.

II. THE INTERVIEW SAMPLE

From the perspective of the social scientists, the sample may appear rife with flaws, which will be enumerated here presently. However, one might view the following as virtues:

- Every one of the interviews consisted of an extended personal conversation. More than half (forty) took place in a face-to-face situation, completed in a few instances by a follow-up telephone conversation. The others were conducted by telephone.[12]
- This writer personally conducted all sixty-seven of the interviews, insuring uniformity of technique, approach, and evaluation.
- More than two-thirds of the interviewees were personal acquaintances of the writer.[13]
- Those in the sample who were not personal acquaintances were approached on the basis of referrals by persons who were.

Some might consider the personal relationship element a flaw, based on the premise that interviews with acquaintances lack an impersonal character desirable for the purity of an interview. I would disagree, at least in this case. The issues raised in *Herbert* v. *Lando* are hot and emotional, as seen through the eyes of many reporters. Given a subject of that character, I relied on my belief that candid answers are the most valid, and that I was far more likely to get candor from reporters and editors who knew me, or of me, well enough to be confident that they could speak freely.

---

12. Of the twenty-seven interviews conducted strictly by telephone, twenty-one were with individuals with whom the interviewer had a substantial personal acquaintance. Thus, it was possible in most of these interviews to be assured of the desirable degree of ease and candor.
13. These relationships were formed during ten years as a newspaperman and another eighteen years in the public relations business.

Confidence in the interviewer was an important consideration in view of the fact that in a few instances there was a degree of what some in the legal profession might have regarded as paranoia. Several newsmen and women, even though well known to the interviewer, would submit to an interview only after assurances that nothing they said would be attributed directly to them in the context of any article or paper that might ensue. They were concerned that in some unforeseeable way their words or opinions might be used against them or their respective news organizations in some future legal proceeding.[14]

Where requested, the assurances were given and honored.

The sampling, this writer would contend, represents a good cross section of newsmen and women who must face at the practical, work-a-day level any problems that might be raised by the threat of state-of-mind questioning. Besides the previously cited representation of editors, reporters, women, men, older and younger journalists, there are in the sample a significant number of reporters or editors who work in jobs which, by standards of that profession, one would consider prominent. There are others whose jobs, by contrast, are less prominent or, by some definitions (usually those of the reporter), obscure. There are ten editors or publishers of weekly newspapers, all in New Jersey. There are seven people from the television industry, a number which, by ratio in the news industry, is probably not far out of line with national totals. Five of the seven are based in New York.

What may arguably be considered flaws in the sample are not hard to identify. For one thing, it is clearly a sampling of views held within what some derisively refer to as the "Eastern Establishment Press." That is a point worthy of concern. Perhaps the findings of this study would be different if the sampling had been obtained from a group of journalists based along a general line running from Houston through Oklahoma City, Kansas City, and Des Moines, to Minneapolis. Even if that is true, however, any evidence of intimidation of the press in its functions, or of what both the press and the courts like to refer to as "chill," is to be taken seriously even if it is found only within that eastern group. That group, after all, is considered to be in the mainstream of the press "action," even by its detractors. Beyond that, even the Eastern Establishment Press qualifies for the protections of the First Amendment, whatever they are.

Another possible flaw is the shortage of blacks among those inter-

14. This is a tangible consideration for a reporter or editor who is concerned that such words or opinions might be thrown back at him should he or she, in the future, have to face state-of-mind inquiry. In at least two instances, reporters who asked not to have their words attributed to them noted that they or their news organizations were in the midst of libel litigation.

viewed,[15] a fact which merely reflects a deficiency in this writer's range of relationships among news personnel and not an intended omission.

Still another shortcoming in the sampling is its failure to reflect any of the views held among journalists representing what are commonly referred to as "radical" publications. Again, the writer did not believe this deficiency could be responsible for any serious distortion of the picture that emerges from the sampling actually obtained, but that subjective judgment may be a legitimate target for criticism.

One other factor, and possible flaw, should be noted. There are no radio newsmen or women included. They were not purposely eliminated, but radio people, it seemed to this writer, do not generally face the same editorial decision-making problems or go through the same news-gathering or news-editing processes as are common to a newspaper staff with its beat reporters, a magazine writer, a television investigative reporter, or a news documentary staff member. There are, of course, exceptions to that generalization, but it did not seem to be of significance to the findings contained here.

III. INTERVIEW TECHNIQUE

The interviews were conducted along informal lines, designed to foster confidence in an easy, conversational climate. All the same, basic questions were asked, although they were expressed in a variety of ways, depending on the course of the conversation.[16]

Each individual was asked whether he or she recognized the case by name[17] and what he or she knew about it. If there was no recognition of the case by name, the interviewee was asked what he or she knew about "the Supreme Court's state-of-mind decision." Interviewees were then asked whether they had been affected in their functions as reporters or editors by the knowledge that they could, at some future time, face state-of-mind questioning. If the respondent said he had been affected, he was then asked to elaborate.

Next came the future. Did the respondent anticipate being affected in the future?[18] Could he or she hypothesize circumstances under which,

---

15. There were two.
16. In some instances it was not necessary to specifically ask one or more of the questions, because the person being interviewed, speaking freely and elaborating on his or her thoughts, had already provided the answer.
17. It became clear early in the project that whether or not one recognized the case by its name was not much indication of the person's knowledge of the holding in Herbert v. Lando.
18. If, before this question was asked, it had become clear that the individual's familiarity with the case was not generally complete, the missing elements were explained prior to the inquiry about possible future effects.

because of the threat of a possible state-of-mind inquiry, he might do things differently? Those who expected such an effect were asked to elaborate.

The discussion then moved from the practical realm to the philosophical. Regardless of possible practical effects, how did the person feel about *Herbert* v. *Lando*? Was his or her general attitude one of approval or disapproval? In either case, what were the specific views upon which his or her feelings rested?

The purpose of exploring the realm of feelings and opinion about the decision was to try to detect any possible correlation between certain attitudes and whether the individual believed he or she would be affected in a practical way.

Finally each respondent was asked to offer a general assessment of the state of relations between the courts and the news media. Here again, the object was to look for possible relationships between some of the previously expressed views and the respondents' overall attitudes on the subject of the courts and a free press.

A deliberate effort was made to avoid giving those journalists who disapproved of *Herbert* v. *Lando* a laundry list of items to choose from as reasons for disapproval. It was thought that it would be more valid if the reasons for dissatisfaction with *Herbert* v. *Lando* were freely offered by those being interviewed, without benefit of coaching.

IV. TABULATION OF THE RESPONSES

From each written interview summary[19] was extracted all of the specific information that could be set down in chart form. Included were the following:

Did the interviewee recognize the case by name? (This piece of data, as footnoted earlier, proved superfluous to the purposes of the inquiry.)

What was the extent of the individual's knowledge about *Herbert* v. *Lando*?

Had the interviewee been affected, and if so, how? (Particularly, did the "effect" run only to an inhibition of the idle banter or gossip which can mark easy newsroom conversation, or did it run deeper than that?)

Did the interviewee expect future effects from the threat of state-of-mind inquiry, and if so, in what form?

Did the person interviewed generally approve or disapprove of *Herbert* v. *Lando*? If there was approval, what was the basis? Because the

19. Notes were taken by the interviewer during each interview. These were written up in a summary during the next day or two.

decision was the inevitable consequence of the protection given the press in *New York Times* v. *Sullivan*?[20] Because the threat of state-of-mind questioning might raise standards of reporting and editing? Because the journalist thought that press power ought to be curbed, and *Herbert* v. *Lando* would help do it?

If there was disapproval, what were the supports for that? Did the interviewee think *Herbert* v. *Lando* made it more difficult to protect sources or that it hampered investigation of public officials? Did the issues of mind invasion or the growing threat of harassment by suit contribute to the disapproving attitude, or was the view based on the perception of *Herbert* v. *Lando* in the overall context of recent Supreme Court decisions? Or, were somewhat different reasons articulated?

Whether the journalist approved or disapproved of *Herbert* v. *Lando,* there were numerous instances where two or more of the above reasons for doing so were given. Sometimes other reasons were cited, and though not included in the data compilation, they were noted.

Also charted was more general information about the person interviewed.[21] This included whether the individual was generally younger or older,[22] stated either an adherence to the ideal of objective reporting or said something indicating he or she had a perception of self as an "investigative reporter."[23] The study also charted whether the person considered *Herbert* v. *Lando* to be of theoretical importance only and of no real practical significance. Also tracked was whether the person believed or feared that an inquiry into "actual malice," as permitted under the *New York Times* v. *Sullivan* standard, would be transformed in many instances to an inquiry into whether there was bias on the reporter's part, not limited to actual malice. Another point charted was whether the journalist mentioned that "getting" someone is sometimes a part of the process of investigative reporting, at least as practiced by some. Reference by an individual to that idea in no way connoted approval of any effort to "get" a public official, only a recognition that it is an issue in the minds of some. Indeed, many said that there are a few,

---

20. New York Times Co. v. Sullivan, 376 U.S. 254, 84 S. Ct. 710, 11 L Ed. 2d 686 (1964). The court defined "actual malice" as a libelous story or statement published "with knowledge that it was false or with reckless disregard of whether it was false or not." 376 U.S. at 280, 84 S. Ct. at 726.
21. This information also was derived from gratuitously offered remarks or assertions during the course of the interview, excepting of course the person's age category and sex. *See also* this study, at 68.
22. *Supra* note 10.
23. Whether one stated a perception of self as "investigative" turned out to be of limited significance. Few referred to themselves in that way, although many were personally known to the interviewer to have distinctly investigative functions.

isolated examples of reporters who do, in fact, indulge in trying to "get" someone. No one approved of that idea in its worst sense; some, however, said that a reporter who, in the course of proper news-gathering activities, accumulates information that is clearly damning to some public official might very legitimately proceed on the assumption that he or she would, in fact, ultimately "get" that official.

It was clear that many of those interviewed regarded the problem of "getting" an official to be at the heart of the state-of-mind issue which went to the Supreme Court.

One reporter (who insisted on anonymity because libel litigation affecting that individual is still in progress) expressed it this way:

> When, out of feelings I get and judgments I make in the course of my work as a reporter, I think that someone is a goddamned thief, I set out to prove it. Suppose I were asked later on the stand about the thoughts which led me to do the story? Some jury could easily ascribe my work to malice.
>
> A good reporter has hackles that sometimes stand up. Like a scholar, a reporter must make assumptions and set out to work on them. Good editors keep check on those assumptions.
>
> I need freedom to make some judgments about people which might look bad later on. I have to be able to follow up on what may be nothing more than suspicions.

One other significant product of the interviews also charted was each individual's view of the current state of relations between the courts and the press.

It should be emphasized that most of the above categories of "data" were not derived from answers to direct questions on these points. Those interviewed were not asked specifically if they considered "getting" someone as part of the investigative process or central to the *Herbert* v. *Lando* case. Where made, that observation was offered in the context of general conversations stemming from those questions which actually were asked. Interviewees were not asked specifically whether they regarded *Herbert* v. *Lando* as the logical consequence of *New York Times* v. *Sullivan,* whether they thought news media power should be curbed, whether *Herbert* v. *Lando* could improve standards of reporting, whether they feared mind invasion, compromise of sources, an increase in harassment suits, or whether they considered *Herbert* v. *Lando* to pose any real threat at the practical level. All of this information was derived from what was said by the person being interviewed, without coaching or leading.

Newspeople need little prodding to get started on this subject. As long as they are not concerned about being hung up on their own words in some future legal proceeding, they stand ready to talk freely about the implications of state-of-mind questioning, many of them at great length. The charted information showed that this is true whether the respondent knew only a little or a great deal about *Herbert* v. *Lando.*

V. THE CASE

To some, there is irony in the fact that the state-of-mind issue was forced to the surface by a case involving television rather than a newspaper or magazine article.

Television news organizations are extremely sensitive to the dangers of being brought to task in libel actions. There are sufficient resources in a major television organization to provide happy hunting for any number of successful libel plaintiffs. For that reason, and because the public is generally so sensitive to what appears on television, the networks have developed extensive screening systems, or "fail-safe" mechanisms, designed to minimize the chance that they will be exposed to such suits.[24] The best defense against such a suit is to be sure that what you are running is true. Truth is generally regarded as an absolute defense to a libel suit.[25]

Smaller television stations, lacking in the resources to withstand the pressures of substantial libel actions or to provide fail-safe defenses against being wrong, are even less likely candidates for the distinction of producing a landmark libel case.[26]

Newspapers and magazines, however, are old hands at the problem. Some have gone to the mat many times. It would have been more logical to expect that the state-of-mind issue would have come out of the much greater volume of litigation generated by what appears in print.

The case that produced the state-of-mind issue never, itself, had reached the open courtroom, and it still has not seen the light of open court.

The case involved Col. Anthony Herbert, who first reached public attention in 1971 when he claimed that he had tried to bring about an

---

24. Interviews with Av Westin, ABC-TV News, Nov. 20, 1979, and Elliott Frankel, NBC-TV, Jan. 2, 1980.
25. While no Supreme Court decision stands for that proposition alone, *see* Fowler v. Donnelly, 358 P.2d 485 (1960), where a newspaper's demurrer to a libel allegation was sustained because the charge failed to allege the falsity of the published material; Garrison v. Louisiana, 379 U.S. 64, 85 S. Ct. 209 (1964), where the Supreme Court struck down a Louisiana statute that made truthful criticism of a public official punishable if published with ill-will, hatred, enmity, or wanton desire to injure; *see also* 50 Am. Jur. 2d, §386.
26. Interviews with Westin and Frankel, *supra* note 24.

army investigation of alleged U.S. war crimes in Vietnam.[27] He claimed that authorities tried to keep his charges out of public view and that reprisals were taken against him including dismissal from command. Considerable news attention, most of it placing the colonel in a favorable light, was focused on him in 1971. In 1972, however, Barry Lando, then producer of the CBS television program "60 Minutes," took a new interest in the story based on what he believed to be new information about the colonel. His investigation led "60 Minutes" to do a segment in 1973 entitled "The Selling of Colonel Herbert."

It was that program which produced the suit. Defendants were CBS itself, Barry Lando, producer of the program, Mike Wallace, who was the narrator, and *Atlantic Monthly Magazine,* which ran an article by Lando containing some of the material that Colonel Herbert alleged was libelous.

The case appeared to pose a minimum of legal difficulties. Colonel Herbert conceded that he was a "public figure" within the meaning of decisions of the Supreme Court and therefore subject to the rule of the *New York Times* v. *Sullivan* case,[28] and that in order to win his action he would have to prove to the satisfaction of the trial court that defendants published the libel with "actual malice."[29]

"Actual malice" was defined in the *Sullivan* case as a reckless disregard of the truth, or at least "serious doubts as to the truth" of what was published.[30] Also a part of that standard, according to a subsequent decision of the Supreme Court,[31] is that the publisher of the allegedly

---

27. The facts are reviewed in greatest detail in the court of appeals, decision of Judge Kaufman, Herbert v. Lando, 568 F. 2d 974 (2d Cir. 1977), at 980, 981, 982. Judge Kaufman's opinion was subsequently reversed by the Supreme Court.
28. Colonel Herbert actively sought the publicity he received in 1971, a fact which established his qualification as a "public figure" as defined in Curtis Publishing Co. v. Butts, 388 U.S. 130 (1967) and Gertz v. Robert Welch, Inc., 418 U.S. 323 (1974), at 342 and 345.
29. *Supra* note 20.
30. This standard for "actual malice" has been modified since the Supreme Court restated its definition in Times v. Sullivan. In St. Amant v. Thompson, 390 U.S. 727, 88 S. Ct. 1323 (1968). The Court said that a showing that the defending publisher had entertained "serious doubts" as to the truth of the material could be found as "actual malice." In that same case, and in Rosenblatt v. Baer, 383 U.S. 75, 86 S. Ct. 669 (1966), the Court stated the mere negligence would not, alone, serve to show actual malice. The Court may have further relaxed the requirement for showing actual malice in the majority opinion of the case under study here, Herbert v. Lando. It was stated: "To be liable, the alleged defamer of public officials or of public figures must know or have reason to suspect that his publication is false." 99 S. Ct., at 1641. Whether this signals a change from a "serious doubts" standard to a "reason to suspect" standard is not discussed further. The latter might suggest a broader area of liability for defending journalists.
31. Gertz v. Robert Welch, Inc., supra note 28.

libelous material can be held to have published with actual malice if he or she had a "subjective awareness of probable falsity"[32] of what was published, or if there were "obvious reasons to doubt the veracity of the informant or the accuracy of the reports."[33]

Whether CBS and its personnel could be held guilty of actual malice in this case is a long way from being decided. The entire action, filed in the District Court for the Southern District of New York,[34] was sidetracked during the process of discovery when Lando, during questioning by Herbert's attorney, refused to answer questions relating to what he believed to be true at the time the story was being produced for television. In other words, he declined to answer questions about his state of mind at the time the story was being done. He contended that he was protected from any such inquiry by the First and Fourteenth Amendments to the Constitution.[35]

Lando's claim, alone, had to be adjudicated. The district court rejected it, finding that Lando's state of mind was at the heart of Colonel Herbert's allegation of actual malice and that nothing in the Constitution denied access to information about that.[36] On appeal, a divided court of appeals panel overruled the district court, holding that the First Amendment gives the press absolute protection from inquiry into editorial processes as they relate to thoughts, opinions, or conclusions about material obtained in the course of news gathering.[37] The appeals court majority contended that the Constitution also protects the entire editorial process from undue inquiry, barring compelling needs in a criminal prosecution.[38]

The Supreme Court, in the case under review here, reversed that finding. The Court majority flatly rejected the claim that the First and Fourteenth Amendments give editorial processes absolute immunity from inquiry in libel actions by public officials.[39] The heart of the Court's position denying Lando's claim was stated in these words:

> If inquiry into editorial conclusions threatens the suppression not only of information known or strongly suspected to be unreliable but also of truthful information, the issue would be quite different. But as we have said, our cases necessarily contemplate examination of

32. *Id.*
33. *Id.*
34. Herbert v. Lando, Wallace, CBS, Inc., Atlantic Monthly Co., 73 F.R.D. 387 (1976).
35. Herbert v. Lando, *supra* 99 S. Ct., at 1637.
36. *Supra* note 34.
37. Herbert v. Lando, 568 F.2d. 974 (1977).
38. *Id.; see also* Herbert v. Lando, 99 S. Ct., at 1645.
39. Herbert v. Lando, *supra* 99 S. Ct., at 1645.

the editorial process to prove the necessary awareness of probable falsehood, and if indirect proof of this element does not stifle truthful publication and is consistent with the First Amendment, as respondents seem to concede, we do not understand how direct inquiry with respect to the ultimate issue would be substantially more suspect.[40]

The Court made clear that not only the mind, but also what the mind had recorded on paper, was to be viewed in the same light:

The privilege as asserted by respondents would also immunize from inquiry the internal communications occurring during the editorial process and thus place beyond reach what the defendant participants learned or knew as the result of such collegiate conversations or exchanges.[41]

The Court majority rejected all of the requests by Lando for editorial process privileges.[42]

The Court appeared to suggest a qualification, however slight, on the right of legal process to push into the realm of editorial process when it stated: "This is not to say that the editorial discussions or exchanges have no constitutional protection from casual inquiry."[43] What constitutes "casual inquiry" was not defined.

The Court took note of press concerns that the discovery process out of which state-of-mind inquiry arises can be costly, and that by not protecting the press from such inquiry it is opening the door to great increases in the expenses the press will have to bear to deal with libel claims that depend on a showing of actual malice. The Court appeared to assert a tough-luck stance on that question:

If plaintiffs in consequence now resort to more discovery, it would not be surprising; and it would follow that the costs and other burdens of this kind of litigation have escalated and become much more troublesome for both plaintiffs and defendants. It is suggested that the press needs Constitutional protection from these burdens if it is to perform its task, which is indispensable to a system such as ours.

40. *Id.* at 1647.
41. *Id.*
42. *Id.* at 1648, 1649.
43. *Id.* at 1648.

. . . mushrooming litigation costs, much of it due to pretrial discovery, are not peculiar to the libel and slander area. There have been repeated expressions of concern about undue and uncontrolled discovery, and voices from this Court have joined the chorus. But until and unless there are major changes in the present rules of civil procedure, reliance must be had on what in fact and in law are ample powers of the District Court to prevent abuse.[44]

The Court then suggested that it is the job of district court judges to keep the discovery process, and costs, within reasonable limits.[45, 46]

Justice Brennan's dissent was actually only a dissent "in part."[47] While he joined the majority in rejecting the call for an absolute protection for all editorial processes in such cases, he suggested instead a "qualified privilege":

The inquiry need not reach an inflexible result: the justifications for an editorial privilege may well support only a qualified privilege which, in appropriate instances, must yield to the requirements of "the administration of justice."[48]

Justices Stewart and Marshall each wrote separate dissents. Justice Stewart called for remand to the district court to determine whether the discovery sought by Colonel Herbert through state-of-mind questioning was actually relevant under constitutional standards previously set by the Court.[49] Justice Marshall, citing *St. Amant* v. *Thompson*,[50] urged the absolute privilege view.[51]

This is where it stands today as far as the outside world of the press is concerned. Mr. Lando, in the course of subsequent depositions, has been questioned as to his state of mind at the time he did the story. There is, at this writing, no available public record of his answers. The case has yet to come to trial, where his responses to any and all state-of-mind questions may or may not get on the record.[52]

---

44. *Id.* at 1649.
45. *Id.* at 1649.
46. *Id.* at 1649, footnote 25.
47. *Id.* at 1651
48. *Id.* at 1653.
49. *Id.* at 1663.
50. *Supra* note 30.
51. 99 S. Ct., at 1667.
52. Telephone interview with Jonathan W. Lubell, counsel for Colonel Herbert, Jan. 16, 1980.

VI. THE FINDINGS OF THE SURVEY

To get general agreement among sixty-seven journalists on one proposition is as unlikely as arriving at a unanimous conclusion in the United Nations on how the Middle East issues should be resolved. Reporters and editors tend to be as independent of mind as a collection of Frenchmen at a seminar on politics.

It is not surprising, therefore, that this study did not uncover unanimity of view on anything. But that was not the object; the object was to try to find evidence of effect, and assuming the truthfulness of all answers, the evidence was there.

The key to the findings is in the answers to three of the questions asked of those interviewed:[53]

- Have you been affected in your functions in any way by the knowledge that at some future time you might be subjected in court to state-of-mind inquiry?
- Can you hypothesize circumstances in the future in which you would expect to be affected, or in which you would do things differently, because of the threat of state-of-mind questioning?
- Regardless of possible effects at the practical level, how do you feel about *Herbert* v. *Lando*? Do you approve or disapprove, and why?

The closest to a unanimous response in the survey is to the first of these questions: fifty-six of the respondents, or 84 percent, said that they have not yet been affected in any way, shape, or form in their activities because of concern about *Herbert* v. *Lando*. Of the eleven who said that they have been affected in their activities, only one individual said that the effect had gone beyond the mere exercise of greater care with facts, or a restraint on the easy wisecracking about public officials and public figures which commonly abounds in the off-hand atmosphere of the city room.

That one individual,[54] a member of the Washington press corps, said that he has taken great care to see that his written communications with his own editors do not contain any material which could later be used to pry into what might have been on his mind.

If one is to judge the question of the real effect of *Herbert* v. *Lando* on the basis of what has happened so far, as against what might happen,

---

53. *Supra* note 16.
54. The individual asked not to be identified on this point.

those who say that the decision does not amount to "a hill of beans" at the practical level win the argument hands down, at least on the basis of this survey.

Further support for the proponents of that point of view is found in an analysis of the answers to the second key question, that of possible future effects. Only twelve others, beyond those who say they already have been influenced in their activities by the decision, foresee that they will be affected in the future.

It was among those who predicted future effects that suggestions were made that the decision will influence editorial activity beyond merely inhibiting either unkind or good-natured banter around the newsroom, or encouraging a reporter to check out the facts with much greater care. About half of them expected to be forced to censor in advance their intra-editorial office communications or their notes, or expected to have difficulty in providing confidential sources of information with iron-clad assurances that the confidentiality could be protected.

What is probably more significant is what is to be found on the other side of the ledger. About two thirds of all respondents—forty-four—say they have neither been affected nor expect to be affected in any way.

So much for the agonized editorial outcries of the press, the proponents of the "hill-of-beans" theory might argue. But, in the view of this writer (who now shares the hill-of-beans argument when the problem is viewed only at the practical level, for reasons to be elaborated upon later), this is only where the argument about *Herbert* v. *Lando* begins.

Of those forty-four individuals who have been unaffected and do not expect to be, thirty-seven or over 80 percent, clearly disapprove of the Supreme Court's holding in *Herbert* v. *Lando*, most of them very strongly.[55] In fact, forty-eight individuals in the overall sample (74 percent) disapproved of the Court's holding in the case. Nine were neutral, and only ten (15 percent) gave their approval to state-of-mind questioning.

An effort was made through the process of data compilation to track the issues which were most responsible for the strong feelings in opposition to the decision.

The biggest concerns expressed by those who disapproved can be summarized in the words "mind invasion" and "chill."

Mind invasion is not, strictly speaking, a legal issue. That it is an emotional one, however, was evident not only in the editorials which greeted *Herbert* v. *Lando* last April but in the responses at the interviews.

---

55. "Strong disapproval" was inferred from such characterizations as "outrageous," "dangerous," "crazy," to name but a few, or a reference such as: "I strongly disagree," or "it's a very bad decision."

"*Herbert* v. *Lando* may be the ultimate invasion of privacy," suggested Av Westin, vice-president and executive producer of ABC-TV News.

"Orwellian" was the characterization of Neil Cocchia, chief editorial writer of the *Newark Star Ledger.* "It's got 1984 overtones."

Charles McDowell, the principal investigative reporter at the Washington News Bureau of Media General, views it as a problem of "rummaging around" in a person's mind.

"I have always felt I've had the First Amendment behind me, not as a protection against specific inquiries, but against a general rummaging around in my mind and my notes," he said. "I feel slightly troubled that this decision can lead to questions which would, in effect, be such a rummaging."

"This involves trying to pick a brain in a very dangerous way," suggests Nancy Keefe, editor of the *Mount Vernon* (N.Y.) *Daily Argus,* one of the integrated Westchester, Rockland Counties newspaper group. "I think it violates fundamental rights. In the American tradition, you just don't go poking around in people's minds."

These are not arguments with a legal foundation,[56] but they certainly contain a clue as to where battle lines are being drawn.

The idea of "chill" is imprecise, perhaps beyond legal definition, but everyone seems to know what it means. Of those who disapproved of the idea of state-of-mind questioning, seventeen used the word "chill" to describe the problems they think it poses for the press. More specifically, most of them saw the chill as something that would hamper investigative reporting.

Among those who disapproved, there was also considerable mention of the problem of protecting notes from a later inquiry aimed at proving what was in the mind, and concern about the problem of facing harassment by lawsuit. Nine of those in the "disapprove" category disapproved of *Herbert* v. *Lando* simply because the decision seems to create further problems and conflict in the overall context of issues between the press and the courts.[57]

---

56. The Supreme Court has, in recent decades, found a number of "Fundamental Rights" which, though not specified in the Bill of Rights, fall within Constitutional protection.
57. Four respondents expressed fear that their organization, or others, might be driven into a corner by suits encouraged by the idea that the decision gives a plaintiff a crack at what was on the reporters' mind. Six saw the decision as a threat to the ability to protect sources. Those numbers may seem insignificant, except when it is recognized that these specific mentions of problems arose in every case in an impromptu conversation in which the interviewer avoided making any suggestions, or offering any list of ideas, as to why the journalist might or should be disturbed by Herbert v. Lando.

The reasons given for their disapproval of the decision illuminated a more general perception of the sixty-seven persons interviewed that the courts and the press are headed in the direction of greater, indeed bitter, conflict. "I believe this decision is absolutely an attempt to remove from the Fourth Estate what I consider to be its inalienable privileges under the Constitution," said Bruce Reynolds, managing editor of the *New Haven Register*. "We're now arming ourselves for what we might face in court."

"The courts are encroaching more and more on the rights of reporters," said Jody Calendar, a reporter and bureau chief for the *Asbury Park Press*. "There is a growing watchdog mentality, and it's getting to the point where the press seems to be under siege."

"Any tinkering with First Amendment rights will inevitably be translated into rights of the government to control the press," said Alan Emory, Washington correspondent for the *Watertown* (N.Y.) *Daily Times*. "That control will only grow."

He was supported in that view by Don Warshaw, a courthouse reporter for the *Newark Star-Ledger,* who said he regards the courts as "government's chosen instrument for slapping the press down, not just on its own behalf but on behalf of the other two branches of government, as well."

"The courts want their powers and prerogatives, and they want to expand them," he asserted.

Vincent Zarate, New Jersey Statehouse correspondent for the *Star-Ledger* had a similar view: "The decision may have sounded very nice in theory to the judges but that decision could be a dangerous lever in the hands of anybody, at any time." Judges, he noted, are "after all, launched by the political process."

Jean Joyce, New Jersey editor of the *New York Daily News,* had this view of the growing conflict: "When I was a reporter I saw attempts by judges to control things. I don't think the press should be subject to that control. The courts have power—too much of it—and they like to use it. The problem is really one of power and its exercise by the courts."

Vince Slavin, suburban editor of the *Elizabeth Daily Journal,* put it less delicately: "This is one more thing on the Supreme Court list for screwing people."

Bernard Izes, city editor of the *Atlantic City Press,* said that *Herbert* v. *Lando* threatens the press with "bullying" in court. "We can be browbeaten too, especially a young reporter trying to do his job."

Robert Dubill, chief of the Gannett National News Service, based in Washington, D.C., shares the general view that the conflict is heated and getting hotter. Contrary to most, however, he welcomes it. "It's a confrontation that's long overdue," said Dubill, who is also an attorney.

"The press has long held the courts in awe, partly because the press has feared the courts' contempt powers. When it comes to criticism of the courts, there has been a conspiracy of silence on the side of the legal profession."

An issue related to the extent to which a press-courts confrontation will generate greater coverage of the courts is that of the secrecy in which the deliberations of the courts, and especially those of the Supreme Court, are conducted. David Hess, a general investigative reporter for the Knight-Ridder News Bureau in Washington, said that he foresees intensification of the secrecy issue in the near future. (As one might suspect, this interview was conducted shortly before the appearance of the advance stories on the subsequent publication of *The Brethren* by Woodward and Armstrong.)

"After all, the American people pay for this system," Hess said. "They have a right to know, after the fact, how and why the judges arrive at their decisions, beyond their written opinions." He drew an analogy to a legislature expressing its views, not through a record of debate, but only in the legislation that it publishes. He believes that an after-the-fact record should be available to the public, other courts, the press, and to law schools.

Warshaw also stated his concern over the secrecy issue. "You put those guys in closed courtrooms and there'll be all kinds of chicanery and crazy decisions, some of which the public will never even hear about."

In fact, some forty-three of the sixty-seven persons interviewed said that they regarded the overall current state of relations between the courts and the press in a very negative light. This assessment, of course, took into account not only the state-of-mind issue but also the many other points of contention between these two major forces in our society. They include such problems as the closing of certain pretrial proceedings,[58] unannounced searches of newsrooms for evidence relating to crimes in which the newsroom personnel themselves may have had no involvement,[59] gag orders,[60] and the power of courts to subpoena the notes of reporters as possible evidence relevant to a criminal trial,[61] to mention

---

58. *Supra* note 8.
59. *Supra* note 9.
60. Nebraska Press Assoc. v. Stuart, 427 U.S. 539, 96 S. Ct. 2791, 49 L. Ed. 2d 683 (1976), where the Supreme Court reversed a lower court gag order but declined to find an absolute right for the press to publish, in all circumstances, what it heard in a courtroom.
61. *In re* Farber, 78 N.J. 259, 394 A.2d 330 (1978), cert. denied, New York Times Co. v. New Jersey, 439 U.S. 997 (1978). This was the celebrated case of *New York Times* reporter Myron Farber, whose notes were held to be subject to subpoena by the defense in a murder trial, despite the New Jersey Shield Law. The Sixth Amendment of the Constitution was held to apply and to have priority over a shield law, if criminal defense required it.

only those with the most potential for further aggravation of the situation.

Beyond the forty-three who had a negative view of the state of the courts-press relationship, six considered the relationship not to be a special problem, while two saw nothing particularly wrong with the relationship and in fact considered it to be quite healthy. (Both of those individuals, however, were two of the three in the entire sampling who stated a belief that the power of the news media is too great and it is the power of the press that ought to be curbed, not the power of the courts.) Of the six who saw no overall problem in the relationship between courts and news media, four were recorded as disapproving of *Herbert v. Lando*. That may be significant in that it adds to the number of those who have reason to think that all is not healthy between the press and the courts.

There were sixteen in the sampling who simply did not give a clear answer, or gave no answer at all, when queried on their view of the situation between the courts and the press.[62]

Among the forty-three who clearly believed that the relationship between the courts and the press is in a negative state were six who made special mention of their intention to take whatever steps may be necessary to insure that a court can never get at any of the notes they have taken.

Also among the forty-three were three individuals who strongly approved of the state-of-mind holding; in each case the person thought the press should be held fully accountable for its use of facts and information, and that the decision might have the salutary effect of making better reporters of some who, because of the threat of state-of-mind inquiry, might otherwise treat their facts with less care. "It forces me to be accurate and very sure of what I am writing," said Bob Hetherington, a general news reporter for the *Star-Ledger*. "There's too much bad reporting in the world, and if this stops some of it, it's probably a good idea." Hetherington's view of the courts, however, indicated strong negative feelings over what he said is a "very superior attitude to everything and everyone else in government. With their [the judges'] attitudes, the idea of equal branches of government is a joke."

George Kentera, assistant news editor of the Knight-Ridder Bureau in Washington, was of the opinion that the threat of state-of-mind questioning probably "will make better reporters out of us." His approval of *Herbert v. Lando* did not extend to other areas of the courts-press relationship. He noted that the decision which authorized the Stan-

---

62. No special attempt was made to press a response on this point from those interviewed. If the question was not clearly answered after a couple of tries, it was dropped.

ford newsroom raid[63] opens up what he referred to as "bizarre possibilities." Kentera conjured up the situation that will ensue when warrantless raiders arrive in a newsroom looking for notes and other materials and find that most of what they want is already stored in the computers which are utilized by the editorial department. "Are editors going to have to give them the codes they would need to get at what they want?" he asked. "How could they ever have the remotest idea of whether they are being given what is really in the computer?" Because such searches will inevitably delve into material that relates to other matters, leads on to other stories, other investigations, and the like, he believes that the potential for bitter conflict in this area is limitless.

It is in the area of notes protection that many reporters expressed a special concern. One who disagrees with the prevailing view among the journalists surveyed is Clark Mollenhoff, a reporter for the Jack Anderson column and a columnist for the *Des Moines* (Iowa) *Register.* Mollenhoff, who also is a journalism professor at Washington and Lee University, offered the opinion that "anyone who keeps notes uncoded, or in a computer, is a damned fool."

Mollenhoff was another who approved generally of the state-of-mind holding. For him, the equation is simple: If *New York Times* v. *Sullivan,* then *Herbert* v. *Lando.* "To have *Times-Sullivan* without *Herbert* v. *Lando* is to leave the plaintiff in a Catch-22 situation," he said.

A number of others shared Mollenhoff's understanding of the equation, but were not necessarily as happy with the current legal order of things.

John McLaughlin, a columnist and reporter for the *New York Daily News,* said that he originally was very enthusiastic about the protections afforded by that decision. Now, he said, he has his doubts. "Logically I don't see much to quarrel with. If you have *Sullivan,* then you have to have *Lando.* Maybe the press would have been better off if there had still been some accountability for our own shortcomings as newsmen."

"I don't need the protection of *Times-Sullivan,*" stated Warshaw, the court reporter from the *Star-Ledger.* "But don't do me that favor and then say that you've got free access to my mind and my notes. Just judge me by what I put in the paper."

Sandra King, a reporter and narrator of news programs for Channel 13, principal public television outlet in the New York area, echoed Warshaw's judge-me-by-what-I-print argument. "If a libel case can't be won by proof based on the facts available, then it shouldn't be won at all," she said.

63. *Supra* note 9.

Zarate, the Statehouse correspondent for the *Star-Ledger,* had the same view: "You have to prove a crime by facts, even the intent of a crime. The same principle should apply here."[64]

The *New York Times* v. *Sullivan* standard for actual malice, as noted earlier, involves deliberate or reckless disregard of the truth by the libeler of the public official or public figure, or willingness to ignore the facts which the publisher of libel should have known would have produced the truth. There exists a general misconception among many newsmen about that standard, at least among those interviewed in the survey. Some mentioned malice in terms of ill-will, or a hostile attitude, and the Supreme Court had expressly rejected that brand of malice as a factor in a libel suit involving a public official.[65]

In any event, when the malice standard was explained to those who seemed to hold that mistaken view, they, and some of the others who had a proper understanding of the standard, were not noticeably comforted. Ten of the individuals interviewed specifically stated a concern that when a case is laid before a jury, and regardless of any standard that might be explained to the jury, a malice inquiry could easily degenerate into a bias inquiry, at least as far as the jury is concerned. Joe Rush, former news editor of the now defunct *Newark News,* and presently associate editor of the *Millburn and Short Hills Item,* was concerned that "if juries get into the question of malice based on what was in someone's mind, then it becomes a subjective inquiry. That could lead almost anywhere."

In fact, that concern relates closely to another which many newsmen think is really at the bottom of the Supreme Court's state-of-mind decision. Although the Court made no reference to it, it is the issue of the reporter who, in the vernacular of the profession, is out to "get" someone, usually a public official. Some twenty-two of the respondents gratuitously raised the point. Nearly all articulated it in some form of the verb "to get," and two or three who didn't use that word specifically did use words which clearly expressed the same point.

"The Supreme Court thinks that many reporters are out to screw people," was the assessment of Ginny Sederis, a New Jersey Statehouse correspondent for the *Passaic Herald News.*

"In investigative work there are times when you don't interview your subject until near the end of an investigation, that is, until you have gathered enough information to have concluded that, rightfully, I'm going to 'get' that individual. The fact that I thought that way now might get me in trouble."

According to Andrew Stasiuk, managing editor of the *Star-Ledger,*

---

64. For further discussion of this issue, *see* this study, at 89.
65. *Supra* notes 20 and 30.

"The thought process in an investigation inevitably leads to: 'Aha, I've got the SOB!' You would be hard pressed to justify that if a smart lawyer for a plaintiff got you to admit that."

Mark Stuart, writer and general investigative reporter for the *Bergen Record* in Hackensack foresees difficulties for investigative reporters when it all gets down to real life cases: "Let's say I'm going after a child abuser; the facts of the story might arouse feelings in me. Those feelings could be interpreted as though I was out to get that guy. The same thing could happen where theft by a public official is involved. I think the decision stinks."

"When you go after someone, of course you make him a target," said Harvey Fisher, chief of the Statehouse Bureau for that same paper. "Someone could see that as trying to 'get' the target, and impute malice. That worries me."

Jana Thompson, the Trenton Statehouse correspondent for New Jersey's two Gannett newspapers (*Camden Courier News* and *Bridgewater Courier News*) has the same conception of the investigative process. "In the course of an investigation a reporter is going to consciously *target* someone and make a decision to go after him," she said. "If state-of-mind questioning gets at that fact, a jury might not understand, and might think instead that the reporter took aim at the individual in advance." The targeting of an individual by an investigative reporter is a natural, inevitable part of the investigative process, she said.

Robert Thompson (no relation) of the Associated Press Statehouse Bureau shares Jana Thompson's concern: "My thought process in an investigative situation would be: 'I've got the goods on this SOB; I'm going to use it.' Is that malice? What I know within myself to be an honest job of reporting and digging out of facts might be construed by someone else as malicious." That "someone else," he added, could be a jury.

John McLaughlin, of the *New York Daily News,* shared the view of those who thought that a reporter can pretty much decide what he wants to remember about his state of mind. "What you write is what you remember," he said. "What you think is what you forget."

Richard Heymann, editorial page editor of the *Morris Record,* thinks for that same reason that "the decision borders on the irrelevant. The further one gets from the moment, the more the state of mind is lost."

"I think it is more a theoretical than a practical matter," he said, "but it is in the theoretical realm that I object to it."

A few who do not feel so immune from the possible threat of state-of-mind questioning are convinced, nonetheless, that for an entirely different reason they will not be caused to change their way of doing things. Two are publishers, one is a managing editor. All oppose the decision, and all three believe that it is a very real threat to people on their respective staffs. Yet they insist they will not be affected in what they do for a reason that can be summed up in the word "defiance."

Robert Ebener, managing editor of the *Atlantic City Press,* expects reporters and editors at some papers to be inhibited by a decision which he characterized as "scary, intimidating, upsetting." Yet, he said, "We can't let ourselves be inhibited by it. If we're honest reporters, we don't let it bother us. We'll still do our job in a practical way."

"I'm just not going to let it affect us in any way," was the response of William Worrall, publisher of the Worrall Newspapers, based in Orange. "If we let it worry us, we could never do our job."

Bert Kersen, publisher of the *Paterson News,* sounded an even more determined tone: "We're going to do our job. We're aware of the damn decisions. There is great expense and strain on a paper in defending these suits, even when they are frivolous and we win on summary judgment. But some papers might well have to say, 'maybe we better stay away from this; we can't afford it.' That's frightening."

Hostility to the state-of-mind decision aside, few in the news media who hold antagonistic viewpoints toward it really feel in any way truly threatened by it. "This is a law that is impossible to enforce," said Palmer Bateman, publisher of the *Somerset Messenger-Gazette.* "A law is useful only if it is enforceable. This one [meaning the law embodied in the decision] isn't."

Arthur Swanson, executive editor of the Recorder Publishing Company in Basking Ridge, New Jersey, although a supporter of the *Herbert v. Lando* holding in principle, has the same view of the impracticability of the decision. "It's farfetched," he said. "Who can really recall a state of mind at any particular time in the past?"

Swanson hinted at a problem that Bruce Bailey, a general assignment reporter for the *Star-Ledger,* met head-on: "A reporter won't tell you what he was thinking, but what he wants you to think he was thinking."

Guy Savino, a reporter for the *Newark News* before it ceased to publish and now editor of a Lyndhurst, New Jersey-based chain of weeklies, the Leader Newspapers, is another who considers the decision to be "nonsense" on a practical level. "It's like dancing on the head of a pin. How can you really tell, long after the fact, what the real state of mind was? It's a tricky, legalistic decision. The judges have made jackasses of themselves here. It's one of those things that you just can't prove. You show malice from the net results (i.e. what was written or broadcast), not from the unprovable question of state of mind."

Garrick Utley, a reporter for NBC-TV, thinks the Court, in *Herbert v. Lando,* has raised a nonissue. "What is state of mind anyway?" he asked. "Usually your state of mind on almost anything consists of a whole set of feelings about the subject, most of them conflicting. I don't know how I could get a clear understanding of my own state of mind on anything; how could anyone else?"

Harry Weingast, editor of the *Jewish News* in New Jersey, was "outraged" by the decision, despite the fact that he also considered state of mind to be beyond the ability of a court to prove. "No judge or court should be given the authority to probe the psyche of a reporter," he said. "Even psychiatrists would have great difficulty in agreeing on what was in a person's mind. Certainly that should not be left to the courts. State of mind is something between a reporter and his or her conscience. There is great potential for abuse in that authority."

On the approval side of the ledger, that is, referring to the nine individuals who said they approved of the state-of-mind holding, the idea that it could force a higher standard of objectivity and care in the news business was the reason most often stated. The second principal reason, cited by three of those who approved, was that state-of-mind was a natural and inevitable extension of the "actual malice" rule of the *Sullivan* decision which gave the press such broad protection.

But there was another reason given for approval of the decision, this one by Robert Dubill, the Gannett National News Service chief, who, as already indicated, sees considerable threat to the press from the courts.

Dubill, a lawyer, outlined this possible courtroom scenario where the libel-plaintiff, public official meets the defending reporter:

> Through his attorney, plaintiff focuses on the supposedly quivering defendant's state of mind. Attorney quizzes defendant about his beliefs, opinions, and conclusions at the time he wrote the offending article. When plaintiff's attorney finishes, defendant's attorney rises. The subject of state-of-mind has now been opened. Defendant's attorney now has the right to examine further on that point, and he does it with a vengeance. Defendant spews forth with all that was in his mind when he did the story, all the gossip, rumor, innuendo, and any other suggestive and unpleasant thoughts he may have had hidden away in his mind.

Not a very inviting prospect for a plaintiff, Dubill suggests.

"If you are going to go into the mind, then you are going to have to bare all," he said. "Plaintiffs should know that newspapers are now going to go that extra mile to get all the information possible—even gossip. Plaintiffs must now recognize that once they open the doors on state of mind, just about anything is fair game."

The purpose of issuing forth with all of that material so potentially devastating to a plaintiff, he said, is not maliciousness or viciousness. "The purpose will be to prove the good faith of the reporter when he did his story," he noted.

An effort was made in this study to determine whether the attitudes generally held by the press differ in any material way from those held in certain subgroups, including those who are generally younger,[66] senior editors, women, those who approved of the decision, weekly newspaper editors and publishers, and journalists based in New York. Accordingly, the responses given by each of these distinct groups was charted separately from the master survey.

Each of these groups was examined for the answers of its members to certain key questions, or for responses which provided significant information. For example, all "generally younger" reporters and editors were studied to determine how many had mentioned an adherence to the objective standard, how many foresaw no effects from the decision and had experienced none, how many had basically complete knowledge of what *Herbert v. Lando* said, and how many approved of the decision, or were neutral about it. The same inquiry was made as to women, weekly editors and publishers, and so forth.

It would be a mistake to place too much stock in some of the findings that follow here pertaining to those subcategories, because the samplings in most instances are probably too small to be fully trustworthy. Nevertheless, for the possible interest there may be in them, these significant differences from the overall norm for the sample are noted:

Senior editors, more than any other single group, anticipate that they will be affected by the threat of state-of-mind questioning in one way or another. About 33 percent of the entire sample expect that in one way or another they will be affected. Among senior editors the percentage for that expectation is about fifty-five.

On the other end of the scale, weekly newspaper editors and publishers, as might have been predicted by some, were unanimous in forecasting that they would not be affected at all, and in reporting that they had been free of all effect up to now.

However, weekly editors and publishers are the group in which there is the lowest rate of approval of *Herbert v. Lando*—ten percent. (It should be reported here that neutrality on the issue was accorded a weight of one half a vote for approval. Among the ten weekly editors and publishers, two said they were neutral about *Herbert v. Lando*.) The

66. *Supra* note 10.

overall approval rate, using the weighted method for evaluating expressions of neutrality, was 21 percent.

The lowest overall rate of approval for the decision appeared among women—a mere four percent.

When each group was examined to determine the extent to which its members had generally complete knowledge of the decision, senior editors rated highest, with about 70 percent showing that level of familiarity with *Herbert v. Lando.* At the other end of the knowledge scale as it pertained to the decision were the editors and publishers of weeklies, women, and journalists based in New York City—each at about 30 percent, against an overall percentage for the sample of 45 percent.

More individuals who approve of the decision also profess the objective standard of journalism than in any other group. Those who are in the "younger" group, by percentage, profess the objective standard in less than half the number of instances for the total sample.

VII. CONCLUSION—THE FUTURE OF STATE-OF-MIND INQUIRY

This paper, in its introduction, offered only one conclusion—that the Court has provided the plaintiff with a harmless weapon, and the press have reacted as patriots whose homeland has been invaded.

It is an article of faith with most in the legal profession that state of mind, as it relates to intent, is a legitimate subject for inquiry in a courtroom proceeding.

Most journalists consider what is in their minds to be related to a right that is fundamental, in the realm of higher law and transcending anything a court might decree on the subject.

The Supreme Court, by its majority holding in *Herbert v. Lando,* has chosen to challenge the press on this basic issue; those in the press community, as shown by this study, are prepared to do whatever is necessary to beat off the challenge.

What, then, can be anticipated about the future of state-of-mind inquiry as a serious factor in libel suits by public officials seeking to show actual malice? Is it a mere teapot tempest?

It is not within the scope of this paper to attempt to predict with certainty future state-of-mind inquiry in public officials' libel suits. The findings of this survey, however, indicate some interesting possibilities.

For one thing, it is clear that while many journalists are sore about the subject, very few are fearful that they will be affected by it in any tangible way. They are well aware of the fact that what is in their minds is in their total possession. If someone wants to use it for evidence, that someone, if it is a trial court, is going to have to take the word of the journalist giving testimony that what he says was on his mind is what in fact was on his mind. The evidence is not of the type that one readily challenges or corroborates. Either challenge or corroboration would have to be accomplished with factual evidence.

In fact, the clue to the future of state-of-mind questioning may have been handed to the press in the very majority opinion that so many journalists found to be threatening. That clue was contained in a cursory reference in Footnote 20 of the majority decision. It read as follows:

> The kind of question respondents seek to avoid answering is, by their own admission, the easiest to answer. See Tr. of Oral Arg., at 31:
> "They are set-up questions for our side.
> . . . These are not difficult questions to answer."

That notation does not take into account the boomerang theory advanced by Bob Dubill, but it certainly would seem to support the idea.

Tactically speaking, the plaintiff is asked to invite the defendant to do either or both of two things: (1) to respond to state-of-mind questioning with the bombshells that might be hidden away in the defendant's mind—bombshells that the public official did not know were in the journalist's possession, or (2) to respond with all manner of self-serving assertions attesting to the very highest of motives in pursuing the story that offended.

In neither instance can it be imagined that a journalist would feel very much threatened. In neither instance can it be imagined that a public official suing for libel would be eager to test either the reporter's hidden store of information or his willingness to take advantage of the opportunity to serve his own cause.

Nevertheless, there might still be isolated instances where the hardy plaintiff is willing to brave these risks and press the issue of the journalist's state of mind. Colonel Herbert was willing. In instances where state-of-mind inquiry is pressed, the plaintiff is still not guaranteed direct access to what he or she may be looking for. There is still the problem of the memory of the journalist, a problem which increases as the time gap widens between the preparation and publication of the story and the actual courtroom trial of the libel action.

There also are some interesting legal questions which are certain to be examined further before the future of state-of-mind inquiry becomes clear. Under the accepted rules of evidence,[67] the plaintiff has the burden of going forward to prove actual malice, or in other words, to break through the protective barrier built for the press by the Supreme Court in

67. *Abbott's Proof of Facts,* at 763, 764; see note, at 818.

New York Times v. *Sullivan.* It is an anomaly that the effort to prove actual malice, even if successful in the eyes of a jury, is all for naught if the defending journalist can provide evidence that would convince a court of the truth of what was published. Truth is an absolute defense to libel.[68] Although the truth issue might preempt the whole question of actual malice, the burden of going forward on the truth issue, and of persuading the court that the material was true, rests on the defending journalist. He does not get his chance to meet that burden until the complaining public official already has taken a crack at him on the issue of actual malice, and its corollary access to the question of the state of the mind.[69]

Perhaps a review of the burdens, or of the order of evidence presentation, would provide a solution to that problem.

It was noted in the findings that a number of the journalists have come to have second thoughts about the protection afforded by the actual malice rule in the *Sullivan* case. The entire rationale for the state-of-mind holding of *Herbert* v. *Lando* rests squarely on the foundation of *New York Times* v. *Sullivan.* If the rule of actual malice in the *Sullivan* case had never been set down by the Court, there would be no *Herbert* v. *Lando.* Some journalists now wonder whether there ever should have been a Times-Sullivan rule for actual malice. Indeed, the rule itself is now not the all-encompassing protection that it might have appeared to be at first.[70]

One possible way for the press to avoid the threat of state-of-mind questioning, if indeed it constitutes any real threat, is to surrender its protection under the *New York Times* v. *Sullivan* rule. That surrender, an idea not novel with this writer,[71] could be accomplished by the introduction at the outset of pretrial proceedings of a "judicial admission"[72] of actual malice by the defending journalist. This judicial admission would not mean that the journalist agrees for all the world to know that he was guilty of actual malice, that he recklessly disregarded the truth or information that he should have known would produce the truth. Rather, the judicial admission says to the court and to the plaintiff that the defendant makes a technical admission for the purpose of removing from himself one of the protections now available to him in a libel action by a public official. That protection is not a defense but a requirement on the plaintiff—the requirement that the plaintiff prove actual malice. The judicial admission by the journalist merely says that the

---

68. *Supra* note 25.
69. *Supra* note 67.
70. On the status of the "actual malice" rule, *see* note 30.
71. The idea was explained to the writer, and discussed at length, by Prof. Michael Risinger of Seton Hall University Law School.
72. *Wigmore on Evidence,* § 2588, 2589, 2590.

public official does not have to prove actual malice. It is hard to imagine a rationale for state-of-mind inquiry if actual malice is not at issue.

Now the journalist has a choice. He can retreat behind the protections afforded in *New York Times* v. *Sullivan* and invite the plaintiff to risk all the hazards that go with a state-of-mind inquiry, or he can surrender the protection of *New York Times* v. *Sullivan.*

Could a court refuse to allow a journalist to waive his rights under *New York Times* v. *Sullivan?* That may bear extended study, but it seems that by doing so a court would be telling the defending journalist that he *must* cloak himself with the protections of *New York Times* v. *Sullivan* and he *must* expose himself to the consequences that flow from it. That rationale, it might be argued, would run counter to the rationale which allows a criminal defendant to refuse to testify, thereby affording himself the right to avoid cross-examination on the issue of intent.

Lawyers are fond of pointing out that libel suits are civil actions, not criminal trials. Journalists are fond of pointing out that the libel action, criminal or not, has the defending journalist "on trial" in a very fundamental way. As some of the journalists see it, intent is the real question a court is getting at by allowing state-of-mind questioning. One of them in this survey made the criminal action analogy directly.[73]

It is not intended to suggest here that, while the state-of-mind issue at the practical level may be a tempest in a teapot, the debate that has ensued is a useless exercise. On the contrary, the debate may be important in that it will cause both the press and the courts to review the philosophical foundations for their mutual relationship. Maybe, as some of the journalists interviewed in this survey suggested, the fact that the relationship seems certain to be more adversarial in the future is a very healthy prospect. Individuals in each institution would possibly benefit from a better understanding of how they are viewed by those in the other.

Perhaps the debate will do no more in the long run than mark off some new general boundaries between the functions of the courts and the free press. If those boundaries can be better understood, then both sides can proceed to the problems generated by the more immediate and practical issues that they face—those related to the openness of all courtroom proceedings, the right of the press to publish whatever information is in its possession, or the right of police and the courts to get at intranewsroom notes and memos, and the limits on those rights.

If the view is correct that there is no practical threat in state-of-mind inquiry, either to the newsroom or to the reporter, then it is unlikely that the courtroom will see very much of the state-of-mind exercise in connection with public officials' libel suits. The Supreme Court will have given

73. Vincent Zarate, *Newark Star-Ledger,* at 81.

the plaintiff a weapon he cannot, or dares not, use. And the press, secure in the belief that their minds have not, after all, become courtroom property to be marked as exhibit A, B, or C, can divert their attention and troops to the other issues, to the front lines of the continuing contest between the courts and the press.

IX. APPENDIX A — LIST OF PERSONS INTERVIEWED

Mike Ascolese, Assistant City Editor, The Star-Ledger, Newark, N.J.

Bruce Bailey, General Assignment Reporter, The Star-Ledger, Newark, N.J.

C. Palmer Bateman, Jr., Publisher, Somerset Messenger-Gazette, Somerset, N.J.

Gordon Bishop, Investigative Reporter, The Star-Ledger, Newark, N.J.

Jody Calendar, A Reporter & Bureau Chief, The Asbury Park Press, N.J.

Sylvia Chase, News Correspondent, ABC-TV News

Neil Cocchia, Chief Editorial Writer, The Star-Ledger, Newark, N.J.

Robert Comstock, Managing Editor, The Record, Hackensack, N.J.

Thomas Connolly, Executive Editor, Daily Record, Morristown, N.J.

Miles Cunningham, Trenton Statehouse Correspondent, Evening Bulletin, Philadelphia, Pa.

Joseph R. Daughen, Investigative Reporter, The Bulletin, Philadelphia, Pa.

Robert Dubill, Chief, The Gannett National News Service, Washington, D.C.

Amy Duncan, Financial Reporter, The Record, Hackensack, N.J.

Louise Easton, Editor and Writer—Local Public Affairs, Madison Eagle, Madison, N.J.

Robert Ebener, Managing Editor, The Press, Atlantic City, N.J.

Alan Emory, Washington Correspondent, The Times, Watertown, N.Y.

John Farmer, National News Editor, The Bulletin, Philadelphia, Pa.

Harvey Fisher, Bureau Chief—Statehouse, The Record, Hackensack, N.J.

Jane Foderaro, Managing Editor, The Daily Register, Red Bank, N.J.

Elliott Frankel, Producer—Documentaries, NBC-TV News

Saul Friedman, Political Correspondent, Knight-Ridder News Bureau, Washington, D.C.

David Hardy, Reporter, Daily News, N.Y.

Charles Harrison, City Editor, The Star-Ledger, Newark, N.J.

Diana Henriques, Investigative and Statehouse Reporter, Trenton Times, N.J.

David Hess, Investigative General Reporter, Knight-Ridder News Bureau, Washington, D.C.

Bob Hetherington, Reporter, The Star-Ledger, Newark, N.J.

Richard Heymann, Financial Editor and Editorial Page Editor, The Record, Morristown, N.J.

Bernard Izes, City Editor, The Press, Atlantic City, N.J.

Jean Joyce, New Jersey Editor, Daily News, N.Y.

Arthur Z. Kamin, Editor & Publisher, The Daily Register, Red Bank, N.J.

Nancy Keefe, Editor, The Argus, Mount Vernon, N.Y.

George Kentera, Assistant News Editor, Knight-Ridder News Bureau, Washington, D.C.

Fred Kerr, Suburban Editor, The Asbury Park Press, N.J.

Bert Kersen, Publisher, Morning/Evening News, Paterson, N.J.

Sandra King, News Reporter and Newscaster, WNET-TV Channel 13

Edward J. Mack, Editor, The Hunterdon County Democrat, Flemington, N.J.

Malcolm Manber, Reporter, Medical World News, N.Y.

Charles McDowell, Chief Investigative Reporter, Media General News Bureau, Washington, D.C.

John McLaughlin, Columnist and Reporter, Daily News, N.Y.

Clark Mollenhoff, Reporter, Jack Anderson Column; Columnist & Correspondent, The Register, Des Moines, Iowa; Journalism Professor, Washington and Lee University

Donald Mulford, Publisher, Montclair Times, Montclair, N.J.

Tim O'Brien, Supreme Court Reporter, ABC-TV

Aric Press, Associate Editor, Newsweek

Bruce Reynolds, Managing Editor, The Register, New Haven, Conn.

Donald W. Rosselet, Editor, The Forum, Hackettstown, N.J.

Joe Rush, Associate Editor, Item of Millburn & Short Hills, N.J.

Guy Savino, Editor, The Leader Newspapers (Weekly Newspaper Chain), Lyndhurst, N.J.

Morton Silverstein, Producer—Documentaries, NBC-TV News

Vincent Slavin, Suburban Editor, Daily Journal, Elizabeth, N.J.

Ginny Sederis, Statehouse Correspondent and Investigative Reporter, The Herald News, Passaic, N.J.

Andrew Stasiuk, Managing Editor, The Star-Ledger, Newark, N.J.

Damon Stetson, Labor Reporter, The New York Times

Mark Stuart, Writer and Investigative Reporter, The Record, Hackensack, N.J.

Joseph Sullivan, Statehouse (N.J.) Correspondent, The New York Times

Mary Stolberg , Reporter, The Press, Pittsburgh, Pa.

Arthur Swanson, Executive Editor, Recorder Publishing Company, Bernardsville, N.J.

Gerald terHorst, Washington Columnist, Universal News Syndicate, The News, Detroit, Mich.

R. Brierly Thompson, Reporter, Trenton Bureau, The Associated Press

Jana Thompson, Trenton Correspondent, Courier-News, Bridgewater, N.J. and Courier-Post, Camden, N.J.

Garrick Utley, Reporter, NBC-TV

Donald Warshaw, Courthouse Reporter, The Star-Ledger, Newark, N.J.

Av Westin, Vice President, ABC-TV News

Harry Weingast, Editor, The Jewish News, East Orange, N.J.

William Worrall, Publisher, Worrall Newspapers, Orange, N.J.

Randy Young, Magazine Writer, New Jersey Magazine, New York Magazine, etc.

Vincent Zarate, Statehouse Correspondent, The Star-Ledger, Newark, N.J.

DONNA LEE DICKERSON

Fashioning a New Libel Defense: The Advent of Neutral Reportage

Donna Lee Dickerson, Ph.D., Southern Illinois University, is Assistant Professor in the Department of Mass Communications at the University of South Florida (Tampa). She is co-author of *College Student Press Law* and author of soon-to-be published *Florida Press Law.*

Libel law has been developing for the past 700 years in response to a need to protect reputation as well as to a need to protect the press from libel suits. This balancing has resulted in a complex system of damages, rules of evidence, mitigating factors, remedies and defenses. Libel prosecutions can be traced to the 1275 seditious libel statute *Scandalum Magnatum* and to the famous case *de Libellis Famosis* in 1606.[1] However, four centuries of such prosecutions passed before any tangible defenses made their way into the courtroom. Truth slowly gained acceptance by the late 1600s,[2] qualified privilege in the late 1700s[3] and

---

1. 3 Edw. I, c. 34 (1275); Levy, *Freedom of the Press in England* 118 (1952).
2. Case of the Seven Bishops, 12 State Trials, p. 183.
3. *Curry v. Walter,* 170 Eng. Rep. 419 (1796).

fair comment in the early 1800s.[4] Of course, the *New York Times v. Sullivan* defense of actual malice, a spinoff of fair comment, was adopted in 1964.[5]

During the past several years, a new defense has surfaced. The defense of "neutral reportage" makes the reporting of public matters more open and less susceptible to libel suits. Neutral reportage, first adopted in *Edwards v. National Audubon Society,* states that the First Amendment protects the accurate and fair reporting of false charges made by prominent and responsible individuals and groups regardless of the reporter's private views regarding their validity.[6] This new defense does not protect those reporters who espouse or concur in the charges, or who deliberately distort the charges for the sake of personal attack. So far this defense has been recognized by only a handful of federal and state courts.[7]

Neutral reportage is an extension of the traditional defense of qualified privilege which states that the First Amendment protects the fair and accurate reporting of official acts, records and meetings whether the information is true or false.[8] Qualified privilege stretches over the broad spectrum of judicial,[9] legislative[10] and administrative proceedings[11] as well as the acts of public officers empowered to perform public duties.[12] Qualified privilege, like most common law defenses in libel, is administered differently in every state and therefore its limitations are difficult to generalize. The majority of states, however, hold that privilege attaches only to official acts, records and proceedings that are necessary or required for the proper functioning of government.[13]

The theory behind neutral reportage parallels that of qualified privilege in that much social and political debate is indulged in by persons who are not public officers, and by officers who are not performing requisite duties. Nonetheless, these are responsible spokespersons

4. *Carr v. Hood,* 170 Eng. Rep. 983 (1808).
5. 367 U.S. 254 (1964).
6. 556 F.2d 113 (2d Cir. 1977), *cert. den. sub mom. Edwards v. N.Y. Times,* 434 U.S. 1002 (1977).
7. *Krauss v. Champaign News Gazette,* 375 N.E.2d 1362 (Ill. App. 1978); *Orr v. Lynch,* 401 N.Y.S.2d 897 (N.Y. App. 1978); *Henderson v. Van Buren Public School,* 4 Med. L. Rptr. 1741 (1978).
8. *E.g., Barr v. Mateo,* 360 U.S. 564 (1959).
9. *E.g., Cox Broadcasting Co. v. Cohn,* 420 U.S. 469 (1975).
10 *E.g., Coleman v. Newark Ledger,* 149 A.2d 193 (1959).
11. *E.g., Mack, Miller Candle Co. v. Macmillan Co.,* 269 N.Y.S. 33 (1934).
12. *E.g., Coleman v. Newark Ledger,* 149 A.2d 193.
13. A full discussion of the variations in state laws is found in Nelson and Teeter, *Law of Mass Communications,* 131-45 (1979).

and statements from them should be reported by the media with the same vigor and the same immunity as are privileged comments and activities.

This new defense finds its heritage not only in the doctrine of qualified privilege, but also in the descendants of *Sullivan* which stretched the actual malice standard of liability to public libel cases involving public figures. In *Curtis Publishing Co. v. Butts,* Justice John Harlan said that public figures will receive less protection from libel laws because they command sufficient continuing public interest and sufficient access to the media for countering attacks.[14] Thus the Court acknowledged that persons who become public figures either because of their position or their activity command no less media interest than do public officials. This observation would seem to warrant equal protection for the fair and accurate reporting of public figure comments. For, as an Illinois court said, it may not be just the content of a person's comment that is newsworthy, but the fact that the statement was made and whom it was made by.[15]

The first hint that this new defense existed was voiced in *dictum* in *Time, Inc. v. Pape.*[16] *Pape* involved a libel suit by a policeman against *Time* magazine. *Time* printed an article about a Commission of Civil Rights report entitled *Justice.* The report enumerated several alleged instances of police brutality against blacks including one incident involving a New York detective and a black family. In reporting the commission's findings, *Time* failed to state that the incident was only alleged and was not an actual finding of the commision. The detective sued *Time.* The U.S. Supreme Court determined that the omission of the word "alleged" was not evidence of actual malice considering the circumstances of this case, particularly in light of the ambiguities which ran throughout *Justice.*

Justice Potter Stewart's opinion reasoned that the third-hand nature of the story should virtually erase any charges of knowing falsity or reckless disregard. He went on, "... a vast amount of what is published in the daily and periodical press purports to be descriptive of what somebody *said* rather than of what anybody *did.* Indeed, perhaps the largest share of news concerning the doings of government appears in the form of accounts of reports, speeches, press conferences and the like."[17] Despite the fact that *Pape* involved the inaccurate report of an official document, Stewart was pointing out that greater protection should be had when the press publishes the false remarks of another

14. 388 U.S. 130 (1967).
15. *Krauss v. Champaign News Gazette,* 375 N.E.2d 1362.
16. 401 U.S. 279 (1971).
17. *Id.* at 285-86.

‚responsible party, rather than when it actually makes the false statement itself.

The first case to formulate the neutral reporting defense was *Edwards v. National Audubon Society.*[18] The Society's magazine, *American Birds,* carried an editorial accusing scientists who were proponents of the use of DDT of making "false" and "misleading" statements about the effects of DDT on birds. The distortions, said the editorial, were "for the most self-serving of reasons," noting that the scientists, who were all connected with the chemical industry, were "being paid to lie." The scientists had stated that the Audubon Society's Christmas Bird Count was proof that bird life was thriving despite the use of DDT. The truth, said the editorial, was that more birds were counted because there were more birders who were better equipped and more knowledgeable about species identification. A *New York Times* science reporter spotted the editorial and asked an Audubon officer for the names of the scientists. The reporter was given the names of the five scientists, but allegedly was told that while these five were not necessarily paid liars, they had persistently distorted the bird count. The reporter contacted three of the scientists who vehemently denied the charges. The *Times* ran the article, quoting the editorial, naming all five scientists and reporting the denials of the three.

Three of the named scientists sued the *Times* for libel in a U.S. district court in New York. The trial judge ruled the article to be libelous *per se.*[19] The court also found the scientists to be public figures who must establish actual malice. The jury found that although the *Times* reporting was accurate, it had acted recklessly by printing the article after the three scientists had vigorously denied the charges. Such denials, said the court, would leave serious doubts about the truth in the reporter's mind. The jury returned a verdict against the *Times* and awarded $20,000 apiece to two scientists and $21,000 to the third.

The Second Circuit Court of Appeals reversed the judgment, adopting the defense of neutral reportage.[20] Plaintiffs argued that the district court was correct in applying the *St. Amant v. Thompson* interpretation of malice, which says "recklessness may be found where there are obvious reasons to doubt the veracity of the information or the accuracy of the reports."[21] The Court of Appeals countered, " ... when a responsible, prominent organization like the National Audubon Society makes serious charges, against a public figure, the First Admendment protects the accurate and disinterested reporting of those charges,

18. 556 F.2d 113.
19. *Edwards v. National Audubon Society,* 556 F.2d at 118.
20. 556 F.2d 113.
21. 390 U.S. at 732.

regardless of the reporter's private views regarding their validity."[22] The court reasoned that the public interest that swirls around sensitive issues demands that the press be afforded the freedom to report such charges without assuming responsibility for them. A reporter should not be forced to withhold a story until a full-scale investigation is completed.

Edwards sets out several conditions for neutral reporting which must be met: 1) The source must be "responsible and prominent;" 2) The subject of any such third party charges must be a public figure or public official; 3) The report must reflect accurately the charges made and; 4) The reporting must be "fair," "disinterested," "reasonable" and done with "good faith."

While all the reported cases utilizing this new defense have involved public figures or public officials, the sources have not necessarily been "responsible and prominent." One case involves inaccurate reporting of charges and one questions the "fairness" of a magazine article.

Since the defense of neutral reporting does not fit snugly into either the traditional or the constitutional defenses, lower federal and state courts are understandably reluctant to adopt it. The Third Circuit Court of Appeals had an opportunity to use the defense in *Dickey v. CBS,* but refused because it did not adhere strictly enough to the rules for determining actual malice.[23]

In *Dickey,* an incumbent congressman appeared on a television public, affairs program and accused local politician Sam Dickey of accepting payoffs for favors. The 79-year-old Dickey asked the station to cancel the program, saying the charges were false. The station sent a reporter to investigate who reported that there was a "good probability (the congressman's) charges were true." After the program was aired, Dickey sued for libel claiming substantial evidence of actual malice. The trial court held that while the station may have been indifferent to the truth, it did not entertain serious doubts about the facts. The court entered judgment for the station.[24] Plaintiffs appealed and the defendant television station asked the Third Circut to consider the *Pape* and *Edwards* precedents and to adopt the constitutional privilege of neutral reportage. The court rejected this notion, stating that to interpret *Pape* as an argument in favor of neutral reporting was too ambitious. The court said *Pape* was merely pointing out that the accurate reporting of third-party statements was difficult without quoting all of the information. Neutral reporting "is not created merely because an individual newspaper or television or radio station decides that a particular state-

22. 556 F.2d at 120.
23. 441 F. Supp. 1133 (D.C. Pa 1977) *aff'd.,* 583 F.2d 1221 (3d Cir. 1978).
24. 441 F. Supp. 1133.

ment is newsworthy."[25] This notion, continued the court, was dismissed when the U.S. Supreme Court overruled the *Rosenbloom v. Metromedia* "matters of public concern" test in *Gertz v. Robert Welch, Inc.*[26]

A comparison of neutral reporting with the *Rosenbloom* test of general and public concern is exaggerated in view of the strictures placed on the new defense (ie. source, subject, accuracy and fairness). The *Edwards* definition of neutral reporting specifically refers only to statements by responsible and prominent persons about public persons, not to all newsworthy statements. Unlike *Rosenbloom,* it also refers only to accurate and fair reporting of third-party comments and not to information originating with the media.

Krauss v. Champaign News Gazette is typical of the type of case where neutral reportage has been adopted.[27] Dr. Fred Krauss was a psychologist who developed and directed a youth services program for juveniles. The *News Gazette* published a story quoting an assistant state's attorney that drugs were very accessible at the youth home where the program was administered. Krauss claimed that the article insinuated he was at fault because he directed the program.

An Illinois district court used the neutral reportage defense to find for the newspaper. The court said that if a journalist accurately conveys information "under circumstances wherein the mere assertion is, in fact, newsworthy, then he need inquire no further."[28] The court was not asking that the assertions made by the state's attorney be investigated before they were published, but only that the story be a fair and accurate report of what the state's attorney had said.

While *Edwards* involved a prominent and responsible organization, *Krauss* involved an undisputed public official. However, the newspaper was not able to defend itself under the traditional defense of qualified privilege because the interview could not be considered an act necessary to the proper functioning of the state's attorney's duties. By adopting the neutral reporting defense in this case, the Illinois court was erasing that bothersome gray line that has existed in qualified privilege between statements and actions that are necessary to the performance of public duty and those that are merely accepted activities of that office such as news interviews, speeches and press conferences. Of course, privilege would attach only if the statements or activities involved the concerns and duties of the public official.

25. 583 F.2d at 1223.
26. 403 U.S. 29 (1971); 418 U.S. 323 (1974).
27. 375 N.E.2d 1362.
28. *Id.* at 1363.

Henderson v. Van Buren Public School, decided by a federal district court in Michigan, used the neutral reporting defense not only where public officials were the source, but where the statements were held to be opinion rather than facts.[29] The *Ypsilanti Press* had been covering a controversy at a local high school that involved changes in the school's Student Services Center to better deal with drug problems. The reporter accurately quoted various school officials who charged that the plaintiff, a 17-year-old student leader and a peer counselor at the Student Services Center, was "not very intelligent," was "a hatchet man" and was "in the bottom 10 per cent of his class." The quotes also insinuated that the plaintiff was difficult to work with. The district court held that the statements were opinions and neither demonstrably true or false. "In such a case, the mere fact that these statements were made is a newsworthy event with respect to both the author (of the statements) and the subject."[30]

The traditional defense of fair comment, albeit rarely used because of its absorption by *Sullivan,* allows the media to comment upon public officers, works of art and literature, products and anybody who places himself before the public as long as no falsehoods are published and the opinions are expressed fairly.[31] The comment protected under this defense is that which is initiated by the media, rather than merely gathered and reported from a third party. *Henderson* takes this defense of fair comment one step further and applies it to third party opinions published by the media. The only element the court felt it had to concern itself with was whether the statements were quoted accurately and fairly.

If neutral reporting is to be seen as an extension of qualified privilege, or in this case, fair comment, the fairness of the report should not be judged by the actual malice standard because it forces a reporter to make judgments about the truth or falsity of the charges. The determination of whether the reporting was fair should be judged by the traditional standard of common law malice or ill will. The distinction between an unfair comment made with common law malice and one that is made with actual malice is historically clear. Common law malice involves personal ill will and motive to do personal harm to the subject of the charges. This ill will is usually manifested in the omission or addition of material favorable to a person, or it may also be found when the communication is used for purposes other than what is in-

29. 4 Med. L. Rptr. 1741
30. *Id.* at 1744.
31. *E.g., Letter Carriers v. Austin,* 418 U.S. 264 (1974); Restatement of Torts 2d, sec. 566. p. 172 (1977).

tended, which is public information.[32] Actual malice, on the other hand, rarely reaches to personal motivation, but to how an article was prepared and researched. Actual malice is tantamount to a conspiracy which revolves around the handling of news. Evidence accepted by courts to find actual malice centers around the reporting procedures rather than around the relationship between defendant and plaintiff.[33] Unlike common law malice, actual malice is not interested in the attitude of the publisher toward the plaintiff.

In neutral reporting, fairness is the question, not actual malice, since neither knowledge of falsity nor reckless disregard for the truth can be considered. The reporter's sole duty is to report information, true or false, of a public nature that comes from responsible third parties.

In *Henderson,* the reporter tape-recorded the meeting at which the statements were made, transcribed the quotes accurately and gave the defendant a chance to refute the charges.[34] It was, according to the court, a fair and accurate report of the opinions of responsible third party public officials and the newspaper "had an absolute privilege to publish the articles when they did."[35]

In one recent case, *Cianci v. New Times,* the Second Circuit held that neutral reporting did not attach itself where the reporting was neither fair nor neutral — where, in fact, the plaintiff "did not simply report the charges, but espoused or concurred in them."[36] *Cianci* involved an article in *New Times* magazine which accused the Mayor of Providence, R.I. of raping a woman at gunpoint and "paying her off" to avoid a criminal charge. The sources of information for the story were varied, including the alleged rape victim herself, a friend of Cianci's, a policeman and another journalist. *New Times* attempted to raise the defense of neutral reporting, claiming that the information was from knowledgeable third persons. However, the court was unwilling to apply neutral reporting to this case where the magazine went beyond the mere reporting of facts.

The court noted, for example, that the title of the magazine article, "Buddy, We Hardly Knew Ya," implied that the mayor was not a man of character, but in fact a rapist and obstructor of justice. The article, in its own words, concluded that for a "nominal sum of $3,000 Cianci

32. *Cantrell v. Forest City Pub.,* 419 U.S. 245, 251-52 (1974).
33. *Id.*
34. 4 Med. L. Rptr. 1741.
35. *Id.* at 1744; however, see *Medina v. Time, Inc.,* 439 F2d 1129 (1st Cir. 1971) and *Thuma v. Hearst Corp.,* 340 F. Supp. 867 (D.C. Md. 1972) where the courts used the actual malice test to determine the fairness of reported third party opinion and fact.
36. 6 Med L. Rptr. 1625 (2d Cir. 1980).

had managed to buy his way out of a possible felony charge." Also, the "ingenious construction of the article" would lead a reasonable person to believe that the $3,000 settlement was made before the charges were dropped (in fact, settlement was made to offset a contemplated civil suit and made after and independent of the decision to drop criminal charges).

The court also noted that the magazine never spoke to Cianci and never reported Cianci's denial of the accusation at the time of the alleged incident. In sum, the court found the magazine did not report the charges fairly. To be protected by neutral reporting, the defendant must establish that the report was balanced, presenting all sides.

While the fairness of the report is mandatory, the beliefs or doubts of the reporter are not important. The reporter is merely a conduit for the assertions and should not assume the responsibility for determining the truth of charges.[37] *Orr v. Lynch,* a New York Supreme Court case, involved Robert Korth who was shot in the back by a policeman. Following an investigation, the police department ruled that the shooting was justified. Afterwards, Korth was interviewed in the hospital by the defendant radio station. Korth claimed the police were involved in a "coverup." The interview along with the police's conclusions was aired several times during the next three days. The policeman sued the station for libel. The New York court said the victim's claims and allegations were newsworthy and legitimate matters of public concern. It was not the station's duty to prove their truth because the station was clearly serving its information function. "The belief or doubt of the reporter is not important since he is reporting the news event, not assuming responsibility for the veracity of the quoted remarks."[38]

Orr involved a private citizen who might not be considered by some courts to meet the *Edwards* requirement that the source be "responsible" and "prominent."[39] Korth was not prominent, and considering that he was the victim of the policeman, might not be considered by some as "responsible." Perhaps the *Gertz* definition of public figure would suffice better in determining who is a privileged source in neutral reporting.[40] *Gertz* defined a public figure as one who achieves "such pervasive fame or notoriety that he becomes a public figure for all purposes and in all contexts."[41] Also, an individual may become a public figure for a limited range of issues by voluntarily injecting himself or being drawn into a public controversy.[42] With such a defini-

37. *Orr v. Lynch,* 401 N.Y.S.2d 897
38. *Id.* at 902.
39. 556 F.2d at 120.
40. 418 U.S. 323
41. *Id.* at 351
42. *Id.*

Defamation: Libel and Slander 51

tion, Korth would be considered a public figure for the limited issue of the shooting and because he voluntarily gave the interview which initiated the controversy and promoted the continuing public interest.

If a reporter quotes an individual whom he believes is a public figure or is a responsible spokesman on the issue, but the court determines otherwise, the defense of neutral reporting would give way and the case would be decided by the *Sulllivan* actual malice rule. Such a possibility makes it incumbent upon the reporter to weigh the source's position, knowledge and responsibility carefully before assuming that privilege attaches.

According to a holding in the Tenth Circuit, not only does the source have to be a public person, but so also does the subject of the third party remarks. *Dixson v. Newsweek* lends authority to the idea that the media will enjoy no protection when they publish third party defamatory comments concerning private individuals.[43] Although the facts of *Dixson* are not directly to the point of neutral reporting, its conclusions are. *Newsweek* published an article quoting the new president of Frontier Airlines, saying that the plaintiff, a scheduling officer, lied about scheduling planes and was fired for incompetence. The record presented to the jury indicated that the *Newsweek* reporter had quoted the president inaccurately, had used quotes out of context and had misrepresented the facts given him. Although the court distinguished this case from *Edwards,* it noted that even if the reporting had been accurate, the fact that the plaintiff was a private individual would preclude any protection from neutral reporting.

CONCLUSION

Although this new defense of neutral reporting has been accepted by only four courts, its advent is timely. With more citizens becoming involved in important public issues such as economy, energy, education and religion, it is important that the media be able, without fear of libel suits, to interview and quote business leaders, civic leaders, educators and religious leaders in order to give the public a broader perspective on problems and to give all sides of the debate which up to now has been one-sided. It is also important that private citizens who become public only for a limited range of issues or events be heard by the public, thus increasing the public's voice in the press.

The widespread adoption of the neutral reporting defense will be slow, as it will call for an exception to the *Sullivan* requirement of actual malice in cases of third party statements by public figures. It will also call for an extension of the traditional defenses of qualified privilege and fair comment.

43.   562 F.2d 626 (10th Cir. 1977).

F. DENNIS HALE

The Future of Strict
Liability in Libel*

F. Dennis Hale is Associate Professor and
head of the News-Editorial Sequence in
the School of Journalism at Bowling
Green State University in Ohio. He
received his BA from the University of
Puget Sound in Tacoma, Washington, MS
from the University of Oregon, and Ph.D.
from Southern Illinois University at
Carbondale and was recipient of a fellow-
ship from LEAA of the U.S. Justice
Department for his dissertation on newspaper coverage of decisions of the
California Supreme Court.

> We hold that, so long as they do not impose liability without
> fault, the States may define for themselves the appropriate
> standard of liability for a publisher or broadcaster of defama-
> tory falsehood injurious to a private individual.[1]

With that sentence, the U.S. Supreme Court in 1974 dramatically altered the
law of libel. Henceforth, all libel plaintiffs would be required by the
Constitution to prove fault.

Fault traditionally has not been a necessary element of libel. A 1934 handbook on legal rights of reporters provided this summary of libel elements:

---

*Study was made possible by an associateship for the summer of 1981 which was
awarded by the Faculty Research Committee of Bowling Green State University. This
paper was presented to the Law Division, Association for Education in Journalism
and Mass Communication, Ohio University, Athens, Ohio, July 25–28, 1982.

---

1. Gertz v. Robert Welch, Inc., 94 S. Ct. 2997, 418 U.S. 323, 41 L. Ed. 789, 1 MED.
   L. RPTR. at 1642 (1974).

> Three elements must be established in both civil and criminal libel: (1) the words must be defamatory; (2) they must be published; (3) the person or persons libeled must be identified.[2]

Over twenty years later another handbook on reporters' rights made the same point:

> Intent, except as a part of express malice, is immaterial in libel. When the press issues a story, it accepts full responsibility for any error or mistake which results in injury to reputation.[3]

Previously, strict liability had been the rule in libel, particularly in libel *per se* in which the defamatory statements were libelous on their face. *Black's Law Dictionary* defines strict liability as "when neither care nor negligence, neither good nor bad faith, neither knowledge nor ignorance will save defendant."[4]

Some question remains about the permanence of the new federal fault requirement. For one thing, it was propounded in an opinion that commanded only a bare majority. The fifth vote was provided by a justice who conceded, in a brief concurring opinion, that he joined merely to provide a majority.[5] Secondly, some lower courts applying the fault standard have specified that it applies to private persons involved in matters of general or public interest or concern. This public interest test was not a provision of the five-judge *Gertz* majority. But its invocation by lower courts creates the impression that some courts, contrary to Supreme Court doctrine, favor strict liability for defamation concerning private persons involved in matters judged not to be of public interest. If it were to review such a case, the Supreme Court would be writing on a clean slate. All the libel and privacy cases that the Court has decided since it first extended Constitutional protection to libel in 1964[6] have involved matters that clearly were of public interest. For these and other reasons, as well as the changing membership of the Supreme Court, the future of the fault requirement is questionable.

2. FREDRICK S. SIEBERT, THE RIGHTS AND PRIVILEGES OF THE PRESS (New York: D. Appleton-Century, 1934), p. 122.
3. FRANK THAYER, LEGAL CONTROL OF THE PRESS, 4th ed. (Brooklyn: Foundation Press, 1962), p. 275.
4. HENRY CAMPBELL BLACK, BLACK'S LAW DICTIONARY, 4th ed. (St. Paul, 1968), p. 1591.
5. 1 MED. L. RPTR. at 1645.
6. New York Times Co. v. Sullivan, 84 S. Ct. 40, 375 U.S. 803.

I. THE 1971 PLURALITY RULE

Any analysis of the uncertainty concerning the abolishment of strict liability and the establishment of fault must start with an examination of the *Rosenbloom* decision.[7] Plaintiff Rosenbloom was a distributor of nudist magazines who was arrested and then acquitted of obscenity charges. A radio station repeatedly broadcast stories that falsely accused Rosenbloom of distributing obscene materials and being involved in the smut literature racket. In 1971 the Supreme Court reversed a $275,000 libel judgment that favored Rosenbloom. The Court ruled that actual malice should have been required in the case because Rosenbloom, although a private figure, was involved in a matter of public interest (his arrest). The Court significantly expanded the application of the actual malice rule, which previously had been required in libel cases involving public officials and public figures. In justifying this expansion, the Court said that the concept of free public discussion pertains to all issues about which information is needed to enable citizens to cope with the exigencies of the period; and the debate of public issues should be uninhibited, robust and wide-open.[8]

The plurality decision in *Rosenbloom* was written by Justice Brennan and signed by two other Court members, Justice Blackmun and, surprisingly, Chief Justice Burger. Brennan wrote that not every newsworthy development was a matter of public interest. He said that some aspects of the lives of even the most public persons fell outside the area of matters of public interest. In a footnote he observed:

> We are not to be understood as implying that no area of a person's activities falls outside the area of public or general interest. We expressly leave open the question of what constitutional standard of proof, if any, controls the enforcement of state libel laws for defamatory falsehoods published or broadcast by news media about a person's activities not within the area of public or general interest.[9]

Concurring and dissenting opinions signed by five other justices in *Rosenbloom* did not shed much additional light on the abolishment of strict liability or the scope of public interest (Douglas did not participate in the

---

7. Rosenbloom v. Metromedia, Inc., 91 S. Ct. 1811, 403 U.S. 29, 1 MED. L. RPTR. 1597 (1971).
8. 1 MED. L. RPTR. at 1601.
9. *Ibid.* at 1604.

case). Black, concurring, repeated his often–expressed objection to libel because of its use to harrass the press.[10] White, also concurring, wished to define public interest narrowly, limiting it to private individuals affected by official actions.[11] Three justices (Harlan in one dissent[12] and Marshall joined by Stewart in the other dissent[13]) strongly objected to strict liability. The three dissenters also objected to restricting the actual malice rule to matters of public interest because it involved the Court in judging the legitimacy of public interest in particular subjects. Thus *Rosenbloom* reflected fragmented thinking concerning the concepts, public interest and strict liability.

II. COURT RULES AGAIN IN 1974

It was this fragmentation and the existence of a plurality rule in *Rosenbloom* that prompted the Court to re-examine the matter two years later in *Gertz*.[14] A federal jury awarded attorney Elmer Gertz a libel verdict of $50,000 after a magazine falsely accused him of being a communist. Attorney Gertz, like magazine dealer Rosenbloom, was involved in a matter that obviously was of public interest. Gertz was serving as legal counsel to the parents of a youth who was shot and killed by a policeman. The five-judge majority in *Gertz* remanded the case back to the Illinois courts because the jury had been allowed to impose liability without fault and to presume damages without proof of injury.

The five-judge majority (author Powell joined by Justices Stewart, Marshall, Blackmun and Rehnquist) created a broad set of rules to govern libel suits involving private figures. (The majority said it was necessary to create rules of general application rather than engage in case-by-case, *ad hoc* balancing because the latter "approach would lead to unpredictable results and uncertain expectations, and could render our duty to supervise the lower courts unmanageable."[15]) The first provision of the holding was that states were permitted to define for themselves the standard of fault for private libel, so long as they did not permit liability without fault. This gave the states the option of requiring ordinary negligence as a standard, or a higher standard such as gross negligence or actual malice. Second, the possibility that the statement may be defamatory must be apparent to a reasonably prudent editor. This covered defamation of the 'libel *per se* variety'– statements that are defama-

---

10. *Ibid*. at 1608.
11. *Ibid*. at 1609.
12. *Ibid*. at 1611.
13. *Ibid*. at 1616.
14. 1 MED. L. RPTR. at 1633.
15. *Ibid*. at 1641.

tory on their face. Third, punitive damages were prohibited without evidence of actual malice. And fourth, presumed damages were disallowed — compensation in private libel must be supported by competent evidence of injury.

The majority in *Gertz* objected to the *Rosenbloom* plurality because of the difficulty of determining which issues were of public interest. The majority said it doubted the wisdom of committing that task to the conscience of judges.[16]

A major purpose of *Gertz* was to clear up the uncertainty in the law engendered by the fragmented *Rosenbloom* plurality. This purpose was only partially achieved. *Gertz* had six separate opinions (a majority and a concurring opinion and four dissenting opinions) compared to *Rosenbloom's* five. A majority would not have been achieved in *Gertz* had it not been for Justice Blackmun who provided the critical, fifth vote. Blackmun, one of the two signers of the *Rosenbloom* plurality, wrote in his brief *Gertz* concurrence that he joined the new majority to create a clearly defined majority position because a definite ruling was paramount.[17] Blackmun apparently did not object to involving the courts in deciding what matters were of public interest. He wrote that extending the actual malice rule to events of public interest was logical and inevitable. But he said he was willing to withdraw to the less protective position of *Gertz* in the interest of a clearly defined majority position, and because it eliminated the specter of presumed and punitive damages.

Gertz presented the press with a mixed blessing. It weakened press libel protection by reversing the *Rosenbloom* rule that extended the actual malice rule to all matters of public interest. But it strengthened libel protection by abolishing strict liability and requiring fault in all private libel suits. These two points attracted much of the attention from the four dissenters.

Dissenters Burger and White saw the *Gertz* majority as unnecessarily infringing on state libel law. Burger, in a short opinion, said that private libel should be allowed to continue to evolve as it had to that time.[18] White, in a lengthy dissent, accused the majority of scuttling the libel law of the states in a wholesale fashion and emasculating state libel law for the benefit of the news media. He particularly objected to the abolishment of strict liability, saying it totally ignored history and settled First Amendment law. The old doctrine, according to White, posed no realistic threat to the press and its service to the public. White went on to say: "To me, it is quite incredible to suggest that threats of libel suits from private citizens are causing the press to refrain from publishing the truth."[19]

16. *Ibid.*
17. *Ibid.* at 1645.
18. *Ibid.*
19. *Ibid.* at 1659.

Gertz dissenters Douglas and Brennan expressed an opposing view. Brennan, the *Rosenbloom* majority author, favored a continuation of the public interest test. He said the *Gertz* rule would significantly weaken press protection because it would merely require private citizens involved in public controversies to prove negligence by the preponderance of the evidence, leading to self–censorship by the press.[20] He also said that the public interest is necessarily broad. Douglas objected to any libel liability in defamations concerning public affairs, which he defined expansively in a footnote as any matter of sufficient general interest to prompt media coverage.[21] He objected to any fault standard in public affairs matters—ordinary negligence or actual malice. He cited two specific problems. First, jury determinations by either fault standard are virtually unreviewable by higher courts. And second, appellate courts have no way of knowing to what extent the subject matter of the libel influenced a jury to find fault.[22]

III. CHANGING MEMBERSHIP OF COURT

How likely is it that the doctrines adopted by five justices in *Gertz* will survive? To some extent that depends upon the composition of the Court.

Five members of the Supreme Court are over 70 years old. And three of the 70-year-olds (Powell, Marshall and Blackmun) belonged to the *Gertz* majority. A fourth member of the majority, Potter Stewart, retired in 1981. Thus of the five judges who created the *Gertz* doctrine eight years ago, one has retired and three could retire in the near future. (*Gertz* dissenters Burger and Brennan are the other two Court members who are over 70.)

It is difficult to predict how the justices new to the Court since *Gertz*— Justices John Paul Stevens and Sandra O'Connor—would vote on fault and the other *Gertz* requirements.

Stevens' record on libel cases since he joined the Court in December 1975 provides few clues as to how he might vote. He did not participate in *Time, Inc. v. Firestone*,[23] decided about two years after *Gertz*. And in 1979 he voted with 8-1 majorities in two decisions that limited the public figure doctrine[24] (Brennan was the lone dissenter in both cases). Also in 1979, Stevens joined a 6-3 majority in the *Herbert* decision[25] in refusing to protect the editorial

20. *Ibid.* at 1650.
21. *Ibid.* at 1646.
22. *Ibid.* at 1647.
23. 96 S. Ct. 958, 424 U.S. 448, 47 L. Ed. 2d 154 (1976).
24. Hutchinson v. Proxmire, 99 S. Ct. 2675; Wolston v. Reader's Digest Association, Inc., 99 S. Ct. 2675.
25. Herbert v. Lando, 99 S. Ct. 1635.

process from judicial inquiry in actual malice libel cases. It should be noted that in *Herbert* the Court was not as divided as it appeared on the surface. Two of the dissenters, Brennan and Marshall, only dissented in part. Thus Stevens went along with a fairly unified Court in that decision. It also might be noted that Stevens did not write a separate opinion for any of the three libel cases, or for *Cantrell*,[26] a case decided in late 1974 involving actual malice and false light privacy.

Stevens is a fairly strong supporter of free expression and civil liberties. A 1978 analysis found that he had supported free expression on 14 of 15 occasions during his first two terms on the Court. Although Stevens supported parties invoking freedom of expression almost as often as did Brennan and Marshall, he often did so with more qualifications than the other two Court members. During his five years on the 7th Circuit of the U.S. Court of Appeals, Stevens similarly supported free expression. There was not one instance in which he rejected a freedom of expression claim when another Court of Appeals judge favored it.[27]

However, Stevens also has a strong regard for *stare decisis* and precedent; thus he might be unwilling to reverse the holding of the *Gertz* majority. This was demonstrated in the Seventh Circuit *Gertz* decision[28] which Stevens authored. He applied the Brennan plurality from *Rosenbloom* in reversing the jury verdict favoring Gertz, even though he conceded that the magazine article in question was libelous *per se*. This regard for precedent and rather limited involvement in libel cases on the Supreme Court make Stevens an unlikely person to overturn the *Gertz* doctrine. Additionally, as a result of his long involvement with federal courts and federal law, Stevens probably disagrees with the dissenting positions of Burger and White in *Gertz* which viewed the case as an unjustified federal encroachment on state defamation law and state prerogatives.

It is even more difficult to predict how the newest Court member, Sandra O'Connor, would vote on *Gertz*. She has a conservative, Republican background, including holding public office as a Republican, attending a private elementary school and a private university and law school, and being a president of the Junior League. She also has extensive experience with state government, including a short stint as a deputy county attorney, four years

26. Cantrell v. Forest City Publishing Co., 94 S. Ct. 2997, 418 U.S. 323, 41 L. Ed. 2d 1156 (1974).
27. F. Dennis Hale, "A Comparison of Court of Appeals and Supreme Court Decisions of John Paul Stevens on Freedom of Expression Cases," paper, Association for Education in Journalism, Law Division, August 1978, Seattle, Washington.
28. Gertz v. Robert Welch, Inc., 471 F. 2d 808 (1972).

as an assistant state attorney general, five years in a state senate, five years as a state trial judge, and 18 months as an intermediate state appellate judge.[29] In a 1981 law review article she argued strongly that federal judges should avoid interfering with the administration of justice by state judges.[30] As a state legislator and a state judge, O'Connor generally favored press access to government.[31] However, it is one thing to create press privileges as a prerogative of state government; it is quite another thing to create press rights by expanding the federal Constitution. In his *Gertz* dissent, Justice White lamented the federal interference with state libel law. White might find an intellectual ally in O'Connor because of her background in state government.

IV. SUPREME COURT RECORD ON ACTUAL MALICE

In *Gertz*, the majority clearly stated that the fault standard applied to all private libel cases, those involving matters of public interest as well as those not involving such matters. However, the facts of *Gertz* — litigation over a youth killed by a policeman — clearly concerned matters of public interest. And every actual malice case that the Supreme Court has decided has dealt with a matter that quite clearly was of public interest. These decisions include libel and slander and privacy cases, news and advertising cases, and cases both before and after *Gertz*.

Public officials and significant public interest have been present in every actual malice decision of the Supreme Court since *Sullivan*,[32] which involved an advertisement that criticized local police reaction to integration. *Henry*[33] concerned spoken criticism of public officials, and *Pickering*[34] concerned published criticism of public officials. Other actual malice decisions concerned public officials or persons directly influenced by public officials, candidates

29. John Huffman and Denise Trauth, "Assessing the Impact of the Reagan Landslide on the Courts," paper, Speech Association, Mass Communication Division, November 1981, Anaheim, California.
30. Sandra D. O'Connor, *Trends in the Relationship Between the Federal and State Courts from the Perspective of a State Court Judge*, WILLIAM AND MARY LAW REVIEW, 22:801–815 (1981).
31. Lyle Denniston, *Sandra O'Connor to be Tested Early and Often*, QUILL, October, 1981, Pp. 15–18.
32. *Supra* note 6.
33. Henry v. Collins, 85 S. Ct. 298, 380 U.S. 356 (1965).
34. Pickering v. Board of Education, 88 S. Ct. 1731 (1968).

for public office, or matters clearly of public interest.[35] This also was true of the Court's two actual malice decisions in false light privacy. *Cantrell*[36] concerned a story about a man, his wife and four children that was published five months after the husband was killed in a bridge collapse. And *Time, Inc. v. Hill*[37] concerned a news account of the opening of a play which fictionalized a much publicized event in which a family was held hostage by prison escapees. Douglas, concurring in *Time*, favored a rule barring the press from any liability in reporting matters in the public domain:

> The episode around which this book was written had been news of the day for some time. The most that can be said is that the novel, the play, and the magazine article revived the interest. A fictionalized treatment of the event is, in my view, as much in the public domain as would be a water color of the assassination of a public official. It seems irrelevant to talk of any right of privacy in this context. Here a private person is catapulted into the news by events over which he had no control. He and his activities are then in the public domain as fully as the matters at issue in *New York Times Co. v. Sullivan.*[38]

35. Garrison v. State of Louisiana, 85 S. Ct. 209, 379 U.S. 64 (1964) (district attorney's criticism of local judges); Rosenblatt v. Baer, 86 S. Ct. 669, 383 U.S. 75 (1966) (criticism of government ski director); Curtis Publishing Co. v. Butts, 87 S. Ct. 1975, 388 U.S. 130 (1967) (allegation that university athletic director fixed a football game); Associated Press v. Walker, 88 S. Ct. 13, 389 U.S. 889 (1967) (participant in university, anti-integration demonstration); St. Amant v. Thompson, 88 S. Ct. 1323 (1968) (public official accused of criminal conduct by candidate); Greenbelt Cooperative Pub. Assoc. v. Bresler, 90 S. Ct. 1537, 398 U.S. 6 (1970) (land developer seeking zone change from city council); Monitor Patriot Co. v. Roy, 91 S. Ct. 621, 401 U.S. 265 (1971) (fitness for office of political candidate); Time, Inc. v. Pape, 91 S. Ct. 642, 401 U.S. 265 (1971) (government report on police brutality); Ocala Star-Banner Co. v. Damron, 91 S. Ct. 642, 401 U.S. 265 (1971) (public official accused of perjury); Herbert v. Lando, 99 S. Ct. 1635 (1979) (conduct of Vietnam War); Hutchinson v. Proxmire, 99 S. Ct. 2675 (1979) (government research grants); Wolston v. Reader's Digest Assoc., Inc., 99 S. Ct. 2701 (1979) (contempt citation for failure to appear before grand jury); Time, Inc. v. Firestone, 96 S. Ct. 958, 424 U.S. 448, 47 L. Ed. 2d 154 (1976) (controversial divorce trial of wealthy couple).
36. *Supra* note 26.
37. 86 S. Ct. 1911, 384 U.S. 995 (1967).
38. *Ibid*, 1 MED. L. RPTR. at 1801.

V. STATE COMPLIANCE AND CIRCUMVENTION

There is some evidence that the fault requirement, as it has been applied by lower courts, poses only an incidental burden on libel plaintiffs.

For one thing, the standard of evidence has generally been a preponderance of the evidence, not the clear-and-convincing proof that the Supreme Court has required in actual malice cases.

For another thing, the Supreme Court in *Firestone* indicated that it would not be very rigorous in regard to finding fault. Justice Rehnquist, writing for the majority, said that fault could be established by a jury as well as by the trial judge, and that the finding could be made in the first instance by an appellate rather than a trial court.[39]

One purpose of *Gertz* was to eliminate presumptions in libel such as presumed fault and presumed damages. However, in two cases judges appear to have presumed negligence based on the nature of the message. Both involved headlines. In *Sprouse*,[40] the West Virginia Supreme Court of Appeals said that the heart of the case was not the newspaper articles, but the dramatic and misleading headlines which would lead ordinary, reasonable minds to false conclusions. The decision said that actual malice would be presumed because of evidence the newspaper became a participant in a plan to destroy a candidate using grossly exaggerated and patently untrue headline assertions. And in *Forrest*,[41] a Louisiana Court of Appeals upheld a libel judgment resulting from the headline, "Bid Specs Reported 'Rigged,' " over an accurate and nonlibelous newspaper story. The judge concluded that the headline by an unidentified copyeditor manifested a poor and erroneous choice of words and thus constituted fault.

Most state and federal courts that have applied *Gertz* have recognized that it rejected the public interest test. For example, in *Jacron*,[42] a unanimous Maryland Court of Appeals stated that it was a misreading of *Gertz* to limit it to private libel cases involving matters of public interest. The alleged slander involved comments made about an employee by one employer to another employer. The court concluded that the negligence standard applied to both slander and libel, and media and nonmedia defendants. It supported its conclusion by citing the Blackmun concurring opinion and the White dissent from *Gertz*. This is one of the few instances in which a court since *Gertz* has reviewed a defamation case involving a purely private matter.

---

39. *Supra* note 35; 1 MED. L. RPTR. at 1670.
40. Sprouse v. Clay Communication, Inc., 211 S. E. 2d 674, 1 MED. L. RPTR. 1695 (1975).
41. Forrest v. Lynch, 347 So. 2d 1255, 3 MED. L. RPTR. 1187 (1977).
42. Jacron Sales Co., Inc. v. Sindorf, 350 A. 2d 688 (1976).

A handful of courts, however, have specifically included public interest in summarizing *Gertz*. Included are the Virginia Supreme Court in 1976,[43] the Washington Supreme Court in 1976,[44] a U.S. District Court in 1977,[45] and the appellate division of the New York trial court in 1977.[46] An example is *Lake Havasu*:[47]

> In *Gertz, supra*, the Supreme Court said that, within certain guidelines, the states could decide for themselves the appropriate standard of liability for a publisher of defamatory falsehoods which involved a matter of public concern as long as they did not impose the common law rule of liability without fault.

Such a characterization of *Gertz* may result from a misreading of the case in conjunction with *Rosenbloom*, since the facts of both concerned matters of obvious public interest. Or, judges may be leaving the door ajar in anticipation of future Supreme Court changes because of the unsettled nature of the *Gertz* five-judge majority.

VI. DEFINING THE PUBLIC INTEREST

Judges who include a public interest test with *Gertz* may be anticipating an evolution in libel law to a doctrine that combines *Rosenbloom* and *Gertz*. Such change could take any of a number of forms. It could extend the actual malice rule to matters of significant public interest, leaving the states free to choose standards of fault or strict liability for private libel cases involving nonpublic matters. Or, a fault standard could be retained for private libel cases involving matters of public interest, and the states would decide between fault or strict liability for nonpublic concerns. With either change, the courts become involved in defining public interest.

In resurrecting a public interest test for private libel, the Court would have a range of definitions and a variety of legal sources from which to choose. Douglas offers a very broad definition. He said that the First Amendment provided an unconditional right to say what you please about public affairs.

---

43. Newspaper Publishing Corp. v. Burke, 224 S. E. 2d 132 (1976).
44. Taskett v. King Broadcasting Co., 1 MED. L. RPTR. 1716 (1976).
45. Lake Havasu Estates, Inc. v. Reader's Digest Assoc., Inc., 3 MED. L. RPTR. 1433 (1977).
46. Wehringer v. Newman, 3 MED. L. RPTR. 1708 (1977). *See also*, Velella v. Benedetto, 57 N.Y. 2d 788.
47. *Supra* note 45 at 1435.

He defined public affairs as politics, science, economics, business, art, literature, and all matters of sufficient general interest to prompt media coverage.[48]
White favored a narrower definition that resembled the concept of political
speech. He said he was not prepared to extend actual malice protection to
"such matters as the health and environmental hazards of widely used manu-
factured products, the mental and emotional stability of executives of business
establishments, and the racial and religious prejudices of many groups and
individuals," all topics of public concern.[49] Instead, he favored moving ahead
slowly and extending the protection to reports of the official actions of public
servants with no requirement that the reputation or the privacy of an individual
involved in or affected by the official action be spared from public view.[50]

Libel cases decided during the three years between *Rosenbloom* and *Gertz*
provide considerable guidance in defining public interest. White, in his *Gertz*
dissent, indicated that 17 states and several federal appeals courts had defined
public interest in 30 decisions since *Rosenbloom*.[51] The fact that in only one-
tenth of those instances was a matter deemed not of public interest indicates
that both state and federal courts were defining the concept quite expansively:
the Virginia Supreme Court determined that a private individual's failure to
join a labor union was not of public interest;[52] the Florida Supreme Court
ruled that the divorce of industrial heiress Mary Alice Firestone was not of
public interest because it was not related to the health, well-being and general
comfort of the public as a whole;[53] and the Pennsylvania Supreme Court ruled
that an overcharge by a one-man snow-plow operation "was by no stretch of
imagination a matter of public concern."[54]

In libel cases resulting from mistaken identification, most judges have
applied the public interest test to the event in the news rather than the libel
plaintiff. In five cases the press was covering a matter of public interest, but
the libel plaintiff was a private person uninvolved in the matter of public
interest. In a Massachusetts case involving false identification of a bookmaker,[55] and a District of Columbia case involving mistaken identification
of a disbarred attorney,[56] the post-*Rosenbloom* courts required evidence of
actual malice because of the involvement of matters of public interest. The

---

48. *Supra* note 1; 1 MED. L. RPTR. at 1646.
49. *Supra* note 7; 1 MED. L. RPTR. at 1608.
50. *Ibid.* at 1609.
51. *Supra* note 1; 1 MED. L. RPTR. at 1654.
52. Old Dominion Branch No. 496 v. Austin, 192 S. E. 2d 737, 213 Va. 377 (1972).
53. Firestone v. Time, Inc., 271 S. 2d 745 (1972).
54. Matus v. Triangle Publications, Inc., 286 A. 2d 357 (1971).
55. Dwyer v. Globe Newspapers, 6 MED. L. RPTR. 2177 (1980).
56. Ryder v. Time, Inc., 3 MED. L. RPTR. 1170 (1977).

Puerto Rico Supreme Court ruled similarly in a mistaken identification case concerning a person arrested for drug violations.[57] And a Louisiana Court of Appeals ruled similarly in a case concerning a man arrested as a drug distributor.[58] The one contrary decision is a 1972 ruling by the Louisiana Supreme Court involving the false identification of a person as a criminal defendant on a peeping Tom charge. Applying *Rosenbloom*, the court said there was no factual connection between the event of public interest and the falsely identified individual: "The keystone of the privilege is actual involvement, not the unsupported association of a name and an event."[59]

Various states have used the concept of public interest to determine which communications are privileged and which deserve the protection of actual malice or gross negligence. One of the first state courts to act in this fashion was the Alaska court, which extended the actual malice rule to matters of public interest in 1966.[60] In response to *Rosenbloom*, the Colorado Supreme Court and the Indiana Court of Appeals adopted similar rules.[61] In Michigan, state and federal courts have extended the qualified privilege defense to matters of public concern.[62] A Florida trial court in 1980 applied the actual malice rule to matters of legitimate public interest.[63] And since 1975, courts in New York have applied a gross negligence standard to stories "reasonably related to matters warranting public exposition."[64]

For additional guidance on the public interest test, the Supreme Court could turn to its own and other federal court decisions on false light privacy, or copyright and commercial speech, both of which include such a test. In *Rosemont*,[65] the U.S. Circuit Court of Appeals prevented the copyright laws from being used to interfere with the public's right to be informed about a matter of general public interest, specifically Howard Hughes. Some 26 years earlier in a classic decision on the privacy tort of disclosure, the same federal court used a public interest test to prevent a former child prodigy, William J. Sidis, from suing the *New Yorker* for its profile about him.[66] More recently, the Supreme Court, in a series of decisions on commercial speech, has invoked

---

57. Torres-Silva v. El Mundo, Inc., 3 MED. L. RPTR. 1508 (1977).
58. Wilson v. Capital City Press, 315 S. 2d 393 (1975).
59. Francis v. Lake Charles American Press, 262 La. 875, 265 S. 2d 206 (1972).
60. Pearson v. Fairbanks Publishing Co., 413 P. 2d 711 (1966).
61. Walker v. Colorado Springs Sun, Inc., 538 P. 2d 450 (1975).
62. Schultz v. Reader's Digest Assoc., Inc., 4 MED. L. RPTR. 2356 (1979); Peisner v. Detroit Free Press, Inc., 4 MED. L. RPTR. 1062 (1978).
63. Sobel v. Miami Daily News, Inc., 5 MED. L. RPTR. 2462 (1980).
64. Chapadeau v. Utica Observer-Dispatch, Inc., 341 N. E. 2d 569, 1 MED. L. RPTR. 1693 (1975).
65. Rosemont Enterprises, Inc. v. Random House, Inc., 366 F. 2d 303 (1966).
66. Sidis v. F–R Publishing Corp., 1 MED. L. RPTR. 1775 (1940).

First Amendment protection for information of public interest in decisions invalidating a ban on advertisements of prescription drug prices,[67] a ban on the use of corporate spending to influence ballot issues,[68] and a ban on factual ads for legal abortion services.[69]

VII. CONCLUSIONS

The only thing certain about the fault requirement is that it has an uncertain future. This is true even if fault continues to receive support from a majority of Court members. Fault may not provide the press with significantly greater protection than strict liability. For one thing, the Court has not imposed rigorous standards. The lesser, civil standard of evidence is required – preponderance of evidence rather than beyond a reasonable doubt – and fault may be established by a judge or jury or even an appellate court. For another thing, because the existence of fault is a finding of fact, it is difficult for appellate courts to scrutinize it. As Douglas pointed out, it is impossible to determine whether a jury has found fault based upon the actions of the defendant or because of the offensive nature of the published defamation.

It is questionable whether fault will be endorsed by a strong majority of the current Supreme Court. The doctrine barely received majority support when it was created seven years ago. One of the five supporters, as he explained in a concurrence, signed primarily to create a majority rule. Of the original supporters, one has retired and three others are over 70 years old. It is difficult to predict how the two justices new to the Court since *Gertz* might vote on the matter. One thing that would make it easier for the Court to reverse itself is that fault, and some other provisions of the *Gertz* holding, did not emerge from the fact situation in that case. If the Court were to review a case involving a matter clearly outside the public interest, it would be writing on a clean slate.

The current Supreme Court has no free speech absolutists such as Douglas who advocate press immunity to law suits for reports of public affairs or any matters commanding public attention. Current members believe that defamation laws protect values that are worthy of some protection, and they are attempting to balance the right to a reputation with the right to press freedom.

Gertz resulted because some justices felt that the Court went too far in *Rosenbloom* when it extended the actual malice rule to all matters of public interest. A broad definition of public interest would have largely immunized the press to libel suits.

67. Virginia State Board of Pharmacy v. Virginia Citizens Consumer Council, Inc., 425 U.S. 748, 1 MED. L. RPTR. 1930 (1976).
68. First National Bank of Boston v. Bellotti, 3 MED. L. RPTR. 2105 (1978).
69. Bigelow v. Virginia, 421 U.S. 809, 1 MED. L. RPTR. 1919 (1975).

But *Gertz* does not strike the proper balance either. At one end of the fault spectrum, people like Gertz and Rosenbloom who are directly involved in government actions merely have to prove negligence – not actual malice – in law suits stemming from press coverage of government. At the other end of the spectrum, some of the truly little people in society who mistakenly are accused of being a peeping Tom, drug dealer or bookmaker are powerless to sue for libel unless they can prove negligence.

A proper balance might be achieved by combining *Rosenbloom* and *Gertz* with some other elements to create comprehensive, constitutional libel protection.

First, actual malice should be extended beyond public officials and public figures to government affairs, adopting at a minimum White's concept of individuals directly affected by the actions of government. Second, fault should constitutionally be required in libels concerning matters of public interest. And third, the states should be free to choose between fault and strict liability for libels involving private individuals in matters judged not of significant public interest. Lastly, expanding *Gertz*, constitutional limits on damages should be strengthened. Punitive or exemplary damages should be made unconstitutional for any defamation, regardless of the existence of actual malice. And in all libel, compensation should be supported by competent evidence of injury. This would permit special damages and reasonable, general damages.

Four members of the *Gertz* majority strenuously objected to the public interest test, saying they doubted the wisdom of committing such a determination to the conscience of judges. One has to question this rationale. State and federal judges had little difficulty developing a definition of public interest during the three years between *Rosenbloom* and *Gertz*. The Supreme Court and other courts have utilized public interest in other First Amendment areas such as privacy, commercial speech and copyright. Public interest should not pose any greater definitional problem that such concepts as actual malice, public figure or fault. In *Gertz*, the Court federalized all libel law; it is only a matter of time before it is drawn into setting constitutional limits – and definitions – for traditional libel elements of identification, publication, defamation and truth.

ANTHONY GREEN

Protecting Confidential Sources in Libel Litigation

Anthony Green, recently graduated from
the Villanova University School of Law,
is now clerk for Pennsylvania Supreme
Court Justice James T. McDermott; in
September 1984 he will join the firm of
Mesirov, Gelman, Jaffe, Cramer & Jamieson
as an associate. Prior to attending law
school, Mr. Green was an award-winning
investigative reporter and an associate
editor for *Philadelphia Magazine*. He has
written for numerous other publications.

I. INTRODUCTION

Every profession has its stereotype. For journalists, the stereotype catches him sitting at a seedy, paper-strewn desk, smoking a cigarette, drinking a cup of coffee. His ear is attached to a telephone. For the reporter to report and write, he must first gather information for his story. He lacks the subpoena power available to a government investigator. He cannot bust down doors, armed with a search warrant.[1] Many records are inaccessible to him. In many instances, the reporter has only one tool at his disposal: people he can talk to, his "sources." Sources are to a reporter what a mouth is to a litigator, what a pair of hands is to an electrician or a dentist or a surgeon, what a yellow automobile is to a taxi driver. Indeed, as Justice Douglas said,

---

1. *See Newsman's Privilege Act of 1971: Hearings*, 92d Cong. 2d Sess. 181 (1972) [hereafter cited as *Hearings*], where Senator Alan Cranston, a one-time reporter, quoted a *Boston Globe* reporter: "Reporters, unlike law enforcement agencies, are not able to subpoena public records, which makes the job of exposing public corruption and malfeasance infinitely more difficult. Confidential sources are the most important tool in a reporter's workshop. To jeopardize this advantage is to handcuff the news media in one of its most important functions."

"A reporter is no better than his source of information."[2] Often, a source will want and require confidentiality. A member of an organized crime family, for example, will desire anonymity to protect his life and/or to protect himself from prosecution. An inside source at a business will desire confidentiality to protect his job.

Discovering sources is not easy; protecting them from exposure if they asked for anonymity is equally difficult, ever since the majority of the Supreme Court chose to disagree with Justice Douglas in *Branzburg v. Hayes*.[3]

Protecting a source's anonymity causes considerable tension in a newsroom. The preliminaries of extracting information from a source can be similar to those involved in negotiating a contract, with a potential source insisting upon a commitment as to how far the reporter and his employers will go to protect his confidentiality. Because the law on the subject is in a state of flux and the risk of an adverse libel judgment is ever present, the reporter does not really know how far he can go. If hit with a libel suit, to what lengths can and will the media outlet go to protect the confidentiality of a source? The question is compelling for the reporter, for the lawyer representing the reporter, and for the reporter's employers.

This article will seek to explore the question of what a reporter, his employer, and their counsel can do to protect the confidentiality of a source in the face of a libel action brought against them within the confines of the First Amendment and statutory protection, the so-called "shield laws."

II. ESTABLISHING A BALANCE OF RIGHTS

The clash of rights is clear-cut; establishing a balance among them is less straightforward. On the one hand, the reporter depends on the First Amendment, in which is specifically set out a right of free press. So far, though, the Supreme Court has not construed this to mean that the press has a special right beyond that of the general public to gain information.[4] Also, the public has a right to know what the press has to report.[5]

On the other hand, a litigant has a right, albeit not a federal constitutional one, to go into court and redress a wrong. In a libel suit, a plaintiff's inability

2. Branzburg v. Hayes, 408 U.S. 665, 722 (1972) (Douglas, J., dissenting).
3. *Id.*
4. *E.g.*, Pell v. Procunier, 417 U.S. 817 (1974); Saxbe v. Washington Post Co., 417 U.S. 843 (1974); Houchins v. KQED, 438 U.S. 1 (1978). *But see* Richmond Newspapers, Inc. v. Virginia, 448 U.S. 555 (1980), upholding the media's right to attend and cover criminal trials. Chief Justice Burger emphasized that when members of the press sought information, they were acting as "surrogates" for the public. 448 U.S. at 572.
5. *E.g.*, Virginia State Board of Pharmacy v. Virginia Citizens Consumer Council, Inc. 425 U.S. 748 (1976).

to get at a reporter's sources can mean the difference between winning and losing. While the libel suit can plead the old rule that a court combatant has a "right to every man's evidence,"[6] this right might not extend so far when it meets the constitutional barrier.

The predicament is especially evident when the plaintiff happens to be a public figure. A public figure in a libel action has a higher burden of proof; he has to show that a reporter was acting with malice or in reckless disregard of the truth.[7] Naturally, one way to show that a reporter was acting recklessly would be to scrutinize the sources of information he drew upon to write or report the allegedly defamatory article. How many sources did he have? Were they credible? Did the source know the divulged information first-hand? If the public figure/plaintiff cannot gain in discovery the answers to such clearly relevant questions, his libel suit may fail. *New York Times v. Sullivan* established that some plaintiffs will not be able to meet their burden of proof; the vitality of the First Amendment is so important, however, that the libel plaintiff's failure to make a case is one of the costs of fortifying all-important First Amendment protection.

A. Constitutionally Based Qualified Protection for Sources

1. *Libel Litigation*

Libel litigation is unique in this area and distinguishable from other civil litigation and criminal cases. The question of protecting sources in the scope of criminal cases was largely resolved in *Branzburg v. Hayes*.[8] *Branzburg* brought before the Court a trio of cases in which reporters had been subpoenaed by grand juries and asked to disclose their sources. They all refused, resting on an implicit First Amendment right to gather the news without interference. The Court put the issue very simply: Do reporters have an obligation "to respond to grand jury subpoenas as other citizens do and to answer questions relevant to an investigation into the commission of crime"?[9] The answer to that very limited question was generally yes, and the Court invited Congress to create a statutory privilege.[10]

In a concurring opinion, Justice Powell was careful to comment on the "limited nature of the holding."[11] Powell, who disagreed with Justice

---

6. 8 J. WIGMORE, EVIDENCE § 2192 (McNaughton rev. 1961); *see also* Winegard v. Oxberger, 258 N.W.2d 847, 851 (Iowa 1977), *cert. denied* 436 U.S. 905 (1977).
7. New York Times v. Sullivan, 376 U.S. 254 (1964); Gertz v. Welch, 418 U.S. 323 (1974).
8. Branzburg v. Hayes, *supra* note 2.
9. *Id.* at 682.
10. *Hearings, supra* note 1.
11. Branzburg v. Hayes, *supra* note 2, at 709.

Douglas's dissent, said that the holding would not "annex" the press as a new "investigative arm of the government." Powell promised that a reporter would have recourse to thwart an unreasonable subpoena and that each case should be decided on the facts, "striking the proper balance between freedom of the press and the obligation of all citizens to give relevant testimony with respect to criminal conduct."[12]

The Court in *Branzburg* glossed over the assertions that sources might dry up and that a reporter's zeal to get out a story might be chilled. In the debate over legislation to erect a statutory privilege, an attorney cited the example of a journalist who refused to report an aspect of the Watergate break-in story for fear of being *"Branzburg-*ed" before a grand jury or one of the congressional investigative committees.[13]

A more recent, highly publicized case involved a *New York Times* reporter who was subpoenaed during the murder trial of one of his story subjects.[14] Neither the First Amendment nor the New Jersey shield law[15] could protect the confidentiality of his sources, and he spent time in prison for contempt. There, notwithstanding New Jersey's very strong shield law, disclosure was mandated because the privilege was qualified by the criminal defendant's constitutional right to compel the attendance of witnesses and the production of evidence in his favor.[16]

Still, *Branzburg* does give a qualified, "conditional," privilege to reporters, with the state having to show that (1) a crime has truly been committed, (2) the reporter possesses relevant information, (3) the information is not available through other sources, and (4) there is a compelling need for the information.

Two other recent cases reveal the Court's reluctance to apply the First Amendment to protect the newsgathering process. In *Herbert v. Lando*,[17] it was held that there was no constitutional barrier limiting a libel plaintiff from delving into the "editorial processes" leading up to the publication of a purportedly defamatory television program. The Court emphasized the fact that the suggested privilege would increase the already heavy burden on public figure libel plaintiffs.

12. *Id.* at 710.
13. *See Hearings, supra* note 1, at 226. Testimony of Attorney Victor S. Navasky. *Also see* statement of Peter Bridge, at 220. Bridge was a New Jersey reporter jailed for defying a contempt order. *In re Bridge*, 120 N.J. Super. 460, 295 A.2d 3 (1972) *cert. denied* 410 U.S. 991 (1973).
      An empirical study on the use of confidential sources by reporters showed that most journalists rely on confidential sources to some extent. BLASI, PRESS SUBPOENAS: AN EMPIRICAL AND LEGAL ANALYSIS (1971).
14. *In re Farber*, 78 N.J. 259, 394 A.2d 330 (1978), *stay denied* 439 U.S. 1301, 1304, 1317, 1331 (1978).
15. N.J. STAT. ANN. § 2A:84A–21 (West 1977).
16. U.S. CONST., amend. IV.
17. 441 U.S. 153 (1979).

As respondents would have it, the defendant's reckless disregard of the truth, a critical element, could not be shown by direct evidence through inquiry into the thoughts, opinions, and conclusions of the publisher....[18]

Furthermore, the Court erected a presumption against privileges: "Evidentiary privileges in litigation are not favored, and even those rooted in the Constitution must give way in proper circumstances."[19]

While *Herbert* clearly illustrates the present posture of the Court with regard to press privileges in the libel litigation sphere, it should not be read to answer the question as to protection for confidential sources. Justice White premised the holding on the assumption that discovery of editorial judgments would not stop the flow of information.[20] A stronger case could be made to suggest that exposure of confidential sources would impede the free flow of information.

In *Zurcher v. Stanford Daily*,[21] it was held that the press could not block a newsroom search warrant by asserting the First Amendment. This case also was fought in the realm of a criminal investigation.

In a particular set of cases, reporters' implicit rights under the First Amendment clash with a court's interest in freely managing the judicial system; in these cases, the court wants to locate an individual who has leaked a story to the press. During the Charles Manson trial in California, a lawyer broke an order dealing with pre-trial publicity; the resulting story, based on material leaked to a newspaper reporter, focused on grisly details of some Manson family threats to skin Frank Sinatra alive. The court charged the reporter with contempt when he refused to disclose the name of his source, and the order was affirmed on appeal.[22]

---

18. *Id*. at 170.
19. *Id*. at 175, *citing* U.S. v. Nixon, 418 U.S. 683 (1974).
20. 441 U.S. at 171.
21. 436 U.S. 547 (1978). *See also In re Roche*, 448 U.S. 1312 (1980) where Justice Brennan granted a stay of enforcement of a civil contempt order against a reporter who refused to divulge sources to a Massachusetts judicial conduct commission. The reporter's story inspired the inquiry into a Massachusetts judge. Brennan insisted that *Branzburg* created some "threshold" First Amendment protection for a reporter and, "Assuming that there is at least a limited First Amendment right to resist intrusion into newsgatherers' confidences, this case presents an apt occasion for its invocation." Brennan considered it important that the information could be gained by other means, "albeit somewhat roundabout." 448 U.S. at 1315–16.
22. Farr v. Sup. Ct. of L.A., 22 Cal. App. 3d 60, 99 Cal. Rptr. 342 (1971) *cert. denied* 409 U.S. 1011 (1972). *See also* U.S. v. Criden, 633 F.2d 346 (3d Cir. 1980), *cert. denied* 449 U.S. 1113 (1980) (where it was held that a Philadelphia *Inquirer* reporter could be held for contempt for failing to affirm or deny that she had a conversation with a particular source in one of the Abscam cases).

2. *Non-Libel Civil Cases*

The plaintiff in a civil action has no analogous federal constitutional right to gain another's evidence. Nevertheless, there is a distinction between a civil action (where the reporter is a third party with relevant information) and a libel action (where the reporter is a defendant). In the former type of action, the reporter has no direct stake in the outcome of the litigation, and his only interest is in protecting his sources, and, more broadly, the First Amendment. In libel cases, on the other hand, the defendant has an interest apart from carrying the gauntlet for the First Amendment; he wants to win the case and can benefit in his defense by thwarting the plaintiff's discovery efforts to get at his sources. The scale, then might be weighed more favorably for the reporter who is a third party in a civil case.[23]

Where the reporter is the plaintiff in a civil action, even the qualified privilege will not hold. The newsman need not disclose his sources, but he also need not seek the aid of the courts in redressing a wrong.[24]

B. The Pre-*Branzburg* Cases: Balancing of Interests

Prior to *Branzburg*, when shield laws were not as prevalent as they are today, the courts were taking a haphazard approach to the protection of sources in libel litigation. Probably the most noteworthy case involved a defamation action brought by the late Judy Garland against CBS and a gossip columnist.[25] The Court, under then-Judge Potter Stewart,[26] decided that there was no privilege implied from the First Amendment, nor from a public policy concern that news not be restricted or chilled. The freedom of the press "must give place under the Constitution to a paramount public interest in the fair administration of justice."[27]

While *Garland* was a loser for the press, the Court nevertheless suggested

---

23. *See* Zerilli v. Smith, 656 F.2d 705, 714 (D.C. Cir. 1981) (where the court said that in a libel case, "the equities weigh somewhat more heavily in favor of disclosure").

    The courts, in civil cases, have been especially certain to protect the interests of the press when it is suspected that a litigant is attempting to harass the media through discovery. *See* Democratic National Committee v. McCord, 356 F. Supp. 1394 (D.D.C. 1973) (where the defendants in one of the Watergate break-in civil cases were indulging in a "fishing expedition" to get at a reporter's sources).

24. *See* Anderson v. Nixon, 444 F. Supp. 1195 (D.D.C. 1978) (where columnist Jack Anderson brought an action against the former president and others to complain about a conspiracy to harass him); Campus Communications, Inc. v. Freedman, 374 So. 2d 1169 (Fla. Dist. Ct. App. 1979).

25. Garland v. Torre, 259 F.2d 545 (2d Cir. 1958) *cert. denied* 358 U.S. 910 (1958).

26. Judge Potter Stewart dissented in *Branzburg*.

27. Garland v. Torre, *supra* note 25, 259 F.2d at 549.

a multiprong test (which was later expanded by subsequent cases) that a trial court should invoke before it forces a reporter to breach confidentiality.[28] The information must be highly relevant, going to the "heart of the matter."[29] The plaintiff must have a viable cause of action, and not one that "is patently frivolous."[30] The information sought must not be available through other sources, and the plaintiff must have exhausted other means of gaining the information before attempting to gain the information from the reporter.[31] Also, the defending party might be required to show that there was in fact confidentiality and a compelling need to preserve confidentiality.[32] This could be important; a reporter may not just presume a desire for confidentiality based on the circumstances—danger to life, fear of dismissal, fear of prosecution, and the like—or on a past history of a confidential relationship.[33]

The *Garland* type of balancing can well fit within the liberal discovery rules envisioned in the Federal Rules of Civil Procedure, which provide that a court may use its discretion to curb discovery if it would cause undue "annoyance, embarrassment, oppression, or undue burden" or when "it is unreasonable and oppressive."[34] The rule should be applied with "heightened sensitivity to any First Amendment implication. . . ."[35] *Garland* was embraced by Justice Marshall's dissent in *Branzburg*.[36] The *Garland* test, which set up a qualified privilege, has endured in libel cases[37] and in civil cases where

---

28. *Id.* at 550–51.
29. *Id.* at 545, 550.
30. Senear v. Daily Journal American, 27 Wash. App. 454, 618 P.2d 536, *rev.* 97 Wash. 2d 148, 641 P.2d 1180 (1982); Bruno & Stillman v. Globe Newspapers Co. 633 Г.2d 583, 597 (1st Cir. 1980).
31. *E.g.*, Greenleigh v. New York Post, 434 N.Y.S.2d 38, 79 A.D.2d 685 (1980); Mize v. McGraw Hill, 86 F.R.D. 1 (1979). The Texas court adhered to its decision to deny the plaintiff discovery on rehearing following the *Herbert* decision. 82 F.R.D. 475 (1980).
32. Bruno & Stillman v. Globe Newspapers Co., *supra* note 30 at 597.
33. *See In re Dack*, 421 N.Y.S.2d 775, 101 N.Y. Misc. 2d 490 (1979); *contra*, Loadholtz v. Fields, 389 F. Supp. 1299 (M.D. Fla. 1975).
34. FED. R. CIV. P. 26 (1970 as amended).
35. Bruno & Stillman v. Globe Newspapers Co., *supra* note 30 at 596.
36. 408 U.S. at 730.
37. *E.g.*, Cervantes v. Time, Inc., 464 F.2d 986, 992 (8th Cir. 1972) *cert. denied* 409 U.S. 1125 (1972); Carey v. Hume, 492 F.2d 631 (D.C. Cir. 1974), *cert. dismissed*, 417 U.S. 938 (1974); Winegard v. Oxberger, *supra* note 6, 258 N.W.2d at 852–53; Bruno & Stillman v. Globe Newspapers Co., *supra* note 30. The newsworthy libel case brought by Mobil Oil president William Tavoulareas against the *Washington Post* recently litigated the issue post-*Herbert*. In denying discovery to the plaintiffs, the court used aspects of the *Garland* test. Tavoulareas v. Piro, 93 F.R.D. 11 (D.D.C. 1981). Later, that holding was affirmed and expanded to cover travel records, telephone bills, and expense vouchers that could lead to the disclosure of confidential sources. 93 F.R.D. 35, 38–39 (D.D.C. 1981). But *Herbert* required disclosure of internal memoranda and the like under the editorial processes doctrine.

reporters are third parties carrying information relevant to the proceeding.[38]

While many courts perform the balancing act suggested by *Garland*, the results are mixed. Even the facts of *Garland* raise questions. The plaintiff was able to narrow the identity of the source to two CBS executives. The Court held that disclosure was required of the reporter, even though the two likely suspects could have been subpoenaed rather than the reporter. Thus, the Court placed little weight on the prong of the test requiring the plaintiff to use reasonable means to gain the information without intruding on the reporter's qualified confidentiality privilege.[39]

At least two courts, though, took *Branzburg* one step further, refusing to protect any confidentiality, and refusing to place any weight on Justice Powell's concurrence.[40]

C. Shield Laws: Statutory Protection for Confidentiality

While Congress failed to accept the *Branzburg* Court's invitation to create by statute a newsman's privilege, many states[41] have done so, and states that already had such shield laws were inspired to strengthen them. The media presumably have been persuasive lobbyists.[42]

The state shield laws take many forms. There are distinctions in defining

38. *E.g.*, Riley v. City of Chester, 612 F.2d 708, 716–17 (3d Cir. 1979); Silkwood v. Kerr-McGee Corp., 563 F.2d 433, 436–38 (10th Cir. 1977); Zerilli v. Smith, 656 F.2d 705, 712–13 (D.C. Cir. 1981); Baker v. F & F Investments, 470 F.2d 778, 783–84 (2d Cir. 1972) *cert. denied*, 411 U.S. 966 (1972); Democratic National Committee v. McCord, *supra* note 23.
39. Similarly, in Carey v. Hume, *supra* note 37, at 638–39, the plaintiff did not have to depose all of the members of the United Mine Workers to find a reporter's source; the court ordered the reporter to breach confidentiality.
40. Caldero v. Tribune Publishing Co., 98 Idaho 288, 562 P.2d 791 (1977) *cert. denied*, 434 U.S. 930 (1977); Dow Jones & Co. v. Superior Court, 364 Mass. 317, 303 N.E.2d 847 (1973).
41. ALA. CODE § 12–21–142 (1975); ALASKA STAT. § 09.25. 150.220 (1973); ARIZ. REV. STAT. 12–2237 (West Supp. 1957–77); ARK. STAT. ANN. § 43–917 (1977); CAL. EVID. CODE § 1070 (Deering Supp. 1978); DEL. CODE tit. 10, § 4320–26 (1974); ILL. ANN. STAT. ch. 51, § 111–19 (Smith-Hurd Supp. 1978); IND. CODE § 34–3–5–1 (1976); KY. REV. STAT. ANN. § 421.100 (Baldwin 1977); LA. REV. STAT. ANN. § 45:1451–54 (West Supp. 1978); MD. CTS. & JUD. PROC. CODE ANN. § 9–112 (1974); MICH. COMP. LAWS § 767.5a (MICH. STAT. ANN. 28.945 (1) Callahan (1974)); MINN. STAT. ANN. § 595.021–.025 (West Supp. 1977); MONT. REV. CODES ANN. § 26–1–901–903 (1979); NEB. REV. STAT. § 20–144 to –147 (1977); NEV. REV. STAT. § 49.275 (1977); N.M. STAT. ANN. § 38–6–7 (Supp. 1980); N.Y. CIV. RIGHTS LAW § 79–h (McKinney 1976); N.D. CENT. CODE § 31–01–06.2 (1976); OHIO REV. CODE ANN. § 2739.04, .12 (Supp. 1977); OKLA. STAT. ANN. tit. 12, § 2506 (West Supp. 1980); OR. REV. STAT. § 44.510–.540 (1977); R.I. GEN. LAWS §§ 9–19.1–1 to –3 (Supp. 1977); TENN. CODE ANN. §§ 24–113 to 115 (Supp. 1977).
42. Following *Branzburg*, no less than fifty-six bills were introduced with the aim of setting up a statutory newsman's privilege. *Hearings*, *supra* note 1.

who can assert the privilege — some protecting only staff reporters, some protecting freelancers, some protecting book authors, some protecting traditional reporters. There are distinctions in defining what the reporter can protect. Some state shield laws protect only the names of sources, while others work to protect a reporter's work product that could reveal the identity of a source. Still other laws protect the type of editorial processes discussed in the *Herbert* case. Most important for the purposes of this inquiry, there are distinctions in setting out the forums in which the statutory privilege may be raised. Some shield laws, responding directly to the *Branzburg* problem, cover only grand juries and criminal proceedings; others cover civil actions, administrative proceedings, legislative hearings, and the like.

1. *Absolute Protection: The* Maressa *Case*

If the spectrum of protection can be described as wide, New Jersey's statutory privilege and the interpretation it has recently received sit at the end of the spectrum most palatable to the press, thanks to *Maressa v. New Jersey Monthly*.[43]

New Jersey is an interesting place to start in that its present shield law had to live two prior lives before reaching its zenith of strength for reporters. The first New Jersey shield law dates back to 1933.[44] Prior to that, New Jersey refused to recognize a common law privilege.[45] The 1933 Act, amended in 1960, applied only to newspapers and failed to define the forums in which it was applicable.[46] The second major revision of the Act came after the New Jersey Superior Court found a loophole: that the reporter waived his privilege by disclosing the name of his source and some of the information received in a story.[47] The 1977 revision of the Act ("1977 Act") was very specific;[48] it covered the "news media," rather than just "newspapers." "News

---

43.   89 N.J. 176, 445 A.2d 376 (1982), *cert. denied*, —U.S. —, 74 L.Ed. 2d 169 (1982). Subsequently cited in KSDO v. Superior Court of Riverside Cty., 136 Cal. App. 3d 325, 186 Cal. Rptr. 211 (1982); Prager v. American Broadcasting Company, Inc., 569 F. Supp. 1269 (D.N.J. 1983).
44.   N.J. STAT. ANN. § 2:97–11 (West 1933).
45.   *In re Julius Grunow*, 84 N.J.L. 235, 85 A. 1011 (Sup. Ct. 1913).
46.   Subject to Rule 37, a person engaged on, connected with, or employed by a newspaper has a privilege to refuse to disclose the source, author, means, agency or person from or through whom any information published in such newspaper was procured, obtained, supplied, furnished, or delivered. N.J. STAT. ANN. § 2A: 84A–21 (West 1960).
47.   *In re Bridge, supra* note 13.
48.   Subject to Rule 37, a person engaged on, engaged in, connected with, or employed by news media for the purpose of gathering, procuring, transmitting, compiling, editing or disseminating news for the general public or on whose behalf news is so gathered, procured, transmitted, compiled, edited or disseminated has a privilege to refuse to disclose, in any legal or quasi-legal proceeding or before any investigative body, including, but not limited to, any court, grand jury,

media" was defined as magazines, press associations, wire services, and electronic media.[49] Further, an amendment sought, in response to the *Stanford Daily* case,[50] to protect the news media from searches and seizures.[51] Despite its definitiveness, the 1977 Act as revised, which was intended to protect confidentiality of sources for the news media "to the greatest extent permitted by the Constitution of the United States and that of the state of New Jersey,"[52] could not keep Myron Farber from jail when information was sought from him in a murder trial.[53]

The extent to which the privilege would go is absolute in civil actions, however, as established by the New Jersey Supreme Court in 1982 in two libel suits brought against *New Jersey Monthly*, a magazine purporting to cover the whole state.[54] In *Maressa v. New Jersey Monthly*, the magazine was "Rating the Legislature," and called State Senator Joseph Maressa, among other things, "sneaky, self-interested, and basically unprincipled . . . callous, stupid, and just plain devious." Maressa sued. The second case was brought by Resorts International, the casino conglomerate, after *New Jersey Monthly* published a story that linked Resorts to the Mafia. The article stated that the company had "the morals of an alley cat," was "mismanaged" and "unscrupulous." Resorts sued.

Both plaintiffs sought the magazine's sources. Both plaintiffs — an elected politician and a highly visible, highly advertised corporation — were public figures and thus were required to meet the reckless-disregard-of-the-truth standard of proof. The difficulty that the plaintiffs would inevitably have in meeting that burden did not trouble the court. No balancing of interests was required; the legislature had already performed the balancing by establishing in the 1977 Act a comprehensive statutory privilege.

The court acknowledged that the holding might be "unfair" to certain defamed individuals[55] but insisted that public-figure plaintiffs would be able to meet the burden by "inferential evidence" of recklessness, solely by "the character of the published statement," by a failure to meet "the standards of responsible journalism."[56]

Unfair or not, the public policy behind the Act would prevail:

---

petit jury, administrative agency, the Legislature or legislative committee, or elsewhere. . . .

49. N.J. STAT. ANN. § 2A: 84A–21 a (West 1977).
50. Zurcher v. Stanford Daily, *supra* note 21.
51. N.J. STAT. ANN. § 2A: 84A–21.9 (West 1980).
52. *In re Farber*, *supra* note 14, 78 N.J. at 270; 394 A.2d at 335.
53. *In re Farber*, *supra* note 14.
54. Maressa v. New Jersey Monthly, *supra* note 43; Resorts International, Inc. v. New Jersey Monthly, 89 N.J. 212, 445 A.2d 395 (1982).
55. *Id.* 89 N.J. at 200; 445 A.2d at 389.
56. *Id.* 89 N.J. at 200; 445 A.2d at 388–89.

> Our constitution grants the press wide freedom because we
> believe that the public interest is served by an informed citi-
> zenry. Those responsible for informing the public can discharge
> their function best when they can publish without anyone look-
> ing over their shoulders. The media must meet stringent dead-
> lines, and it is inevitable that they will occasionally publish
> an inaccurate statement. The State House is no place for the
> meek and thin-skinned. Sometimes published statements will
> hurt. Sometimes they will turn out to be untrue. Nevertheless,
> those regrettable consequences must yield for an informed
> citizenry.[57]

The Maressa court also rejected an argument that there was a constitutional right to maintain a libel action. That suggested right came from the
statement: "Every person may freely speak, write and publish his sentiments
on all subjects, being responsible for the abuse of that right."[58] The broad
interpretation of the New Jersey shield law, according to the dissent, would
eliminate a person's constitutional right of redress for a defamatory statement.[59] The majority also construed the 1977 Act to protect the "editorial
processes" discussed in *Herbert*. "Discovery of editorial processes is especially
threatening to newspersons because it inhibits the exchange of ideas that is
crucial to the functioning of a free and vigorous press."[60]

Pennsylvania's shield law[61] ("1976 Act") resembles the New Jersey 1977
Act[62] and has been liberally construed in favor of the news media. The
Supreme Court of Pennsylvania has used strong language in applying the
1976 Act, even in the scope of a grand jury investigation:

> Newspapers are owned by individuals or private corporations;
> they are run, operated and managed by human beings, and
> consequently are sometimes biased, sometimes unfair, some-
> times inaccurate, and sometimes wrong. Nevertheless, inde-
> pendent newspapers are today the principal watch-dogs and
> protectors of honest, as well as good, Government.... We
> would be unrealistic if we did not take judicial notice of another
> matter of wide public knowledge and great importance, namely,
> that important information, tips and leads will dry up and the

---

57.   *Id*. 89 N.J. at 200; 445 A.2d at 389.
58.   N.J. CONST. art. 1, para. 6.
59.   Maressa v. New Jersey Monthly, *supra* note 43, 89 N.J. at 203, 445 A.2d at 393.
60.   *Id*. 89 N.J. at 188, 445 A.2d at 383.
61.   42 PA. CONS. STAT. ANN. § 5942(a) (1976 as amended).
62.   Maressa v. New Jersey Monthly, *supra* note 43, 445 A.2d at 384.

public will often be deprived of the knowledge of dereliction of public duty, bribery, corruption, conspiracy and other crimes committed or possibly committed by public officials or by powerful individuals or organizations, unless newsmen are able to *fully and completely* protect the sources of their information. It is vitally important that this public shield against government inefficiency, corruption and crime be preserved against piercing and erosion.[63]

2. *Weaker Shields: Qualified Statutory Protection*

Shield laws that are not as mighty as New Jersey's or Pennsylvania's include some or all of the prongs of the *Garland* test as qualifications. Minnesota's shield law[64] extinguishes the privilege in libel cases where there is reason to believe that the source has clearly relevant information and where the information is unavailable through other sources. Other states' shield laws are qualified in that a defendant cannot utilize the "verification" defense — that the reporter relied on other sources in verifying the story — when the defendant refuses to disclose the identity of a source.[65] In four states, the statutes are qualified with language leaving it up to the court to weigh more fungible interests (i.e., disclosure should be denied unless justice would be denied).[66] In some states, the privilege is extinguished when the reporter or news medium is a defendant in a civil case.[67]

Another form[68] of shield law allows only that the reporter or the news medium may not be held in contempt for failing to disclose sources, leaving the door open for other, equally onerous sanctions, such as default judgment.[69] A default judgment, under a shield law, was ordered by an Idaho

---

63. *In re Taylor*, 412 Pa. 32, 40–41, 193 A.2d 181, 185 (1963). *See also* Hepps v. Philadelphia Newspapers, Inc. 3 Pa. D. & C. 3d 693 (1977); Mazella v. Philadelphia Newspapers Inc., 479 F. Supp. 523 (E.D.N.Y. 1979); Steaks Unlimited, Inc. v. Deaner, 623 F.2d 264, 278 (3d cir. 1980). (The Pennsylvania shield law protects extrinsic sources that could pace the trail for the exposure of a reporter's confidential sources. In this case, a television station's "outtakes" were unavailable to the libel plaintiffs.)

64. Minn. Stat. Ann. § 595.025 (West Supp. 1977).

65. Greenberg v. CBS, Inc., 419 N.Y.S.2d 988, 69 N.Y. App. 2d 693 (1979).

66. La. Rev. Stat. Ann. § 45:1453 (West Supp. 1978); N.M. Stat. Ann. § 38–6–7.A (Supp. 1979); N.D. Cent. Code § 31–01–06.2 (1976); Alaska Stat. § 9.25.160 (1973).

67. Ill. Ann. Stat. ch. 51 § 111 (Smith-Hurd Supp. 1978); Or. Rev. Stat. § 44.530 (1977); Tenn. Code Ann. § 24–114 (Supp. 1978). (In Illinois and Oregon, the defending news medium loses the privilege when it erects a defense based on its sources for a story.)

68. *E.g.*, Cal. Evid. Code § 1070(a) (Supp. 1979); N.Y. Civ. Rights Law § 79–h (McKinney 1981 as amended).

69. Rancho LaCosta, Inc. v. Penthouse, 165 Cal. Rptr. 347, 106 Cal. App. 3d 646

lower court but was overturned later.[70] Two other courts handled the problem by instructing the jury that they could conclude, based on the failure to disclose, that the media defendant had no source.[71]

III. CONCLUSION: MORE QUALIFICATIONS, MORE BALANCING

In cases with a constitutional dimension, it is often impossible to arrive at a rule or a test which can act as a crystal ball in predicting how each case will come out. The law does not work that way, nor should it.

Similarly, it is impossible to predict how the Supreme Court would come out on this issue, even with *Stanford Daily* and *Herbert* as indications of the cynicism with which the Court views privileges asserted by the press. The two cases can be distinguished. The *Stanford Daily* case was decided in the sphere of criminal investigation. The "editorial processes" privilege asserted by the media in *Herbert* is much more illusory than the confidential source privilege. With qualifications or not, applying the *Garland* criteria or not, the courts, including the *Branzburg* Court, have recognized the importance of confidential sources for the press and to satisfy the public's right to know.

On the other hand, New Jersey's approach in *Maressa* may go too far.[72] For all practical purposes, it will put many defamed persons out of court. This may surpass the "unfairness" that the Court talks about in the case; it may amount to a deprival of due process of law. The weighing of interests, via the *Garland* criteria, may be the fairest way to go. Case-by-case determinations will continue in the meantime.

(Cal. Super. Ct. 1980) (where the court was persuaded by Herbert v. Lando, *supra* note 17, that a source privilege was ruled out, along with the editorial processes privilege). *See also*, Rancho LaCosta v. Superior Court of Los Angeles County, 165 Cal. Rptr. 347, 106 Cal. App. 3d 646, *appeal dismissed, cert. denied*, 450 U.S. 902 (1981).

70. Sierra Life v. Magic Valley Newspapers, 4 MED. L. RPTR. 1689 (Dist. Ct. Id. 1978) *rev.*, 101 Idaho 795, 623 P.2d 103 (1980).

71. Downing v. Monitor Publishing, 120 N.H. 383, 415 A.2d 683 (1980); DeRoburt v. Gannett, 507 F. Supp. 880 (D. Hawaii 1981).

72. It is interesting that the Court denied certiorari in *Maressa* considering New Jersey's stunning rejection of their *Herbert* logic.

DONNA L. DICKERSON

Retraction's Role Under the Actual Malice Rule

Donna L. Dickerson, who holds a Ph.D.
from Southern Illinois University, is an
associate professor of mass communications at the University of South Florida.
She is the author of *Florida Media Law*
and coauthor of *College Student
Press Law*.

In October 1978, professional golfer Floyd Rood began a cross-country
golfing tour to raise money for a drug rehabilitation program.[1] At the start
of his tour, he was interviewed by a New Orleans UPI reporter. The story
sent over the wires read in part: "For every person he has hit, he has missed
millions, which is quite an accomplishment in 20 years of highway golf, the
sport he invented to help solve *the* drug problem." By the time the story
appeared in the Houston *Chronicle*, the last phrase read ". . .to help solve
his drug problem." Rood sued UPI for $310,000. One of the arguments Rood
made was that UPI's failure to retract the error, which they admitted to,
constituted reckless disregard.[2]

The American law of libel as retranslated by the Supreme Court[3] has
produced a great disparity among states as to how the new interpretation fits
into the traditional legal structure for finding defamation and awarding
damages. States differ as to whether plaintiffs are public or private, as to
what standard of negligence or fault will be used to determine liability, and
as to what degree of proof is necessary to establish actual malice.[4] In addi-

1. Rood v. Finney, 418 So. 2d 1 (La. App. 1982), *cert. denied*, 420 So. 2d 979 (La.
    1982), *cert. denied*, 103 S. Ct. 1254 (1983).
2. 418 So. 2d 1.
3. New York Times v. Sullivan, 376 U.S. 254 (1964).
4. *See* Stonecipher and Trager, *The Impact of Gertz on the Law of Libel*, 53 JOURN.
    Q. 609 (1976); McCarthy, *How State Courts Have Responded to Gertz in Setting
    Standards of Fault*, 56 JOURN. Q. 531 (1979).

tion, courts are having to decide what role the traditional defenses and partial defenses now play.

One of those partial defenses is the retraction, a tool that has been used for over one hundred years to lessen or defeat damages. Despite the changes in standards of proof, newspapers, in particular, continue to print retractions as though their effect will be the same in the 1980s as it was in the 1890s. This article examines the role retraction plays today in determining the existence of actual malice and discusses whether a retraction is a valid mitigating defense under current libel law.

BACKGROUND

Retraction has always been considered the strongest of the mitigating factors because it is believed that a correction will present the truth to many who saw the original charge, thus showing that plaintiff's reputation suffered less than claimed.[5]

The idea of correcting or retracting material is an ancient concept. Defamation originally was a moral offense handled by ecclesiastical courts, and part of the punishment applied by the church was a public apology.[6] The idea of using a printed retraction to forestall damages in a libel suit did not come about until the mid-1800s, when the British Parliament accepted the contention that a retraction could lessen damages.[7] American law first recognized the mitigating effect of a retraction in 1842 when a New York court held that a retraction afforded "proof not only of a disposition to repair the wrong afflicted, but of actual reparation to some extent."[8] Within the next forty years, retraction quickly gained acceptance as a way to lessen punitive and general damages.

Beginning in 1885, legislators and courts agreed that a retraction could do more than just reduce damages; it could be a defense against punitive damages.[9] Other states were willing to go further and allow a retraction to defend against both punitive and general damages, leaving only special damages to be proven in court.[10]

Today, twenty-nine states incorporate some form of written retraction in their libel laws. The most recent retraction law was passed by Arizona

5.   *E.g.*, Holden v. Pioneer Broadcasting Co., 365 P.2d 845 (Or. 1961); Linney v. Maton, 13 Tex. 449 (1855).
6.   *See* Great Britain, Parliament, Sessional Papers (Commons) 1843. Public Bills, 5 *Report from the Select Committee of the House of Lords Appointed to Consider the Law of Defamation and Libel*, 249, 403; V. Veeder, *The History of the Law of Defamation*, in 1 SELECTED ESSAYS IN AMERICAN LEGAL HISTORY 440 (1968).
7.   6 & 7 Vict., ch. 96, § 1 (known as Lord Campbell's Act).
8.   Hotchkiss v. Oliphant, 2 Hill 510, 516 (N.Y. 1852).
9.   *E.g.*, MICH. GEN. STAT. ANN. ch. 268, § 7782a,b,e (1889).
10. *E.g.*, IND. CODE ANN. tit. 35, § 34–4–15–1 (1949).

in 1974.[11] The most recent retraction law to be declared unconstitutional was Montana's in 1978.[12]

No two retraction statutes are identical. Some rewrite the mitigating effect of the common law, allowing the retraction to reduce punitive and general damages;[13] some prescribe various conditions for allowing a full-faith retraction to reduce damages and to defend completely against punitive damages;[14] some allow a full-faith retraction not only to defend against punitive damages, but also to defend completely against general damages.[15] The remainder allow "no more than special damages unless retraction is demanded and refused."[16]

ACTUAL MALICE V. COMMON LAW MALICE

In common law libel, before the *New York Times v. Sullivan* (hereafter *Sullivan*) ruling, general damages were presumed from the nature of the defamation, special damages were awarded on proof of monetary loss, and punitive damages were assessed based on a finding of malice in fact—ill will or bad faith.[17] By publishing a correction and a full-faith apology for the plaintiff, the defendant was seen as holding no such ill will.[18]

The court in *Hotchkiss v. Oliphant*, mindful of the role retraction could play, established the standard that apologies should carry no "hesitation, lurking insinuation and attempted perversion . . . of the language."[19] Subsequent cases held that merely printing the truth was not acceptable in a retraction unless accompanied by a full and forthright apology.[20] In at least two common-law cases, an attempt to explain the circumstances or to justify the inaccurate story was considered evidence of bad faith, for it indicated that the editor was trying to make excuses. In *Ellis v. Garrison*, a Texas court rejected a retraction that explained why the reporter felt the plaintiff had stolen certain goods.[21] In another case, a Kentucky court refused to accept a retraction that attempted to justify a confusion in names.[22] These precedents, which were established for common-law retraction, emphasized the need for

---

11. ARIZ. REV. STAT. ANN. § 12.653–02 (1974 Supp.).
12. Madison v. Yunker, 589 P.2d 126 (Mont. 1978); MONT. CODE ANN. § 64–207.1 (1947).
13. *E.g.*, ME. REV. STAT. ANN. tit. 7, § 173 (1957).
14. *E.g.*, MISS. CODES ANN. § 95–1–5 (1973).
15. *E.g.*, OR. REV. STAT. § 30.160 (1963).
16. ARIZ. REV. STAT. § 12.653–02 (1974 Supp.).
17. *See* M. NEWELL, SLANDER AND LIBEL 810 (4th ed. 1924); C. McCORMICK, LAW OF DAMAGES 422–30 (1935).
18. Dalziel v. Press Pub. Co., 102 N.Y.S. 909 (1906).
19. 2 Hill 510.
20. Lehrer v. Elmore, 37 S.W. 292 (Ky. 1902).
21. 174 S.W. 962 (Tex. Civ. App. 1915).
22. Lehrer v. Elmore, 37 S.W. 292.

an honest, meaningful statement from the publisher that the libel was not instigated by an intent to harm the plaintiff. A retraction that set the facts straight and apologized was simply an affirmation of the publisher's good intentions toward the plaintiff.

A finding of common-law malice required two types of evidence. First was the need for concrete evidence by witnesses concerning the circumstances of publication. Such evidence as source of information, amount of investigation, and typographical problems responded to the question of whether there was recklessness in preparing the story.[23] Second was the need for a public affirmation — such as a retraction, affidavit, or testimony — by the responsible party to indicate lack of intent.[24]

In 1964, the Supreme Court in *Sullivan* defined a new standard of malice to be used by public officials seeking libel damages.[25] The new standard, actual malice, was defined as reckless disregard for the truth or knowledge of falsity.[26] Eventually, actual malice was extended to include public figures[27] and candidates for public office.[28]

In *Gertz v. Robert Welch*, the Court suggested strongly that when punitive damages are being determined in cases of private libel, recovery should be restricted unless there is a finding of actual malice.[29] The Court was attempting to halt the uncontrolled discretion of juries, which were awarding punitive damages based on common-law malice.

Despite new developments in the area of libel, retraction statutes have not been amended to reflect these changes. And a review of cases in those states with retraction laws reveals a confusion where actual malice is being determined. Such confusion and the resulting contradictions are sufficient to indicate that retraction statutes are unworkable under the new interpretations of libel law.

There is an implicit understanding in cases dealing with actual malice that the types of evidence required by common-law malice and actual malice are different. The most significant difference was stated by the Supreme Court in an invasion of privacy case, *Cantrell v. Forest City Publishing Co.*:

> "Actual malice"... is quite different from the common-law standard of "malice" generally required under state tort law to support an award of punitive damages.... [C]ommon law malice — frequently expressed in terms of either personal ill

23. 1 A. HANSON, LIBEL AND RELATED TORTS 151 (1969).
24. *Hotchkiss v. Oliphant*, 2 Hill 510.
25. 376 U.S. 254.
26. *Id.* at 280.
27. *E.g.*, Curtis Publishing Co. v. Butts, 388 U.S. 130 (1967).
28. *E.g.*, Monitor Patriot v. Roy, 401 U.S. 265 (1971).
29. 418 U.S. 323 (1974).

will toward the plaintiff or reckless or wanton disregard for the plaintiff's rights — would focus on the defendant's attitude toward the plaintiff, not toward the truth or falsity of the material published.[30]

In common law, ill will is a varying condition that ebbs and flows with a person's temperament or disposition toward the plaintiff. Prior to the *Sullivan* and *Gertz* decisions, courts were interested in the willingness of the editor to apologize and in his feelings toward the libeled person. The law assumed that, by retracting, the editor would not only be publishing the truth, but would be testifying that he meant no harm toward the plaintiff. Also, by apologizing promptly and fully, the editor was telling the court there was no need for punitive damages.

Unlike common-law malice, actual malice is not as interested in apologies and symbols of good faith toward the plaintiff, nor is it as interested in the attitude of the publisher toward the plaintiff. As the Court stated in *Garrison v. Louisiana*, "Even if [the defendant] did speak out of hatred, utterances honestly believed contribute to the free interchange of ideas and the ascertainment of truth."[31]

Knowledge of falsity and reckless disregard are tantamount to a conspiracy that revolves around the handling of the truth. The courts are requiring very specific and "convincingly clear" evidence that such a conspiracy to defame actually exists or that the degree of care taken in reporting is so reckless that it deserves to be punished.

Evidence accepted by courts to find actual malice centers around the reporting procedures rather than around the relationship between defendant and plaintiff. Several cases have attempted to guide courts in determining actual malice by further defining reckless disregard. In *Sullivan*, the Court stated that recklessness included the publisher's awareness of the likelihood that he was circulating false information.[32] In *Curtis Publishing Co. v. Butts*, a four-member plurality felt that where public figures were involved, recklessness incorporated "highly unreasonable conduct constituting an extreme departure from the standards of investigation and reporting ordinarily adhered to by responsible publishers."[33] Justice Byron White said, in *St. Amant v. Thompson*, that recklessness could be found where there are "obvious reasons to doubt the veracity of the informant or the accuracy of his reports."[34] *St. Amant*, *Butts*, and *Garrison* all agree that publishing with an awareness of probable falsity or with doubts about the truth showed reckless disregard for the facts.

30.　419 U.S. 245, 251–52 (1974).
31.　379 U.S. 64, 73 (1964).
32.　376 U.S. 254.
33.　388 U.S. 130.
34.　390 U.S. 727, 732 (1968).

DONNA L. DICKERSON

REFUSAL TO RETRACT AND ACTUAL MALICE

Only matters known to the defendant when he published the defamation can shed light on the presence of actual malice, and it is for the plaintiff to discover and prove these matters rather than for the courts to lean on the absence of a retraction. This was the opinion of the Louisiana Court of Appeals when it heard golfer Floyd Rood's arguments about UPI's failure to retract.[35]

Under common-law precedent, the refusal to retract could be construed as evidence of defendant's (common-law) malice.[36] In cases where actual malice has been an issue, however, the majority of courts have held that failure to retract could *not* be entered as evidence of actual malice.

In *Sullivan*, a demand for retraction was made by the plaintiff, Commissioner L. B. Sullivan, as required by Alabama's retraction law.[37] Section 914 of the law states that punitive damages are not recoverable "on account of any publication concerning the official conduct of activities of any public officer, or for the publication of any matter which is proper for public information" unless the plaintiff demands a retraction and the defendant fails or refuses to publish one.[38] After receiving the demand from Sullivan, the *Times* instructed two correspondents to check the facts in the advertisement. Both reported that the information in the advertisement was false. The *Times* did not retract, but instead asked Sullivan why he felt the statements, which were "substantially correct," referred to him.[39] The Alabama Supreme Court suggested that the failure of the *Times* to check the accuracy of the advertisement and the refusal to retract were:

> a cavalier ignoring of the falsity of the advertising from which the jury could not have been but impressed with the bad faith of the *Times* and its maliciousness inferable therefrom. The *Times* could not justify its nonretraction as to the plaintiff by fallaciously asserting that the advertisement was substantially true.[40]

The U.S. Supreme Court, in reversing the Alabama court, held that falsity was not sufficient for a finding of malice and the *Times'* failure to retract was "likewise not evidence of malice for Constitutional purposes."[41] The Court qualified this holding by stating that while there may at times be doubt

35.   418 So. 2d 1.
36.   *E.g.*, Dennison v. Daily News Publishing Co., 118 N.W. 568 (Neb. 1908); Augusta Chronicle Publishing Co. v. Arrington, 157 S.E. 394 (Ga. 1931).
37.   376 U.S. at 261.
38.   ALA. CODE RECOMPILED tit. 7, § 914 (1958).
39.   N.Y. Times Co. v. Sullivan, 144 So. 2d 25, 50–51 (1962).
40.   *Id.* at 51.
41.   N.Y. Times Co. v. Sullivan, 376 U.S. at 286.

whether a failure to retract could ever be evidence of malice, it specifically did not in this instance because the refusal was not final and because the editor was not convinced that the advertisement referred to the plaintiff.

In *St. Amant*, the Supreme Court said that a defendant cannot automatically ensure a favorable verdict by testifying that he published in good faith: "Professions of good faith will be unlikely to prove persuasive for example where a story is fabricated by defendant, is the product of his imagination or is based wholly on an unverified anonymous telephone call."[42]

An early Tennessee case, *McNabb v. Tennessean Newspapers, Inc.*, reflects court attitudes toward a retraction's inadequacy as a piece of conclusive evidence.[43] The Nashville *Tennessean* accused Earl McNabb, chairman of the Davidson County Democratic Primary Board, of dereliction of duty. The *Tennessean* refused to retract. Under Tennessee's retraction law, a failure to retract is evidence of common-law malice should liability be found.[44] The Tennessee Court of Appeals found no evidence of actual malice in the preparation or printing of the story, nor did it consider the refusal to retract evidence of actual malice. The story, however, was found to be false.

In *New York Times Co. v. Connor* (hereafter *Connor*), even the plaintiff, Birmingham Police Commissioner Eugene Connor, admitted the weakness of a failure to retract as either conclusive evidence or persuasive evidence.[45] The U.S. Court of Appeals for the Fifth Circuit concluded that the *Times'* failure to retract a statement about Connor did not constitute evidence of actual malice.[46] Again, under Alabama's retraction law, failure to retract would normally be sufficient to support a finding of malice.[47]

A federal district court in Maryland also held that failure to retract was not adequate evidence of malice.[48] After an article appeared falsely stating that a zoning hearing officer had been brought before the Maryland bar on conflict of interest charges, the plaintiff demanded a correction. The Baltimore *News American* refused to retract although the reporter admitted parts of the statement were false. The court, quoting *Sullivan*, said that malice is determined by looking to the time of the publication, not to any latter occurrence such as the refusal to publish a retraction.

In *Dupler v. Mansfield Journal*, the *New Philadelphia (Ohio) Times Reporter* carried an editorial that accused the plaintiff, a private investigator, of misconduct and of ignoring Ohio law regulating the activities of private

---

42.   390 U.S. at 731.
43.   400 S.W.2d 871 (Tenn. App. 1965).
44.   TENN. CODE ANN. § 23-2605 (1955).
45.   365 F.2d 567, 574 (5th Cir. 1966).
46.   *Id.* at 577.
47.   ALA. CODE RECOMPILED tit. 7, § 914.
48.   Samborsky v. Hearst, 2 MEDIA L. RPTR. 1639 (D. Md. 1977).

investigators.[49] Four months after the editorial, the plaintiff requested a retraction according to Ohio's retraction law. The newspaper reprinted the letter of request, but did not meet the technical requirements for placement and heading. Over protest, the trial court permitted testimony concerning the editor's noncompliance with the statute.

The Ohio Court of Appeals held that the judge was in error on this point, noting rather adamantly that when questioning about the editor's noncompliance was allowed, it only served to confuse the jury as to what was the true responsibility of the defendant.[50] "If the jury decided that the defendant did not comply exactly with the reply statute they could reasonably have inferred this satisfied the requirement of 'actual malice.'"[51]

The Ohio Supreme Court agreed with the appeals court, calling the error a prejudicial one.[52] After quoting *Sullivan* (that failure to retract is not adequate evidence of actual malice) the court said, "It has not been demonstrated that [the defendant's] conduct, four months after the editorial, had any bearing on his state of mind at the time of publication."[53]

Finally, in *Pelzer v. Minneapolis Tribune*, a state district court held that the determination of malice is to be made as of the time of the publication of the allegedly defamatory statements, and the failure to retract has no bearing on the issue of malice.[54] In fact, "the existence of the retraction statute and any action taken pursuant thereto is entirely immaterial."[55]

There are three reported cases in which courts have accepted plaintiff's arguments that a refusal to retract was some evidence of actual malice. In the earliest case to confront this problem, *Mahnke v. Northwest Publishers, Inc.*, the Minnesota Supreme Court held that failure to retract was some, but not conclusive, evidence to show actual malice.[56] The case evolved out of a St. Paul *Dispatch* story that accused plaintiff, a Minneapolis detective, of unprofessional conduct in handling a child molesting case. The story, written six days after the event, related a third-hand account of how Detective William Mahnke had refused to arrest a man who had been sexually molesting a six-year-old girl. The story quoted a priest who described Mahnke as flying "into a rage" and not performing his duty of arresting the man.[57]

The plaintiff demanded a retraction. The *Dispatch* refused the demand, and Mahnke brought an action against the newspaper. Evidence provided

49.   5 MEDIA L. RPTR. 2269 (Ohio App. 1979), *aff'd*, 413 N.E.2d 1187 (Ohio 1980).
50.   5 MEDIA L. RPTR. 2269.
51.   *Id.* at 2275.
52.   413 N.E.2d 1187.
53.   *Id* at 1193.
54.   7 MEDIA L. RPTR. 2507 (Minn. Dist. Ct. 1981).
55.   *Id.* at 2509, quoting Hurley v. Northwest Publications, Inc., 273 F. Supp. 967, 975 (D. Minn. 1967).
56.   160 N.W.2d 1 (Minn. 1967).
57.   *Id.* at 5.

at the trial indicated that the priest was not present at the confrontation described, that there was not enough evidence upon which the detective could have based an arrest, that Mahnke had been sympathetic to the mother when confronted with the problem, and that the reporter had failed to verify the priest's account.

The trial court ruled that the failure to retract could not be considered by the jury. On appeal, the plaintiff contended that the refusal was "logically relevant to whether the *Dispatch* was recklessly indifferent to the truth or falsity of the article."[58] The Minnesota Supreme Court agreed, holding that the failure to retract "underscored defendant's reckless attitude as to the consequences of what had been published. . . ."[59] The opinion admitted that this holding was the "only way courts can encourage compliance by publishers with Minnesota's retraction law."[60]

The court's finding of malice in *Mahnke* was based on several pieces of evidence that showed lack of responsible reporting—an intent to sensationalize, reliance on a third-hand source, reluctance to hold the story for further investigation, and a failure to cross-examine the priest as to his source of information. All of these facts were sufficient for a finding of reckless disregard. In fact, the court concluded that actual malice was present even before addressing the absence of the retraction. In other words, the failure to retract was not the only piece of evidence of actual malice, but was merely persuasive. The court saw the failure to retract as a gesture of effrontery—a thumbing of the nose at the truth. *Sullivan* asks for "convincingly clear" evidence of reckless disregard,[61] and the court in *Mahnke* appears to have accepted failure to retract as one of several pieces of "convincing" evidence of actual malice.

In another early case, *Brown v. Fawcett Publishers, Inc.*, the Florida Supreme Court held that the failure of the defendant to print a retraction according to Florida's retraction law would be "some evidence of actual malice on the part of the defendant."[62] This holding is similar to the common-law effect of a refusal. In *Brown*, the editor refused to retract after being notified twice. The court said the editor deliberately spurned the request, figuratively "thumbing its nose at the victim and the world at large."[63]

A Michigan court argued that although the malice must exist at the time of the original libelous publication, the failure to retract was relevant and admissible on the question of that malice.[64] The confusion stems from the

---

58. *Id.* at 11.
59. *Id.*
60. *Id.*
61. 376 U.S. at 285–86.
62. 196 So. 2d 465, 473 (Fla. 1967).
63. *Id.* at 473.
64. Peisner v. Detroit Free Press, 304 N.W.2d 814 (Mich. App. 1981).

court's use of *Sullivan* as well as an 1894 and a 1906 case.[65]

These last three cases appear to be based on the action-inaction theory of liability, which has seen little use, nor has it been well received by most courts. The theory suggests that the failure to retract, in and of itself, could be evidence of knowledge of falsity, and hence be a cause of civil action.

This school of thought, explained in a 1967 *Harvard Law Review* note,[66] suggests that even if an article is not published with actual malice, a defendant could lose his privilege by refusing to retract after learning the truth. A publisher's reluctance to retract after falsity has been shown would be considered an intentional disregard for the truth. The refusal would also signify the publisher's knowing willingness to give currency to a defamatory remark. It is suggested that while knowledge of falsity may not exist during the preparation of the article, falsity is known afterward when the demand for retraction is made by the plaintiff. The defendant, therefore, should lose his *Sullivan* privilege because he evidenced knowledge of falsity by not subsequently retracting. The action-inaction theory is not well received by courts because they are asked to base liability on the inaction (refusal to retract) rather than on the action (defamation) that is the basis for the libel claim.[67]

RETRACTION AND MALICE

In cases where newspapers have refused to retract, most courts have agreed that the refusal was not admissible as proof of actual malice. The logic is that the refusal takes place after the preparation and publication of the article in question. Only the libelous article and the defendant's action leading up to the publication of that article — not actions following the deed — can be judged.

Logically, it would follow that in cases where newspapers did retract, the motivations behind the retraction and the retraction itself also would be inadmissible. In every case where newspapers have retracted, however, courts have agreed that the existence of the retraction was some indication that actual malice did not exist.

Two of these cases are from the District of Columbia. The first, *Hoffman v. Washington Post*, involved an article published by the *Post* but written by a freelance writer.[68] The article accused a weight-lifting coach of selling protein supplements that were nutritionally valueless, and it stated that the weight-lifting team had used anabolic steroids during competition rather than the protein supplements, as claimed. The *Post* ran a retraction of the portions

---

65. Thibault v. Sessions, 59 N.W. 624 (Mich. 1894); Smith v. Hubbell, 106 N.W. 547 (Mich. 1906).
66. Note, *Vindication of Reputation*, 80 HARV. L. REV. 1730, 1741–42 (1967).
67. W. PROSSER, HANDBOOK OF THE LAW OF TORTS 334–46 (4th ed. 1971).
68. 433 F. Supp. 600 (D.C. Cir. 1977).

it felt were inaccurate. The district court stated, "It is significant and tends to negate any inference of actual malice on the part of the Post Co: that it published a retraction of the indisputably inaccurate portions" in the next day's issue.[69]

In the second case, *Logan v. District of Columbia*, the newspaper falsely stated that the plaintiff was one of eight Narcotics Treatment Administration (NTA) patients who showed positive use of drugs.[70] The next day, the NTA said that no drugs were found in the plaintiff, and the *Post* published a correction. Quoting from *Hoffman*, the court stated that the retraction was significant in negating actual malice.[71]

In *DiLorenzo v. New York News*, the paper falsely reported that Judge Ross DiLorenzo was convicted of perjury, but that the charges were later dropped.[72] The story should have read that he had been indicted for perjury. The article was printed in a special Brooklyn section, which was delivered to Brooklyn news dealers to be inserted in the regular Sunday issue of the paper when it arrived. When the *News* discovered the error, it ran a retraction on the editorial page of the regular Sunday news section. Thus, the retraction appeared in the same issue as the charge. The court, noting the retraction in the same issue, held that the simultaneous publication of the retraction negated actual malice.

These three cases involved situations where there was no evidence of actual malice or reckless disregard. Testimony existed that standard journalism practices were used. The existence of the retraction was seen as one more piece of evidence to indicate that when mistakes are made despite careful reporting they will be corrected. The courts seem to be saying that the printing of a retraction is one aspect of how the whole story was handled, particularly when the retraction is run the same or next day. Essentially, this is what *Mahnke* was saying in 1965 when it viewed a refusal to retract as the last of a number of pieces of evidence indicating the existence of reckless disregard.[73]

This was also the attitude of the New York Court of Appeals when it denied a motion for summary judgment in the case of *Kerwick v. Orange County Publications*.[74] An editorial criticized the plaintiff, a tax assessor, for approving tax exempt status for ministers of the Universal Life Church, then becoming a minister himself to avoid paying taxes. After the plaintiff informed the newspaper that he was not a member of the church, owned no real property, and did not grant any tax exemption for himself, the newspaper ran a retraction. Testimony revealed that the editor had relied only on his

69. *Id.* at 602.
70. 447 F. Supp. 1328 (D.C. Cir. 1978).
71. *Id.*
72. 81 A.D.2d 844 (N.Y. Sup. Ct. 1981).
73. 160 N.W.2d 1.
74. 53 N.Y.2d 625 (1981).

memory to write the editorial and that his conduct did not meet the standards of responsible journalism. The New York Court of Appeals denied the defendant's motion for summary judgment, stating that the editor's admission of carelessness was sufficient to require a hearing on the issue of actual malice. On the matter of the retraction, the court said, "That a retraction was promptly published might be considered evidence of lack of malice in certain instances, but would not be sufficient as a matter of law for that purpose."[75] In other words, a retraction is not sufficient in and of itself to establish lack of actual malice, particularly in a case where lack of journalistic standards is evident.

CONCLUSION

Although case law on the evidence question is sparse, the holdings seem to indicate that most courts praise the existence of a retraction, but ignore the absence of one. This contradiction appears to lie in the interpretation of "when" the reckless disregard for the truth occurs. *Sullivan* said that only those matters that occur at the time of the story's preparation are admissible on the question of reckless disregard.[76] However, *Hoffman*, *Logan* and *DiLorenzo* seem to suggest that reckless disregard can be at any time before, during, and subsequent to the preparation of the story. They circumvent the *Sullivan* precedent by arguing that a retraction is like a mirror, reflecting past attitude. Should this be an acceptable argument, then the failure to retract should also be seen as a reflection of the defendant's attitude.

A stronger argument can be made that a retraction reflects only the editor's and publisher's attitude toward the facts after they have been corrected by the plaintiff. Retractions are seldom self-generated; instead, they come about because of a request from the plaintiff to retract. They are seldom written by the reporter who handled the original story. If reckless disregard is to be determined by what occurred at the time of the story's preparation, a retraction simply does not fill that bill. A retraction does not reflect how a story was prepared, the thinking that goes into the selection of facts and quotes, and degree of reliance on sources, etc. In fact, a retraction that includes such information could be more damaging to the newspaper than the refusal to retract. A retraction only corrects errors in facts; it cannot right the wrongs that might have been committed by a reporter. If a reporter has acted responsibly in preparing the story, that evidence alone should be sufficient without giving added weight to the existence or nonexistence of a retraction. If a reporter has acted irresponsibly and with reckless disregard, then, likewise, that evidence alone should be sufficient to find against the plaintiff. A retraction run following an act of responsible journalism should not be

75.   *Id.*
76.   376 U.S. at 286.

given any weight on the question of actual malice.

That is not to say that a retraction has no role in today's libel suits. When a private plaintiff is involved in a libel suit, a retraction may still be useful in determining the amount of general (actual) damages.[77] It can be argued that the sting of the original article is reduced by the presence of a retraction, and some who saw the original article may have also seen the retraction, thus lessening the reputational damages to the plaintiff.[78]

77. Gertz v. Robert Welch Inc., 418 U.S. 323.
78. *Hotchkiss v. Oliphant*, 2 Hill 510.

DONNA LEE DICKERSON

Libel and the Long Reach of Out-of-State Courts

Donna Lee Dickerson, who holds a Ph.D. from Southern Illinois University, is an associate professor of mass communications at the University of South Florida. She is the author of *Florida Media Law* and coauthor of *College Student Press Law.*

In March of 1984, the U.S. Supreme Court again exorcised the "special rights of the press" demon from the first amendment, and refused to conjure up an exclusive constitutional protection for the institutional press. The Court practiced its sorcery in *Calder v. Jones*[1] and *Keeton v. Hustler,*[2] two cases linked together by the legal theory of long arm jurisdiction. *National Enquirer's* editor and president Iain Calder and reporter John South, along with *Hustler* magazine argued that the special role of the institutional press prohibited states from exercising long arm jurisdiction where the connection between the media or its employees and the state was only minimal.

In *Calder v. Jones*, the *National Enquirer* (residence: Florida) published a story alleging that Marty Ingles, husband of actress Shirley Jones, "terrorized his staff" and "has one of the most notorious casting couches in all of Hollywood." The story further stated that Jones "has been driven to drink by his bizarre behavior."

Ingles and Jones (residence: California) sued the *National Enquirer* in Superior Court in Los Angeles for libel, invasion of privacy and infliction of emotional distress. Also named in the suit were Calder and John South, who contended that their contact with California was insufficient and that

---

1. Calder v. Jones, 138 Cal. App. 3d 128, 187 Cal. Rptr. 825 (1982), *affirmed*, 104 S. Ct. 1482 (1984).
2. Keeton v. Hustler, 682 F.2d 33 (1st. Cir. 1982), *reversed*, 104 S. Ct. 1473 (1984).

the first amendment should be taken into consideration when determining the long reach of a state's jurisdiction.[3]

In *Keeton v. Hustler*, Kathy Keeton (residence: New York) brought a libel suit in New Hampshire against the magazine (residence: Ohio) after statutes of limitation had run out in Ohio and New York. The only contact *Hustler* had with New Hampshire was a monthly circulation of 10–15,000 copies of its magazine. A district court dismissed the suit, stating that the due process clause did not allow long arm jurisdiction in cases where the relationship with the state was so tenuous. The Court of Appeals for the First Circuit agreed, suggesting that New Hampshire had no interest in redressing Keeton's injuries where there was little contact by either party.

The controlling laws in these two cases are the states' long arm statutes,[4] which give the states a limited personal (*in personam*) jurisdiction over suits brought by a resident against a non-resident. Jurisdiction in such cases extends only to suits that result from the defendant's activities in the forum state.

Most long arm statutes are similar, having been adopted after the Supreme Court established due process limitations for the exercise of personal jurisdiction.[5] For example, South Dakota's long arm statute provides in part:

> Any person is subject to the jurisdiction of the courts of this state as to any cause of action arising from the doing personally, through any employee, through an agent or through a subsidiary of any of the following acts:
> 1) The transaction of any business within the state.
> 2) The commission of an act which results in accrual within this state of a tort action;[6]

The more recent statutes are modeled after the Uniform Interstate and International Procedure Act. The District of Columbia's law, for example, reads in part as follows:

> A District of Columbia court may exercise personal jurisdiction over a person, who acts directly or by an agent, as to a claim for relief arising from the person's . . .
> 3) Causing tortious injury in the District of Columbia by an act or omission in the District of Columbia;

3. The Supreme Court has heard several cases questioning, among other things, the imposition of long arm jurisdiction on out-of-state newspapers; Polizzi v. Cowles Magazines, Inc., 345 U.S. 663 (1953); N.Y. Times v. Sullivan, 376 U.S. 254 (1964). However, *Calder v. Jones* was the first such case to raise the first amendment arguments in its petition for review.
4. CAL. CODE CIV. PROC. § 410.10 (1973); N.H. REV. STAT. ANN. § 300:14 (1979).
5. International Shoe Co. v. Washington, 326 U.S. 310 (1945).
6. S.D. COMP. LAWS ANN. § 15-7-2 (Supp. 1983).

4) Causing tortious injury in the District of Columbia by an act or omission outside the District of Columbia if he regularly does or solicits business, engages in any other persistent course of conduct, or derives substantial revenue from goods used or consumed, or services rendered, in the District of Columbia.[7]

Historically, a defendant's presence within the geographical jurisdiction of the court was necessary for personal judgment to be binding. That concept has given way with time, however, and the only requirement for personal jurisdiction is that the defendant have a minimum contact with the state.[8]

The theory behind personal jurisdiction over non-resident defendants is as follows. When a business or person purposefully conducts activities in the state such as selling newspapers, soliciting advertising or gathering information for a story, that person enjoys the benefits and protection of that state's laws. Because each state has an interest in protecting its citizens from the actions of anyone conducting business in the state, a non-resident causing an injury or defaulting on an obligation is on notice that he must respond in that state to any suit brought to enforce the due process rights of the resident.

In the leading case on long arm statutes and personal jurisdiction, *International Shoe Co. v. Washington,*[9] the U.S. Supreme Court in 1945 stated that in the name of fair play, personal jurisdiction could only be had over the defendant who had "certain minimal contacts" with the state, thus protecting the defendant from inconvenient or unreasonable litigation in a foreign court. *International Shoe* left the door open for each jurisdiction to establish its own definition of "minimal contacts" and "fair play."

Although not addressed by the Supreme Court, other constitutional limitations beyond the due process requirement may also exist. For example, the commerce clause's[10] limitation of state interference with interstate commerce could place restrictions on the reach of a state's long arm. Also, the first amendment may limit personal jurisdiction to avoid "chilling" newsgathering or distribution of newspapers in foreign states.[11]

It is this latter constitutional limitation that *Hustler* and Calder and South proposed to the Supreme Court and the one this article will examine along with the fourteenth amendment limitations.

7. D.C. CODE § 13-423 (1981).
8. International Shoe Co. v. Washington, 326 U.S. 310, 316 (1945).
9. *Id.*
10. U.S. CONST. art. I, § 8.
11. *See* N.Y. Times v. Connor, 365 F.2d 567 (5th Cir. 1966); in addition, single publication laws may act as statutory limitations to personal jurisdiction. *See* Insull v. World Telegram Corp., 273 F.2d 166 (7th Cir. 1960), *cert. denied,* 362 U.S. 942 (1960).

In the typical case challenging a state's reach over a non-resident publisher, due process requires a court to balance the plaintiff's interest in having the suit tried in the forum state against the defendant's right in not being forced to litigate in a foreign court.[12] This balancing typically begins by asking three separate, but not mutually exclusive, questions: 1) Do the necessary minimal contacts with the forum state exist? 2) Was there notice that the activity would cause the effect? and 3) Is it "fair" to force the defendant to litigate in the foreign court?

MINIMAL CONTACT AND RELEVANCE

The minimal contact rule, as established in *International Shoe*, not only protects publishers from distant and possibly harassing litigation, but also gives the plaintiff a reasonable opportunity to bring suit in the state where his reputation exists.[13]

The only criterium provided by *International Shoe* on the question of minimal contact was that a continuous and systematic presence rather than a casual one is required to justify personal jurisdiction. And the boundary between those activities that justify and do not justify a suit must be judged by their "quality and nature" and not simply by "mechanical or quantitative means."[14]

In defamation cases, like most commercial cases, quantitative measures are more easily applied than qualitative ones, and the results are often sufficient to dismiss a case for lack of jurisdiction.[15] Courts look first at circulation because the physical presence of the damaging material within the forum state is a requirement for conferring jurisdiction. Yet, the Fifth Circuit Court of Appeals stated in 1964 that "mere circulation of a periodical through the mails to subscribers and independent distributors constitutes neither doing business nor engaging in business activity."[16] This holding has not been persuasive in other jurisdictions.

In a New York case, attorney Bonnie Brower sued *The New Republic* magazine for $2.5 million for defamations that appeared in an article titled, "The Hidden Rosenberg Case."[17] The plaintiff was a New York resident; *The New Republic* was a Delaware corporation with offices in Washington, D.C. Based solely upon *The New Republic*'s New York circulation (twelve percent

12. World-Wide Volkswagen Corp. v. Woodson, 444 U.S. 286, 292 (1980).
13. International Shoe Co. v. Washington, 326 U.S. 310 (1945); *see* Shaffer v. Heitner, 433 U.S. 186 (1977).
14. International Shoe Co. v. Washington, 326 U.S. 310, 317 (1945).
15. *E.g.*, American Federation of Police v. Gordon, 8 Media L. Rep. 1393 (Fla. Cir. Ct. 1982).
16. Buckley v. N.Y. Times, 338 F.2d 470 (5th Cir. 1964).
17. Brower v. The New Republic, 7 Media L. Rep. 1605 (N.Y. Sup. Ct. 1981).

of total), the court held that the magazine was subject to personal jurisdiction in New York.

Florida courts have declined to accept jurisdiction where out-of-state magazines had five percent[18] and 3.5 percent[19] of their circulation in Florida. However, .5 percent was considered great enough in Virginia,[20] and in the District of Columbia, circulations as small as one percent,[21] and .7 percent[22] have been found sufficient to establish "minimal contact."

In *Calder*, circulation was not a factor because the *National Enquirer* itself was not challenging jurisdiction. The publisher acknowledged that California's personal jurisdiction over it was legitimate considering that it was a national publication with over ten percent of its circulation in California. However, personal jurisdiction was being challenged by *National Enquirer's* editor and reporter, and the Supreme Court stated that "jurisdiction over an employee does not automatically follow from jurisdiction over the corporation which employs him; nor does jurisdiction over a parent corporation automatically establish jurisdiction over a wholly-owned subsidiary."[23]

In *Keeton*, *Hustler* magazine was challenging personal jurisdiction by the state of New Hampshire because, although it is a national publication, its circulation in that state was only one percent of its total circulation.

Other quantitative measures include advertising solicitation and contract obligations, as well as presence in the forum state of an office, property, employees or bank accounts.[24] In *McBride v. Owens*,[25] the Los Angeles Times Syndicate was retained as a defendant in a Texas suit because it had an office in Houston staffed by a reporter and a researcher, and the syndicate had contracts with Texas newspapers to furnish them material (although no Texas newspaper printed the article in question).

In *Ziegler v. Ring Publications*,[26] the New York publishers of *Ring* magazine testified that 3.5 percent of the magazine's circulation was in Florida. A federal district court ruled that the minimal contacts did not exist because the magazine was not authorized to do business in Florida, did not solicit subscriptions nor did it have a regular reporter assigned to Florida.

18. American Federation of Police v. Gordon, 8 Media L. Rep. 1393 (Fla. Cir. Ct. 1982).
19. Ziegler v. Ring Publications, 9 Media L. Rep. 1303 (D. Fla. 1982).
20. Ajax Realty Corp. v. J.F. Zook, Inc., 493 F.2d 818 (4th Cir. 1972).
21. Founding Church of Scientology v. Verlag, 536 F.2d 429 (D. D.C. 1976).
22. Akbar v. New York Magazine, 490 F. Supp. 60 (D.D.C. 1980); *see also* Samad v. High Society, 10 Media L. Rep. 1930 (D. V.I. 1984) where only 275 copies of the magazine were distributed monthly, but "while not great in absolute terms, it is quite substantial in relation to the population of the territory." (at 1931)
23. Keeton v. Hustler, 104 S. Ct. 1473, 1482, fn. 13 (1984); Calder v. Jones, 104 S. Ct. 1482, 1487 (1984).
24. Gonzales v. Atlanta Constitution, 4 Media L. Rep. 2146 (D. Ill. 1976).
25. McBride v. Owens, 454 F. Supp. 731 (D. Tex. 1978).
26. Ziegler v. Ring Publications, 9 Media L. Rep. 1303 (D. Fla. 1982).

In addition to the strictly quantitative measures, courts must examine the quality of the contact—whether the contact had a relationship to the cause of action. When the senior editor of *Playboy* magazine sued the *Atlanta Constitution* in Illinois for an article that referred to him as a "wetback," a federal district court dismissed the suit for want of jurisdiction.[27] In a hearing on the newspaper's motion to dismiss, the court ruled that Cox Enterprises, owner of the *Atlanta Constitution*, had significant contacts with Illinois: a contract with a Chicago bank to guaranty an obligation of another subsidiary, business negotiations to purchase a printing press, a contract to sell features to the *Chicago Tribune*, as well as deriving one percent of advertising revenue from Illinois advertisers. Nevertheless, the court ruled that those contacts were unrelated to the claimed defamation; the only relevant contact was the newspaper's circulation of thirty-seven copies (less than .001 percent of its circulation) in Illinois, and that fell short of minimal contacts.

In 1975, the Church of Scientology of California sued the *St. Louis Post-Dispatch* alleging that a series of articles about the church contained numerous libels.[28] A federal district court in California granted the defendant's motion to dismiss for lack of personal jurisdiction. The California Church appealed. The Ninth Circuit acknowledged that Pulitzer Publishing Co. had several contacts with California, including the receipt of three percent of its advertising revenue from California and part ownership by Pulitzer in Million Market Newspapers, Inc., an advertising agent licensed to do business in California.

The court found that these contacts had no "nexus" to the cause of action. The only relevant contact between the defendants and California was the distribution of 150 newspapers (.04 percent of total circulation). "Sustaining personal jurisdiction on so tenuous a basis would be inconsistent with the notions of fairness . . . . "[29] In a footnote, Circuit Judge Kennedy foresaw that if personal jurisdiction could be exercised in California based upon mere circulation, the *Post-Dispatch* could be called upon to defend against defamation charges in every state where a Scientology branch is located.[30]

Sending reporters into a state to gather information for an offending article is often the most convincing evidence of "nexus" and is usually sufficient for a finding of personal jurisdiction against the individuals involved. This was Jones' argument for including reporter John South as a defendant in the *Calder* suit.

The trial court stated that South's contacts were insubstantial: South made a few phone calls (one to Ingles) and he visited California only once for pur-

27. Gonzales v. Atlanta Constitution, 4 Media L. Rep. 2146 (D. Ill. 1976).
28. Church of Scientology of California v. Adams, 584 F.2d 893 (9th Cir. 1978).
29. *Id*. at 899.
30. *Id*. at n.3.

poses relating to the article. The judges on the Tenth Circuit Court of Appeals were not as solicitous. The court reinstated South as defendant because "the material had its source in California and South tapped that source both by telephone and by personal visits to California." The court went so far as to hold that one single phone call to the plaintiff "was instrumental in the commission of one of the torts of which plaintiffs complain," thus the call "constituted the doing of a significant act in California."[31]

Iain Calder was also found to be within the long reach of California's courts, although he never entered California in connection with the story nor made any phone calls into the state. Under the rules of personal jurisdiction, even a person who has no contact with a state can be subject to the state's jurisdiction if the injury was caused intentionally.

If the complaint alleges that the defendant acted intentionally, that allegation is enough to warrant jurisdiction. Calder's approval of the story and review of the page proofs in Florida were found sufficient, since the complaint accused him of having acted maliciously and with intent to harm the plaintiff. "It must be presumed that Calder, in participating in the publication of the article as its editor, intended to cause injury to plaintiffs in California where they reside; such injury in fact occurred."[32]

The U.S. Supreme Court readily affirmed this qualitative effects test in *Calder*. Although Calder's and South's physical contacts with California were limited, the Court drew on the effects of those contacts—that the article was drawn from California sources, that the injury was suffered in California, and that the editor and reporter knowingly and intentionally committed an allegedly tortious action expressly aimed at California.[33]

The effects test took a different turn in *Keeton*. Although neither party had contact with the state of New Hampshire outside of the small circulation of *Hustler* magazine, the Court accepted the plaintiff's argument that she was trying to collect for damages suffered in *all* states. Since part of those damages was suffered in New Hampshire, the state had a legitimate interest in adjudicating the suit, although Keeton was a non-resident. In one of the most controversial statements to come out of the Court in recent years, Justice Rehnquist stated that "false statements of fact harm both the subject of the falsehood *and* the readers of the statement. New Hampshire may rightly employ its libel laws to discourage the deception of its citizens."[34] Hence, the readers, by more judicial sorcery, were joined to Keeton as plaintiffs in New Hampshire.

31. Calder v. Jones, 138 Cal. App. 3d 128, 135 (1982). *See* Margolis v. Johns, 333 F. Supp. 942 (D. D.C. 1971) where a first amendment rationale was used in a slander case to deny jurisdiction over a Washington defendant who made slanderous phone calls into Washington, D.C.
32. Calder v. Jones, 138 Cal. App. 3d 128, 134 (1982).
33. Calder v. Jones, 104 S. Ct. 1482, 1487 (1984).
34. Keeton v. Hustler, 104 S. Ct. 1473, 1479 (1984).

To allow intent to be established by the complaint creates a dangerous precedent that could leave every reporter, freelancer, editor or even source open to the reach of personal jurisdiction. Most courts, cognizant of the problems associated with pulling anyone connected with a story into a suit, are likely to dismiss reporters and writers when their contact is tenuous, or at best, unsubstantial.

For example, in *McDonnell Douglas V. N.Y. Times*,[35] a federal district court found that Missouri could not assert personal jurisdiction over a book reviewer. In that case, Robert Sherrill, Washington editor of *The Nation*, freelanced a book review for the *New York Times* about two books dealing with the 1974 crash of a Turkish Airlines DC-10 jetliner. McDonnell Douglas, manufacturer of the DC-10, alleged that the review was not supported by the content of the books and that it libeled both the plaintiff and its product. The court ruled that Sherrill had never been in Missouri and had no control over the distribution of the review.

NOTICE AND RELEVANCE

In addition to "minimal contact," due process also requires that jurisdiction be asserted only over a publication that could anticipate or foresee that its publication would cause an effect in the forum state.[36] With few exceptions, it is well established that sending a defamatory statement into a state and causing an injury is actionable.[37] As Rehnquist said in *Keeton*, "The tort of libel is generally held to occur wherever the offending material is circulated. The reputation of the libel victim may suffer harm even in a state in which he has hitherto been anonymous."[38]

There is disagreement among jurisdictions whether a defendant must purposefully desire the contact with the forum state or whether merely being able to foresee the harm is sufficient for notice.[39] Some authorities suggest that if the defendant conducts activities in the state, then he/she has fair notice that he/she is subject to suit because the defendant could anticipate an actionable effect.[40] In other words, if a newspaper is sent into a foreign state, the publisher should reasonably anticipate that articles in that newspaper might be defamatory to a resident in that state.

In product liability cases, the presence of a single defective product is usually sufficient to establish personal jurisdiction. In such cases, courts ask

35. McDonnell Douglas v. N.Y. Times, 4 Media L. Rep. 1323 (D. Mo. 1978).
36. *See* World-Wide Volkswagen Corp. v. Woodson, 444 U.S. 286 (1980).
37. *See* Rebozo v. Washington Post Co., 515 F.2d 1208, 1214 (5th Cir. 1975).
38. Keeton v. Hustler, 104 S. Ct. 1473, 1479 (1984).
39. Comment. *Constitutional Limitations on State Long Arm Statutes*, 49 U. CHI. L. REV. 156, 169 (1982).
40. World-Wide Volkswagen v. Woodson, 444 U.S. 286 (1980).

whether it is foreseeable by the manufacturer that the product will be introduced into the state.[41] However, in libel cases where circulation of the material is small, most courts agree that the mere likelihood that even one copy of the article might enter a state is not a reasonable measure of notice.[42] The nature of the print medium is such that, if one looks hard enough, copies of most major newspapers can be found in almost every state. Therefore, the due process inquiry requires that the publisher be able to anticipate reasonably a legal liability for defamation by purposefully placing that publication in the state.[43]

Foreseeability can be demonstrated by the presence of a large circulation in the forum state. It is for this reason that the *National Enquirer* did not challenge California jurisdiction over itself, and the reason that the *New Republic*, a Delaware corporation, could be sued in New York.[44] The magazine purposefully solicited subscriptions in New York and twelve percent of its sales were in that state.

Purposefullness and foreseeability were also the underlying justifications in *McBride v. Owens* for retaining the L.A. Times Syndicate and two writers as defendants, but dismissing out-of-state newspapers.[45] In that case, a *Los Angeles Times* syndicated column was published in the *Orlando Sentinel Star*, the *Denver Post* and the *Long Island Press*. The plaintiff, who was allegedly libeled in the column, was a resident of Texas and brought suit in that state. No Texas newspapers carried the questionable article; however, the plaintiff claimed personal jursidiction in Texas because the three out-of-state newspapers had paid circulations in Texas and because the other defendants had purposefully conducted business in Texas.

The court ruled that the newspapers were not national publications nor did they actively solicit what little circulation they had in Texas. The court was instructed by *Curtis Publishing Co. v. Golino*,[46] where the Fifth Circuit stated that the survival of a newspaper depends upon its circulation in the vicinity of publication, and while circulation outside that area is welcome, it is not critical for survival. This out-of-area circulation is the product of the newspaper's excellence rather than of its active solicitation of subscribers.[47] Therefore, since the three newspapers are not national publications and the unsolicited shipment of their publications into Texas was so small, no foreseeability existed.

The L. A. Times Syndicate, however, had engaged in contracts with Texas

41. Gray v. American Radiator & Standard Sanitary Corp., 176 N.E. 2d 761 (Ill. 1961).
42. Church of Scientology of California v. Adams, 584 F.2d 893 (9th Cir. 1978); Buckley v. N.Y. Times, 338 F.2d 470 (5th Cir. 1964).
43. *See* Hanson v. Denckla, 357 U.S. 235 (1958).
44. Brower v. The New Republic, 7 Media L. Rep. 1605 (N.Y. Sup. Ct, 1981).)
45. McBride v. Owens, 454 F. Supp. 731 (D. Tex. 1978).
46. Curtis Publishing Co. v. Golino, 383 F.2d 586 (5th Cir. 1967).
47. *Id*. at 590.

newspapers and could foresee circulation of the damaging article in that state. The last defendants, syndicated writers Robert Owens and Jack Cloherty, were also retained because of their "purposeful act of allowing the Syndicate to sell publication rights of their articles anywhere in the United States . . . from which Owens and Cloherty derived revenue . . . ."[48]

A "state may also exercise personal jurisdiction over an out-of-state publisher who purposefully directs a story toward the forum state in order to exploit the local market." In *Edwards v. A.P.*, the Fifth Circuit emphasized that long arm jurisdiction could be asserted over the Associated Press, which had carried a story primarily for its Mississippi readers and subscribers. Associated Press employed five correspondents in Mississippi and transmitted the article in question only to Mississippi subscribers. Such actions were found to be "purposefully and specifically aimed at Mississippi, as surely as if the proverbial gunman had stood in Alabama and fired into a crowd in Mississippi."[49]

A California appeals court quashed service of process to several out-of-state newspapers not only because their circulation in California was small, but also because the story was not purely of local appeal.[50] In *Sipple v. Des Moines Register and Tribune*, the plaintiff was identified as a homosexual by columnist Herb Caen after he thwarted an assassination attempt by Mary Jane Moore on President Gerald Ford. The court said the story was of national importance and not expected or intended to receive any greater attention in California.

In *Anselmi v. Denver Post*,[51] plaintiffs appealed a district court action dismissing the *Los Angeles Times* as a defendant; the case involved two Wyoming businessmen who alleged that articles in the *Denver Post* and the *Los Angeles Times* implied they were involved in organized crime. The *Times* sold only "five to eight" copies of its newspaper in Wyoming, had $2,000 worth of contracts to sell syndicated material to Wyoming papers, and solicited advertising in the state by direct mail.

The Court argued that in other circumstances, the small amount of business conducted by the *Times* might be insufficient for personal jurisdiction; however, the story was a "special event" which the *Times* knew would be given attention within Wyoming, since there was more reader interest there than in any other state. "So, then, the *Times* developed and prepared a story which had greater reader interest, was colorful, explosive and capable of inflicting injury within Wyoming." This single act became the dominant factor in finding that personal jurisdiction did reside in Wyoming. "We conclude

48. McBride v. Owens, 454 F. Supp. 731, 737 (D. Tex. 1978).
49. Edwards v. Associated Press, 512 F.2d 258, 259 (5th Cir. 1975).
50. Sipple v. Des Moines Register & Tribune, 82 Cal. App. 3d 143 (1978).
51. Anselmi v. Denver Post, 552 F.2d 316 (10th Cir. 1977), *cert. denied*, 429 U.S. 1041 (1979).

that the L.A. Times released a force which took effect in Wyoming and which with the other jurisdictional facts satisfies the minimum contact requirement."[52]

In *McGuire v. Brightman*,[53] defendant Lehman Brightman had visited South Dakota and gathered information for an article published in his organizations' newspaper, *The Warpath*. Plaintiff Dr. David McGuire, director and general medical officer with the U.S. Public Health Service hospital on the Rosebud (S.D.) Reservation, claimed that the article defamed him. He brought suit in South Dakota. Brightman was served process in California but never appeared, resulting in a $100,000 judgment against him by default.

When McGuire went to California to enforce the action, the California Court of Appeals upheld the judgment and ruled that South Dakota's long arm statute gave that state personal jurisdiction over the defendant. *The Warpath's* small circulation in South Dakota was offset by the great interest the article had for residents in South Dakota. The information was gathered by the plaintiff in South Dakota and it was foreseeable that the story would be read and be given substantial attention in South Dakota.

In *Calder*, the Supreme Court countered the defendants' arguments that as employees, they were not responsible for nor had control over circulation activities in California. The Court stated that they could foresee that the article would be circulated and have an effect in that state because their tortious action was intentional and expressly aimed at California. Calder and South wrote an article they knew would have a potentially devastating impact upon Jones. "Under the circumstances, petitioners must 'reasonably anticipate being haled into court there' to answer for the . . . article."[54]

A significant point that separates *Keeton* from *Calder* is that the latter was a suit for damages suffered only in California, whereas Keeton was seeking to recover for damages suffered in all states. The Court was correct in finding that notice and foreseeability existed in *Calder*; however, their finding of notice in *Keeton* seems feeble. Contrary to lower court rulings that mere circulation is not enough to establish personal jurisdiction, the Supreme Court's ruling in *Keeton* suggests that circulation alone is sufficient. *Hustler* magazine, according to the Court, purposefully chose to enter the New Hampshire market and knew its laws; under different circumstances, it could have even claimed the benefit of those laws had it sought redress against a subscriber or distributor. It is without dispute that, had Keeton brought her suit in New York where she lived, *Hustler* could be found to have knowledge and foreseeability of the tort. But could it foresee that the damage would occur in all states where it circulated—particularly in a state where Keeton was unknown?

52. *Id*. at 325.
53. McGuire v. Brightman, 79 Cal. App. 3d 776, 145 Cal. Rptr. 244 (1978).
54. Calder v. Jones, 104 S. Ct., 1482, 1487 (1984).

DONNA LEE DICKERSON

CONVENIENCE

After a court has found minimum contact, notice and relevance, it may then decide whether the rules of fair play require jurisdiction to be dismissed based upon convenience to the parties. Obviously, convenience weighs heavily in favor of the plaintiff, who is bringing the case in his state of residence. And litigation becomes more burdensome for the defendant the further away the forum state is. However, the courts are not asked to balance convenience. In fact, the general rule is "unless the balance is strongly in favor of the defendant, the plaintiff's choice of forum should rarely be disturbed."[55]

A few of the factors that can be used to determine convenience include financial ability of the parties, convenience to witnesses, access to evidence and need for a prompt trial.[56] In a defamation case, the defendant publication is usually better able financially to defend itself in a foreign state than is the plaintiff; most witnesses are already in the plaintiff's state of residence and the burden of bringing reporters and editors to testify is counterbalanced by the financial ability of the publication.[57] Although several libel cases have raised the issue of *forum non conveniens*, it has rarely been used to dismiss or change venue in a libel case. However, as will be seen under the discussion of first amendment limitations, at least one court felt that convenience might play a role in deciding jurisdiction.[58]

FIRST AMENDMENT LIMITATIONS

In *International Shoe*, the Supreme Court required personal jurisdiction to be based upon the fourteenth amendment's due process clause and its standards of essential fairness.[59] It is well established that the liberties embodied in the fourteenth amendment also include the rights guaranteed by the first amendment.[60] Therefore, if the fourteenth amendment is to be used as a limitation on personal jurisdiction, those limitations must include first amendment considerations.

First amendment arguments first surfaced in 1966, when the Fifth Circuit ruled in *N.Y. Times v. Connor*[61] that Birmingham Police Commissioner Eugene Connor could not recover for an alleged libel in the *New York Times*. Circulation of the *Times* in Alabama was .23 percent of total circulation. Although the court held that the circulation met the due process requirements,

55. Gulf Oil Corp. v. Gilbert, 330 U.S. 501 (1947).
56. Fannin v. Jones, 229 F.2d 368 (6th Cir. 1956).
57. Rebozo v. Washington Post, 515 F.2d 1208 (5th Cir. 1975).
58. N.Y. Post Corp. v. Buckley, 373 F.2d 175 (2d Cir. 1967).
59. International Shoe Co. v. Washington, 326 U.S. 310 (1945).
60. Gitlow v. New York, 268 U.S. 652 (1925); Cantwell v. Connecticut, 310 U.S. 296 (1940).
61. N.Y. Times v. Connor, 365 F.2d 567 (5th Cir. 1966).

"jurisdiction based upon minimal contacts . . . when applied to the press will limit the circulation of information to which the public is entitled" and "freeze out of existence . . . publications espousing unpopular positions in a particular locale."[62]

The court felt that the first amendment not only protects the publication, but also preserves the vital interest the state has in assuring that its citizens receive information. The publisher would likely stop distribution in any state "where the size of circulation does not balance the danger of liability."[63] The Connor court used the first amendment to decide whether minimal contacts existed, demanding "greater contacts" than required in other commercial cases.[64]

These first amendment considerations are meant to tilt the scales in the defendant's favor, particularly when the publication is a small one or when there is a risk of a biased jury verdict.[65] This balance is evident when cases from Florida are compared with those from the District of Columbia, where the first amendment has not been a consideration. In similar cases, where the only contact was through circulation, Florida courts have routinely dismissed jurisdiction where circulation was less than ten percent. Florida courts give as their reasoning the chilling effect created when a publisher is forced to defend itself far from home. However, in the District of Columbia, circulations of one percent or less have stood the test of "minimal contacts."[66]

When the defendant is a large national newspaper or magazine, even the first amendment cannot outweigh the defendant's overwhelming presence in the state. In *Rebozo v. Washington Post*,[67] the newspaper ran a front-page article that stated Charles "Bebe" Rebozo, former President Richard Nixon's financial adviser, had cashed $91,500 in stocks he had been told were stolen. Rebozo brought suit in a federal district court in Florida and the *Post* moved to have the case dismissed for lack of jurisdiction.

The Fifth Circuit upheld jurisdiction, stating that while first amendment considerations are important, they do not preclude the assertion of personal jurisdiction over a national publication like the *Washington Post*. The paper actively solicited subscriptions and advertising in Florida and sent reporters into the state to do investigative work on the story. These activities "tend to ameliorate the fear that the prospect of litigation might limit the circulation of information to which the public is entitled."[68]

In *Curtis Publishing Co. v. Golino*,[69] the court noted that first amend-

62. *Id.* at 573.
63. *Id.* at 572.
64. *Id.*
65. *E.g.*, New York Post Corp. v. Buckley, 373 F.2d 175 (2d Cir. 1967).
66. Cases cited *supra* notes 17, 18, 20, 21.
67. Rebozo v. Washington Post, 515 F. 2d 1208 (5th Cir. 1975).
68. *Id.* at 1215.
69. Curtis Publishing Co. v. Golino, 383 F.2d 586 (5th Cir. 1967).

ment considerations did not preclude personal jurisdiction over the *Saturday Evening Post*. In magazine libels, concerns about "chilling effects" are not as compelling as they might be in libels against small newspaper publishers since a national magazine encourages national circulation and occasional suits would not "chill the desire of [the magazine] to actively encourage the widest circulation."[70]

The lack of "greater" contact was one reason the federal district court in Texas dismissed the *Orlando Sentinel Star* and the *Denver Post* as defendants in the case of *McBride v. Owens*.[71] Although the sending of the newspapers into Texas constituted a contact, "the court finds it would not be fair and reasonable to require them to defend this action in Texas. First Amendment considerations enter into this . . . inquiry and dictate this result."[72]

Although courts in the Seventh[73] and Third[74] circuits have followed the reasoning of the Fifth Circuit; the Ninth,[75] Tenth[76] and Eleventh[77] circuits have openly challenged any assertion of first amendment consideration. The Second Circuit[78] stands in the middle, restricting the first amendment to the question of convenience rather than minimal contact.

A year after Connor, the Second Circuit questioned whether the first amendment should be allowed to determine minimum contacts, upholding jurisdiction in *N.Y. Post Corp. v. Buckley*.[79] The plaintiff, a resident of Connecticut, brought suit against the *Post*, a Delaware corporation with offices in Washington, D.C. Judge Friendly dismissed the effects of the first amendment on minimal contacts, but he did agree that convenience might be a better place to assert first amendment arguments. "The First Amendment could be regarded as giving *forum non conveniens* special dimensions and constitutional stature in actions for defamations . . . ."[80] *Buckley* thus acknowledged that the first amendment is a consideration in the due process clause and does play a role in determining whether jurisdiction is properly exercised. Since Connecticut and New York are not an inconvenient distance apart, the argument was of no avail to the *Post*.

Opposition to first amendment restrictions was made by the Tenth Cir-

---

70. *Id*. at 592.
71. McBride v. Owens, 454 F. Supp. 731 (D. Tex. 1978).
72. *Id*. at 735.
73. Gonzales v. Atlanta Constitution, 4 Media L. Rep. 2146 (D. Ill. 1976).
74. Johnson v. Time, Inc., 321 F. Supp. 837 (D. N.C. 1970) *modified on other grounds*, 448 F.2d 378 (4th Cir. 1971).
75. Church of Scientology of California v. Adams, 584 F.2d 893 (9th Cir. 1978).
76. Anselmi v. Denver Post, 552 F.2d 316 (10th Cir. 1977).
77. Army Times v. Watts, 10 Media L. Rep. 1774 (11th Cir. 1984), *overturning* Cox Enterprises v. Holt, 8 Media L. Rep. 1702 (11th Cir. 1982).
78. N.Y. Post Corp. v. Buckley, 373 F.2d 175 (2d Cir. 1967).
79. *Id*.
80. *Id*. at 183–84.

cuit in *Anselmi v. Denver Post*.[81] The court said that any first amendment considerations must be left to the time when the question of defamation is addressed and should not be presented when determination of jurisdiction is made.

In mixed metaphor, the court said that to throw the first amendment "on the scales as an added impediment in media cases gives the media an additional arrow which is not appropriate . . . ."[82]

In *Sipple v. Des Moines Register and Tribune*,[83] the California Court of Appeals refused to allow the press to "encase itself in special armor because a free press belongs to all—not to any definable category of persons or institution." Citing numerous cases ranging from *Pennekamp v. Florida*[84] to *National Bank of Boston v. Bellotti*,[85] Judge Jenkins argued that the institutional press can lay no greater claim to protections under the first amendment than can the general public. Thus, the first amendment does not give "special protection from jurisdiction to defendants whose tortious acts performed out of state arise from exercise of rights arguably protected by the first amendment."[86]

This reasoning was adopted by the California Supreme Court in *Calder v. Jones*. There the court said that the constitutional perimeters of personal jurisdiction were established by the Supreme Court in *International Shoe* with no mention of a special first amendment test. "The right of the California court to assert jurisdiction over [Calder and South] must be determined in accordance with traditional principles unaffected by First Amendment considerations."[87]

Justice Rehnquist agreed and made short shrift of the first amendment arguments, stating that "the infusion of such considerations would needlessly complicate an already imprecise inquiry."[88] Instead, he proposed that first amendment arguments have already been taken into consideration in the substantive law of libel (i.e., *Sullivan* rule for public officials and the *Gertz* negligence rule for private plaintiffs). "To introduce those concerns at the jurisdictional stage would be a form of double counting."[89] Rehnquist ended his opinion by citing other cases in which the Court had banished the "special press protection" arguments from constitutional law.[90]

---

81. Anselmi v. Denver Post, 552 F.2d 316 (10th Cir. 1977).
82. *Id.* at 324. *See also* Buckley v. N.Y. Times, 338 F. 2d 470 (5th Cir. 1984).
83. Sipple v. Des Moines Register and Tribune, 82 Cal. App. 3d 143, 147 Cal. Rptr. 59 (1978).
84. Pennekamp v. Florida, 328 U.S. 331 (1946).
85. First National Bank of Boston v. Bellotti, 435 U.S. 765 (1978).
86. Sipple v. Des Moines Register and Tribune, 82 Cal. App. 3d 143, 149 (1978).
87. Calder v. Jones, 138 Cal. App. 3d 128, 132 (1982).
88. Calder v. Jones, 104 S. Ct. 1482, 1487 (1984).
89. *Id.*
90. *Id.* at 1488.

Aside from Rehnquist's controversial statement that a state may employ its libel laws to discourage deception of readers, nothing surprising came from either opinion.[91] The Court was simply doing what it has been doing since *Branzburg v. Hayes*[92]—trying to purge from first amendment theory the concept that the media, by virtue of their watchdog function, deserve greater protection under the law and the Constitution than do non-media litigants. In cases involving corporate speech, search and seizure in newsrooms, reporter's privilege, access to prisons and jails, and pre-trial discovery in libel,[93] the Court has steadfastly held that the first amendment belongs to all persons wishing to express themselves, regardless of the forum they choose. Chief Justice Burger's concurring opinion in *First National Bank of Boston v. Bellotti* sums up the view of the more conservative members of the Court as to special treatment of the institutional press:

> The very task of including some entities within the "institutional press" while excluding others, whether undertaken by legislature, court, or administrative agency, is reminiscent of the abhorred licensing system of Tudor and Stuart England— a system the First Amendment was intended to ban from this country. In short, the First Amendment does not "belong" to any definable category of persons or entities: It belongs to all who exercise its freedom.[94]

Despite the raging controversy inside[95] and outside[96] of the Court on this sensitive question, the Court has repeatedly stated since *Zemel v. Rusk* that the first amendment does not offer any greater protection to newsgatherers than it does to the average citizen.[97] Just as individuals who commit tortious acts in a foreign state are amenable to jurisdiction in that state, so are reporters, as long as due process is applied equally. It could be argued that the threat of being sued in a forum state could force reporters to use less zeal in gathering information, resulting in inaccurate, incomplete or inadequate reports. If such a result were to come about, the Court would probably see it as a trivial personnel problem rather than a first amendment one.

91. *Id.*
92. Branzburg v. Hayes, 408 U.S. 665 (1972).
93. First National Bank of Boston v. Bellotti, 435 U.S. 765 (1978); Zurcher v. Stanford Daily, 436 U.S. 547 (1978); Branzburg v. Hayes, 408 U.S. 665 (1972); Houchins v. KQED, 438 U.S. 1 (1978); Herbert v. Lando, 441 U.S. 153 (1979).
94. First National Bank of Boston v. Bellotti, 435 U.S. 765, 801–2 (1978) (Burger, C.J., concurring).
95. *See supra* note 93.
96. Blasi, *The Checking Value in First Amendment Theory*, 1977 AM. B. FOUNDATION RES. J. 523; Note, *Examining the Institutional Interpretation of the Press Clause*, 58 TEX. L. REV. 171 (1979); Stewart, . . . *Or of the Press*, 26 HASTINGS L. J. 631 (1975).
97. Zemel v. Rusk, 381 U.S. 1 (1965).

Yet, despite Burger's rigid bias against allowing other agencies, such as state courts or legislatures, to provide special protection, that avenue is still available. It is assumed that states are free to provide greater protection than those minimums guaranteed by the Court's interpretation of the Constitution. The Court stated in *Branzburg* that, should states wish to provide special protection for the media through legislation or through interpretation of their own constitutions, they may do so.[98]

As long as the delicate due process balance between defendant and plaintiff is not upset, states can provide added protection for the media in the area of long arm jurisdiction, just as they have in other areas, such as reporter's privilege. However, until states take the initiative, state and federal courts will follow the *Calder* decision. For example, the Eleventh Circuit (which relies on Fifth Circuit precedent where the circuit has not set its own) rejected the *Connor* "greater contacts" rule soon after the Supreme Court rejected it in *Calder*. In *Army Times v. Watts*, the Eleventh Circuit ruled that the *Federal Time*'s circulation in Alabama (2.1 percent of total), its solicitation of advertising and subscriptions in that state, and its reasonable belief that the article would have its greatest impact in Alabama were all significant enough that the publisher could reasonably anticipate having to answer in Alabama for any tort committed in that state. The court concluded "the circuit's requirement of greater contacts for the finding of personal jurisdiction in First Amendment cases is thus no longer valid law after *Keeton* and *Calder*."[99]

The issue of whether special rights in long arm cases should be sought from state legislatures or Congress must be studied carefully by the media. Again, this question returns to the controversy over the special status of the institutional press: the Burger-Stewart debates, the Abrams-Lewis differences, the institution v. the role arguments.[100] Without elaborating on those various arguments, this writer simply proposes that before the media attempt to seek special protections and rights in this particularly narrow area, they should study what effect such a move would have on the fundamental values and basic underlying principles behind libel laws and long arm jurisdiction and whether traditional first amendment roles are indeed enhanced.

98. Branzburg v. Hayes, 408 U.S. 665, 706 (1972).
99. Army Times v. Watts, 10 Media L. Rep. 1774 (11th Cir. 1984).
100. *See* Sack, *Reflections on the Wrong Question: Special Constitutional Protection for the Institutional Press*, 7 HOFSTRA L. REV. 629 (1979); Abrams, *The Press Is Different: Reflections on Justice Stewart and the Autonomous Press, id* at 563; Lewis, *A Preferred Position for Journalism? id.* at 595.

ERIK L. COLLINS,
JAY B. WRIGHT, and
CHARLES W. PETERSON

Problems in Libel Litigation

Erik L. Collins, Ph.D., J.D., teaches communications law at the College of Journalism, University of South Carolina. Jay
B. Wright, Ph.D., teaches communications
law at the S.I. Newhouse School of
Public Communications of Syracuse
University. Dr. Wright is also Executive
Director of The New York Fair Trial Free
Press Conference. Charles W. Peterson is
a second year law student at the University of Pennsylvania.

In *Gertz v. Robert Welch, Inc.*,[1] the Supreme Court of the United States
renewed its efforts, begun ten years earlier in *New York Times v. Sullivan*,[2]
to strike the proper balance between the first amendment guarantees of open
debate of public issues and the states' interests in protecting reputation. The
"public interest test"—weakly endorsed by the Court in *Rosenbloom v.
Metromedia*[3]—was discarded in *Gertz* in favor of a public involvement index
by which most public officials, a few famous individuals, and persons voluntarily involved in major public controversies would have to meet the actual
malice standard enunciated in *New York Times*. The Court did not define public
controversy in *Gertz*. Subsequent Supreme Court decisions have shed more
light on what a public controversy is *not* than on what it is, or should be. Lower
courts, left to interpret what is meant by a public controversy, have produced
rulings no less "unpredictable" than those feared under the *Rosenbloom* public
interest standard.[4]

1. Gertz v. Robert Welch, Inc., 418 U.S. 323 (1974).
2. New York Times v. Sullivan, 376 U.S. 254 (1964).
3. Rosenbloom v. Metromedia, 403 U.S. 29 (1971).
4. The Court found application of the Rosenbloom test "would lead to unpredictable
   results and uncertain expectations." Gertz v. Robert Welch, Inc., 418 U.S. 323, 343
   (1974).

The lower courts' problems have led judges and commentators to argue that the Supreme Court must resolve the question of what is a public controversy.[5] Meanwhile, judges and scholars who have suggested ways to determine a public controversy in lieu of a definitive pronouncement by the Court follow different courses. Some argue for the (rejected) public interest view, in which almost any public matter is a controversy if it meets a general newsworthiness test.[6] Others, usually legal scholars, argue for some form of a Meiklejohnian political speech doctrine which, as originally formulated, reads the first amendment guarantees of speech and press as protection of communications related to self-governance.[7] Still others, most often judges in lower courts faced with adjudicating the issue, have opted for ad hoc determinations or creative new interpretations of the *Gertz* requirements.

In this article, the authors will first review the problems involved with determining a public controversy and then suggest a set of requirements necessary for finding a public controversy that reflects the current direction of the Supreme Court. Such an approach arguably is the most sensible until the Supreme Court offers clearer guidelines on exactly what it means by the term "public controversy."

I. BACKGROUND: *NEW YORK TIMES* THROUGH *GERTZ*

New York Times marked the initial intrusion of clearly defined first amendment concerns into defamation law. The Court recognized that the "profound national commitment to the principle that debate on *public issues* should be uninhibited, robust, and wide-open. . ."[8] must be secured even at some expense to the states' interests in protecting reputation. In taking this step, the Court (1) stressed the notion that the *publicness* of the information warranted first amendment protection, and (2) gave at least provisional support to a reading of the first amendment's "central meaning" as protection of political speech.

5. *See, e.g.,* Waldbaum v. Fairchild Publications, 627 F.2d 1287 (D.C. Cir. 1980), where the court noted (at 1292) that "Unfortunately, the Supreme Court has not yet fleshed out the skeletal descriptions of public figures and private persons enunciated in *Gertz*."
6. *See, e.g.,* Rosanova v. Playboy, Enterprises, Inc., 580 F.2d 859, 861 (5th Cir. 1978) where the court said, "There is no dispute that appellant has been the subject of published newspaper and other media reports. . . .The nature of his reported associations and activities concerning organized crime, are, without dispute, subjects of legitimate public concern. . . . [Mr. Rosanova is] a public figure, subject to media comment as such."
7. *See* ALEXANDER MEIKLEJOHN, POLITICAL FREEDOM (1960); Meiklejohn, *The First Amendment is an Absolute,* SUP. CT. REV. 245–66 (1961); Meiklejohn, *What Does the First Amendment Mean?* 20 U. CHI. L. REV. 461 (1953); *and generally,* William Brennan, *The Supreme Court and the Meiklejohn Interpretation of the First Amendment,* 79 HAR. L. REV. 1 (1965).
8. New York Times v. Sullivan, 376 U.S. 254, 270 (1964). [emphasis added]

In *New York Times*, first amendment considerations were brought to bear upon factually incorrect criticism of official acts of public servants. Three years later, in *Curtis Publishing v. Butts* and *Associated Press v. Walker*,[9] the court extended the scope of protected public speech by ruling that private individuals who nevertheless have a major impact upon the regulation of society must meet the actual malice requirements to recover damages in defamation actions.[10] The "public figure" test introduced in *Butts* and *Walker* was a logical extension of the ruling in the *New York Times* case, though it is clear that the analogy of seditious libel advanced in *New York Times* does not hold as well in these cases. In a sense, the public figure concept occupies a middle ground between the political speech idea of *New York Times* and the broad public interest standard later articulated in *Rosenbloom*.

Even before the Court entertained the notion of public interest, some lower courts were ruling that plaintiffs needed to show actual malice when a private individual was defamed in relation to matters of public importance. The Court acknowledged this view in *Rosenbloom*, though only two justices joined Justice Brennan in the plurality opinion. The opinion said in part:

> If a matter is a subject of public or general interest, it cannot suddenly become less so merely because a private individual is involved, or because in some sense the individual does not "voluntarily" choose to become involved....We honor the commitment to robust debate on public issues, which is embodied in the First Amendment, by extending constitutional protection to all discussion and communication involving matters of public or general concern, without regard to whether the persons involved are famous or anonymous.[11]

The lack of agreement in *Rosenbloom* led the Court in *Gertz* to reconsider the question of public interest and public involvement in terms of first amendment requirements. The public interest test, while not forbidden, was rejected as unworkable; defining public interest was better "not left up to the

---

9. Curtis Publishing v. Butts, Associated Press v. Walker, 388 U.S. 130 (1967). The *Walker* case was reported with *Butts*.
10. *i.e.*, in effect. In actuality, the ruling contained two different standards, one akin to gross negligence, proposed by Justice Harlan, and the actual malice test, proposed by Chief Justice Warren. Justice Harlan's formulation was based on "highly unreasonable conduct" in the form of "extreme departure from the standards of investigation and reporting ordinarily adhered to by responsible publishers." *Id.* at 155. In subsequent lower court decisions, however, the actual malice test was the preferred standard.
11. Rosenbloom v. Metromedia, 403 U.S. 29, 43–4 (1971).

conscience of judges."[12] The Court reimposed the twin standards of public official/public figure and private person, focusing on the degree of voluntary activity taken by plaintiff in yielding his/her interests in reputation for the benefits achieved through public status.

The *Gertz* Court left the definition of public official untouched but spelled out with greater precision the public figure defamation plaintiff. One major category of public figures, said the Court, was the "all-purpose" or pervasive public figure, so called because this person has achieved a high degree of prominence or power within a community.[13] The other major public figure category was described as a "limited" or "vortex" public figure who, while achieving no general notoriety, "injects himself...into a particular public controversy."[14]

After *Gertz*, it was clear that much would depend on the definition of "public controversy." Under a narrow interpretation of public controversy, the public figure category would be a comparatively limited one, though not as small as the all-purpose public figure category. Under a broader interpretation of public controversy, many plaintiffs would be classified as public figures, even if acting in furtherance of ostensibly private interests.

In the absence of a clear statement by the Supreme Court, the lower courts have been divided over which interpretation to adopt. Among scholars, the debate concerns not simply how broad the reading of "controversy" should be, but which content-based interpretation of the first amendment governs or should govern the concept of public controversy.[15] Some commentators, recognizing that the *Rosenbloom* general public interest test is thoroughly discredited, have suggested alternative definitions of public controversy based

12. Gertz v. Robert Welch, Inc., 418 U.S. 323, 346 (1974). In its most recent pronouncement, however, the Court sems to apply to some aspects of *Gertz* only to cases involving issues of public concern, which apparently means that a lower court will be forced to determine if such an issue exists in each case. *See* Dun & Bradstreet, Inc. v. Greenmoss Builders, Inc. _____ U.S. _____ (1985). The Court clearly is making a distinction between matters of public concern and matters of public controversy, although the differences remain unclear.
13. *Id*. at 351.
14. *Id*.
15. As Lillian BeVier points out in her article, *The First Amendment and Political Speech: An Inquiry into the Substance and Limits of Principle,* 30 STAN. L. REV. 299, 299–300 (1978),

> Disputes about the proper "test" for determining the permissible extent of governmental regulation of speech occupied the first several decades of first amendment theorizing. The early test seekers often implicitly assumed that the only significant first amendment issues were the degree to which, and the circumstances under which, government could regulate speech.

Prof. BeVier adds:

> Recent commentators have begun to recognize explicitly that so long as first amendment values remain obscure, clarity will never emerge from first amendment analysis...the various "tests" [like clear and

on Alexander Meiklejohn's original concept of "political speech."[16] Others, still with reference to the ideas of Meiklejohn (often the later Meiklejohn), have advanced an expanded public interest-political speech test.[17] Before looking at how the courts have dealt with the public controversy question, we should briefly outline this Meiklejohnian theoretical approach and how commentators apply it to define a public controversy.

II. MEIKLEJOHN POLITICAL SPEECH AND SUPREME COURT

The "political speech" basis for interpreting the meaning of the first amendment rests on the historical linkage of important public speech to speech involving government and the democratic process. Meiklejohn theorized that the core meaning of the first amendment is the protection of political speech. According to Meiklejohn, the first amendment, "protects the freedom of those activities of thought and communication by which we 'govern'. . . . All constitutional authority to govern the people of the United States belongs to the people themselves acting as members of a corporate body politic." This is "not . . . a private right, but . . . a public power, a governmental responsibility."[18]

Adopting such a unified theory of first amendment interpretation to help resolve the confusion over the extent of *New York Times* protection of libelous statements is both intellectually and practically satisfying. As Steven Shiffrin points out,

> [T]he attractiveness of a politically based interpretation of the First Amendment is easily understood. . . . As a strategy of communication protection, it offers the pragmatic prospect of preventing the government from intruding into areas where its potential for bias is particularly acute. As a theory of interpretation, it offers the legalistic neatness of permitting the conclusion that the absolute terms of the First Amendment protect absolutely that speech within its scope. It confines the area within which the judiciary may impose subjectively derived values. And, finally, it offers a grand and romantic appeal for

present danger] . . . cannot create a foundation for a theory of the first amendment nor provide adequate justification for first amendment results.
Some other notable commentators focusing on first amendment values include Robert Bork, *Neutral Principles and Some First Amendment Problems*, 47 IND. L. J. 1 (1971), and Anthony Lewis, New York Times v. Sullivan *Reconsidered: Time to Return to the Central Meaning of the First Amendment*, 83 COLUM. L. REV. 91 (1983).
16. *See supra* note 7.
17. *See, e.g.,* Carl Willner, *Defining a Public Controversy in the Constitutional Law of Defamation*, 69 VA. L. REV. 901 (1983) *and* Gerald G. Ashdown, *Of Public Figures and Public Interest—The Libel Law Conundrum*, 25 WM. & MARY L. REV. 937 (1984).
18. *See The First Amendment is an Absolute, supra* note 7, at 253.

conjoining First Amendment theory with the basic theory of
American Government.[19]

   This theoretical attractiveness has led some commentators to suggest that
a political speech rationale should govern the concept of public controversy.
This approach is exemplified by one commentator who notes the "considerable
confusion" engendered by the Supreme Court's public controversy standard.
He suggests "a political speech interpretation of the public controversy requirement, encompassing all core political and some peripheral speech, is
the most coherent rationale for a content-based inquiry."[20] It is speech about
government (and, for some, speech that is governmental by analogy) that falls
within the confines of a public controversy. "There is clearly a public controversy if the actionable speech involves governmental policies or processes.
If not, the secondary inquiry asks whether the speech involved so resembles
or is tied to political speech that a reasonable speaker would see no clear
difference." Collective action, institutional or personal linkage with government, and significant consequences for public policy are proposed as criteria
that "suggest that a dispute falls within the gray area where. . .a public controversy should be found."[21]
   Tidy as these rationales for determining a public controversy are, appealing
in their elegance and clarity as they may be, there remains a major obstacle
to their adoption. That is, the Supreme Court is not following this approach—or
at least not in a form suggested by its adherents. The Court has decided three
cases since *Gertz* where the issue of what is meant by the term "public controversy" played an important part in the ultimate decision. In each case, the
Court sent forth a clear signal that it intends to read the definition of public
controversy very narrowly. What is more, the Court has given little indication that it will base any ultimate definition on the public/private speech distinctions many legal theorists might prefer, and certainly it is not returning to
a general public interest test. However, the Court has still to articulate a working definition of exactly what is meant by public controversy.
   The Court's first interpretation of its own public controversy standard
came in *Time, Inc. v. Firestone.*[22] The Court, in an opinion delivered by Justice
Rehnquist, held that Mary Alice Firestone "did not assume any role of special
prominence in the affairs of society, other than perhaps Palm Beach society."[23] Moreover, the Court said, a divorce proceeding is not necessarily a public
controversy, even when involving prominent people. This, the court said,

19. Steven Shiffrin, *Defamatory Non-Media Speech and First Amendment Methodology,*
    25 UCLA L. Rev. 915, 917–918 (1978).
20. *See* Willner, *supra* note 17, at 931.
21. *Id.*
22. Time, Inc. v. Firestone, 424 U.S. 448 (1976).
23. *Id.* at 453.

seeks to equate "public controversy" with all controversies of interest to the public. . . . Dissolution of marriage through judicial proceedings is not the sort of "public controversy" referred to in *Gertz*, even though the marital difficulties of extremely wealthy individuals may be of interest to some portion of the reading public.[24]

While in *Firestone*, the Court clearly rejected the argument that public controversy equals "public interest" or even "controversies of interest to the public," it left ambiguous its feelings about the "public controversy equals political speech" argument. Reports of formal open judicial proceedings of whatever nature arguably would fall under the heading of political speech, yet the Court said that "the details of many, if not most, courtroom battles would add almost nothing toward advancing the uninhibited debate on public issues thought to provide principal support for the decision in *New York Times*."[25] The Court also made it clear that "imposing upon the law of private defamation the rather drastic limitations worked by the *New York Times* cannot be justified by generalized references to the public interest in reports of judicial proceedings."[26]

However, in its discussion of public controversy, the Court refused to hold that public controversies equate with "controversies of interest to the public."[27] Thus the Court maintained

the core of Meiklejohn's approach in this sense—at least in those cases where the plaintiff has attempted to influence the outcome of a controversy by means of public communication, the extent to which the communication bears upon public issues determines the level of constitutional protection enjoyed by the defendant. Thus, at least in some contexts, speech on public issues is deemed to be entitled to greater first amendment protection than speech which is not.[28]

In *Hutchinson v. Proxmire*,[29] the Court rejected the claim that Dr. Hutchinson's involvement in government-sponsored research made him a limited public figure, partly on the basis that

Hutchinson did not thrust himself or his views into public controversy to influence others. Respondents have not identified

24. *Id.* at 454.
25. *Id.* at 457.
26. *Id.*
27. *Id.* at 454.
28. *See* Shiffrin, *supra* note 19, at 927–28.
29. Hutchinson v. Proxmire, 443 U.S. 111 (1979).

such a particular controversy; at most, they point to concern about general public expenditures. But that concern is shared by most and relates to most public expenditures; it is not sufficient to make Hutchinson a public figure.[30]

This is clear evidence that the Court is not relying primarily on a content-based speech rationale that simply equates public controversy with overt political speech. Plainly, Senator Proxmire's bestowing of his "Golden Fleece" award on Dr. Hutchinson, based on the contention that Hutchinson's research is a wasting of public funds, seems incontrovertably to be an example of political speech or, to quote Meiklejohn, "communication by which we 'govern.'"[31]

In *Wolston v. Reader's Digest Association*,[32] the Court again narrowed the definition of "public controversy" when it questioned whether the issue of Soviet espionage in the United States was a controversy at all. "It is difficult to determine with precision the 'public controversy' into which petitioner is alleged to have thrust himself," said Justice Rehnquist speaking for the Court.

Certainly, there was no public controversy or debate in 1958 about the desirability of permitting Soviet espionage in the United States; all responsible United States citizens understandably were and are opposed to it. Respondents urged, and the Court of Appeals apparently agreed, that the public controversy involved the propriety of the actions of law enforcement officials in investigating the prosecution of suspected Soviet Agents. . . .[33]

While the Court decided it need not address the public controversy issue further because the case could be decided on other grounds, the Court's language appears to raise doubt that even speech related to foreign espionage, clearly subject matter related to political speech, would be judged as creating a public controversy unless such espionage were to be the subject of a reasonable debate.

Both *Hutchinson* and *Wolston* have been criticized by commentators for too narrowly restricting the public controversy definition. Alexander Del Russo notes that in *Hutchinson*

the content of the speech involves a matter of public concern. An obvious societal interest exists in the government's spend-

30. *Id.* at 135.
31. *See The First Amendment is an Absolute, supra* note 7, at 255.
32. Wolston v. Reader's Digest Association, 443 U.S. 157 (1979).
33. *Id.* at 166 n.8.

ing of tax dollars. The ultimate decisions on public expenses are made by our elected representatives whose tenure depends upon popular support. More important, the speech in *Hutchinson* is political speech—it is critical of government funding of what is perceived to be a wasteful study. While the speech may cast a shadow on the professional character of the plaintiff, this would not alter the political character of the speech and subject it to a lesser degree of protection.[34]

And Floyd Abrams, writing in the *Washington Post,* said *Hutchinson* and *Wolston* "limit what the public learns about real criminals, about possible wastes of public funds, and about others whose conduct and misconduct affect us all."[35]

III. PUBLIC CONTROVERSY AND THE LOWER COURTS

The Court's refusal to articulate and adopt an underlying theoretical rationale for defining a public controversy, or at least to set out clear guidelines for determining the boundaries of this term, besides frustrating commentators, undoubtedly has contributed to a confusing series of contradictory decisions by lower federal and state courts. These decisions usually have been ad hoc determinations based on the facts of each case. Unfortunately, this standardless, fact-finding approach provides little predictability in decisions from court to court, as analysis of cases involving similar fact patterns shows.

In *Rosanova v. Playboy Enterprises, Inc.,*[36] one issue on appeal was the public figure status of Mr. Rosanova, whom *Playboy* magazine called a "mobster." The district court held, citing *Gertz* and *Firestone*, that the plaintiff clearly was a public figure, although the court noted that "defining public figures is much like trying to nail a jellyfish to the wall."[37] The circuit court agreed with the lower court's opinion that Mr. Rosanova "voluntarily engaged in a course that was bound to invite attention and comment."[38] The circuit court apparently also found a public controversy in the "reported associations and activities concerning organized crime" of the plaintiff.[39]

In contrast, the California Court of Appeals in *Rancho La Costa v. Superior Court*[40] held that allegations by *Penthouse* magazine that plaintiff

---

34. Alexander Del Russo, *Freedom of the Press and Defamation: Attacking the Bastion of* New York Times v. Sullivan, 25 St. Louis U. L. J. 501, 540–41 (1981).
35. Washington Post, June 27, 1979, at A10, col. 1.
36. Rosanova v. Playboy Enterprises, Inc., 580 F.2d 859 (5th Cir. 1980).
37. Rosanova v. Playboy Enterprises, Inc., 411 F. Supp. 440, 443 (S.D. Ga. 1976).
38. *Id.* at 445.
39. Rosanova v. Playboy Enterprises, Inc., 580 F.2d 859, 861 n.3 (5th Cir. 1980).
40. Rancho La Costa v. Superior Court, 165 Cal. Rptr. 347 (1980).

corporation and individual plaintiffs were connected with organized crime were not enough to push plaintiffs into the public figure category. In part, the court said

> there is no public controversy or debate over the "desirabili-
> ty" of "organized crime." There truly never has been. All con-
> scientious and responsible citizens are opposed to it. There
> was no "controversy" over La Costa itself. At most it was a
> matter of limited press interest. The creation of a large resort-
> spa and attendant facilities created no "public controversy."
> But even if La Costa were deemed *arguendo* a matter of public
> controversy, that fact alone would not and does not make [in-
> dividual] petitioners public figures.[41] [emphasis added]

Similar problems with differing ad hoc determinations have surfaced in a series of cases involving the activities of corporations litigating as plaintiffs in defamation actions. For example, in *Steaks Unlimited v. Deaner*,[42] the Third Circuit agreed with the trial court that an "intensive advertising campaign"[43] and subsequent questions raised about the quality of the corporation's pro- ducts created a public controversy. Yet, in *Vegod Corporation v. ABC*,[44] the California Supreme Court clearly rejected this argument. The court noted:

> While availability of goods for sale and their quality are mat-
> ters of public interest, this is not the test. . . .Criticism of com-
> mercial conduct does not deserve the special protection of the
> actual malice test. . . .We conclude that a person in the business
> world advertising his wares does not necessarily become part
> of an existing public controversy.[45]

Some courts, faced with a limited public figure defamation plaintiff, seem to have thrown up their hands when faced with determining if a public con- troversy exists. A way out is to hold that, because of factual circumstances, the public controversy requirement can be waived. And at least one court simply held that *Gertz*'s limited public figure requirements do not apply to an entire class of defamation plaintiffs. In this latter decision, *Martin Mariet- ta Corporation v. Evening Star Newspaper Company*,[46] a federal district court

41. *Id.* at 354.
42. Steaks Unlimited v. Deaner, 623 F.2d 264 (3rd Cir. 1980).
43. *Id.* at 274.
44. Vegod Corporation v. ABC, 603 P.2d 14, 160 Cal. Rptr. 97 (1980.)
45. *Id.* at 18.
46. Martin Marietta Corporation v. Evening Star Newspaper Company, 417 F. Supp. 947 (D.C. 1976).

judge in Washington, D.C. found that *Gertz* provided "an ill-fitting mold"[47] for determining constitutional protections in cases involving corporations as plaintiffs in defamation suits. The court held that because corporations have no personal reputation to injure they should be

> denied full protection from libel. Stated another way, the "public figure" standards set out in *Gertz* are designed to ascertain whether a person, through his activities, has lost claim to his private life. It makes no sense to apply these standards to a corporation, which, regardless of its activities, never has a private life to lose.[48]

The first circuit, in *Bruno & Stillman v. Globe Newspaper*,[49] categorically rejected the argument that corporations either are not covered by the *Gertz* standards or are public figures for all purposes (the alternative reasoning in *Martin Marietta*). "We know of no support [for that position] in . . . applicable substantive law. . . ." the court said.[50] It added, "We shall therefore follow a more particularized approach. Our first task, following the guidance of *Firestone*, is to determine whether there was 'the sort of public controversy referred to in *Gertz*.'"[51] The court found no public controversy prior to the series of articles criticizing the plaintiff and refused to hold that the plaintiff was a public figure.

Brewer v. Memphis Publishing Company[52] provides an example of a court looking to extenuating circumstances. The court analyzed the notoriety surrounding plaintiffs' lives and held that the extreme extent of publicity generated by their actions obviated the need for a public controversy test in determining limited public figure status. The court admitted that "a sports or entertainment career clearly does not necessarily involve any public controversy." Nonetheless, the court held that both Anita and John Brewer were public figures for comments related to their careers by focusing "on plaintiffs' actions in seeking publicity or voluntarily engaging in activities that necessarily involve the risk of increased exposure and injury to reputation."[53] This led one commentator to note that "in effect, the *Brewer* court found the level of voluntariness so high as to render unnecessary any inquiry into the existence of a public controversy."[54]

In contrast to *Brewer*, a federal district court judge in Wyoming did not

---

47. *Id.* at 956.
48. *Id.* at 955.
49. Bruno & Stillman v. Globe Newspaper, 633 F.2d 583 (1st Cir. 1980).
50. *Id.* at 590.
51. *Id.*
52. Brewer v. Memphis Publishing Company, 626 F.2d 1238 (5th Cir. 1980).
53. *Id.* at 1254.
54. *See* Shiffrin, *supra* note 19, at 951.

find that seeking publicity was sufficient grounds for viewing Miss Wyoming as a public figure of any kind. In *Pring v. Penthouse*,[55] the court said:

> We think it is a matter of general knowledge that our country has a multitude of beauty contests, in each of which there may be dozens or even perhaps hundreds of contestants. It also has countless marching bands, each of which usually enjoys the services of a twirler. But who among us can name or recall their names unless perhaps they have won a major beauty contest like that of the Miss America Pageant? Except for that fortunate person, generally speaking the rest of the contestants fade into the private life enjoyed by most Americans.[56]

Brewer and cases like *James v. Gannett*[57] are often cited by courts that apparently feel a plaintiff is neither a household word nor involved in a matter of public controversy yet "should" be a public figure for purposes of a defamation suit because of plaintiff's own efforts to seek the limelight. The problem with the "publicity" public figure analysis is that it is just another ad hoc method until the Supreme Court recognizes it and suggests guidelines for determining what and how much publicity or publicity seeking is "enough." Until such determination, we are left with decisions like *Brewer* and *Pring*, as well as such recent cases as *Holt v. Cox Enterprises.*[58] In the latter case, a football player for Alabama in the late 50s and early 60s was judged a public figure on the basis of criticism, generated twenty years later, of his on-field conduct. In *Hellman v. McCarthy*,[59] a court held that author Lillian Hellman was not a public figure, rejecting defendant's arguments that were based on a *Brewer*-type analysis.

Frustrations with such a diversity of opinions led the D.C. Circuit Court in *Waldbaum v. Fairchild Publications*[60] to suggest a new test to "flesh out the skeletal descriptions" of public figures suggested in *Gertz.*[61] The circuit court, noting that all participants in defamation litigation would profit from a consistent policy of public controversy determination, suggested that a public controversy be defined as "a specific public dispute that has foreseeable and substantial ramifications for persons beyond its immediate participants. . . ."[62]

---

55. Pring v. Penthouse, 7 Media L. Rep. 1101 (D. Wyo., 1981).
56. *Id.* at 1103.
57. James v. Gannett, 40 N.Y.2d 415, 353 N.E.2d 834 (1976).
58. Holt v. Cox Enterprises, 590 F. Supp. 408 (N.D. Ga. 1984).
59. Hellman v. McCarthy, 10 Media L. Rep. 1789 (1984).
60. Waldbaum v. Fairchild Publications, 627 F.2d 1287 (D.C. Cir. 1980).
61. *Id.* at 1292.
62. *Id.*

The court added that the outcome of this dispute must affect "the general public or some segment of it in an appreciable way."[63]

Waldbaum involved a former head of a large food cooperative in the Washington, D.C., area who sued Fairchild's *Supermarket News* for allegedly defaming him in an article that claimed the cooperative had lost money under Waldbaum's leadership. Waldbaum gained attention within the food service industry by promoting the benefits of food cooperatives and other innovative food-marketing techniques. He received media attention for his activities and admittedly sought to educate the public to the benefits of the co-op form of organization. The court apparently added together the facts of Waldbaum's activities, the innovativeness of the company, and the discussion and debate the court found within the food service industry about the wisdom of co-op policies, to determine that there was an ongoing public controversy about the management abilities of Waldbaum which predated the defamatory reference by *Supermarket News*.[64]

In so doing, the court raised a number of troubling issues for those wishing to adopt the *Waldbaum* test. It seems quite clear that had the court surveyed residents of the Washington, D.C., area, almost no one could have pinpointed the supposed public controversy or Waldbaum's role in it. While large-scale public understanding is not a necessary condition for the existence of a public controversy, it certainly is one indicator that such a controversy exists. Second, the court apparently believed that any action out of the ordinary, and therefore the subject of comment and discussion, raises such action to the level of public controversy. According to the court, it was Waldbaum's activities to encourage "unit pricing, open dating, the cooperative form of business, and other issues" that thrust him into public controversies surrounding these policies.[65]

The question is: What raises the discussion of any new or offbeat proposal to the kind of legitimate public controversy the Supreme Court has in mind? The *Waldbaum* court doesn't tackle this issue, skipping over it by noting that "to determine whether a controversy indeed existed and, if so, to define its contours, the judge must examine whether persons actually were discussing some specific question."[66] The court immediately substitutes the term "debate" for "question" and continues its opinion without further elaboration on how this transformation takes place.

A third, and related, issue is the circuit court's stated refusal to concern itself with the "legitimacy of the public's concern" because, the court said, "such an approach would turn courts into censors of 'what information is relevant to self-government'."[67] The circuit court said that it took this course

63. *Id.*
64. *Id.* at 1299–1300.
65. *Id.* at 1300.
66. *Id.* at 1297.
67. *Id.*

because "no arm of government, including the judiciary, should be able to set society's agenda."[68] Perhaps the court's action was taken to avoid reintroducing a *Rosenbloom*-like test through the back door, reflecting the Supreme Court's criticism of judges determining what constitutes a matter of public interest. There are two problems with this. First, the circuit court, early in its opinion, specifically exempts purely private matters and general criminal proceedings from public controversies based on *Firestone* and *Wolston*.[69] It seems likely that courts following *Waldbaum* will have no better alternative than to continue to make ad hoc exceptions to this refusal to question the legitimacy of the public concern, depending on the latest Supreme Court decision. This severely limits the predictive power of a *Waldbaum* public controversy test. The second problem is that by refusing to limit the scope of concern, the circuit court arguably extends the range of public controversies far beyond that envisioned by the Supreme Court and lower courts which, in fact, seem determined to rein in, rather than expand, the notion of public controversy.

IV. REQUIREMENTS FOR FINDING A PUBLIC CONTROVERSY

Nothing is inherently wrong with courts in different states (or different lower federal courts applying state laws) arriving at different decisions on similar facts. It is troublesome, however, if these differing opinions all purport to be based on attempts to fathom what the Supreme Court means (or may mean) when the Court uses a term like "public controversy."

For whatever reasons, the Supreme Court today does not appear willing to adopt the doctrinal, content-based approach for determining public controversy suggested by legal commentators. The Court seems content to allow some play in the joints of such constructs, perhaps because the justices do not believe the first amendment requires more. Neither does it seem that the Court is going in the direction suggested by the methods or tests seen to date in the opinions of lower courts. If this is so, the efforts taken by most lower courts and commentators to broaden the definition of public controversy might better be turned to convincing state high courts and/or legislators of the worthiness of their approach.

68. *Id.*
69. *Id.* at 1296. The court characterized *Firestone* as "meaning that matters essentially of a private nature do not become public controversies solely because members of the public find them appealing. . . ." Similarly the court said about *Wolston* that "publicity surrounding litigation does not by itself elevate the parties to public figures, even if they could anticipate the publicity, unless they are using the court as a forum for espousing their views in other controversies." While ingenious, these exceptions to the court's wish not to question the legitimacy of the public interest are clearly ad hoc. The Supreme Court has not hesitated to make distinctions from the time Justice Brennan noted in *New York Times* that purely private defamatory speech does not merit an actual malice standard.

While predicting the Court's ultimate determination is chancy at best, it may be somewhat safer to set out those requirements for determining a public controversy that seem to reflect the Court's interpretation to date. It is also important to recognize that each of the procedural and substantive requirements listed below, while perhaps necessary, probably are not sufficient for completing the Court's own definition.

A. Procedural Requirements

1. The controversy must come first, then the defamation, i.e., it must predate the defamatory statements.[70]
2. The discussion of the specific public controversy must be ongoing among a sizable or significant portion of the public, i.e., evidenced by discussion in large segments of the public and frequently engendering media coverage of the issues involved in the controversy. "Public" may mean the general public or a subset of the general public unified by geographic, organizational or other similar ties.[71]
3. There must be clear evidence of ongoing debate.[72] Such evidence might be found in the formation of special interest groups organized to argue for different sides of the controversy. Indicia language could be the reasonable formulation of the sides of the public controversy in formal debate terms, i.e., "be it resolved that. . . ."
4. The public controversy must be beyond the control of the plaintiff, i.e., it has a life of its own. The plaintiff may have set the stage for the controversy through action that initiates the debate (for example advertising a product) but this is not enough to create a public controversy in itself.[73]

B. Substantive Requirements

1. A public controversy must be a genuinely debatable issue, i.e., at least two legitimate sides. Thus, a public controversy is not automatically begun by discussion of important public issues or public questions, even if such questions involve political speech.[74]
2. A public controversy should concern legitimate, important subjects,

---

70. Fitzgerald v. Penthouse International, 525 F. Supp. 585 (D. Md. 1981). *See also* Hutchinson v. Proxmire, 443 U.S. 111, 135 (1979) *and* Wolston v. Reader's Digest Association, 443 U.S. 157, 167–68 (1979).
71. Time, Inc. v. Firestone, 424 U.S. 448, 453 (1976).
72. *See* Hutchinson v. Proxmire, 443 U.S. 111, 135 (1979).
73. *See* Fitzgerald v. Penthouse International, 525 F. Supp. 585, 589–90 (D. Md. 1981). *See also* Waldbaum v. Fairchild Publications, 627 F.2d 1287, 1292 (D.C. Cir. 1980).
74. *See* Hutchinson v. Proxmire, 443 U.S. 111, 135 (1979) *and* Wolston v. Reader's Digest Association, 443 U.S. 157, 166–67 (1979). *See also* Street v. NDC, 645 F.2d 1227 (6th Cir. 1981).

not merely disputes between private parties (even though newsworthy) or arguments discussed publicly about sports, show business or other trivial matters. The Court may follow a policy of first determining that the indicia for a true public controversy exist, with the further stipulation that the subject of the controversy resemble early Meiklejohn-like political speech.[75]

The suggested requirements may be criticized as making it likely that courts adopting such a test will find fewer public controversies, thereby reducing the numbers in the limited public figure category. This is a legitimate criticism, but it seems safe to predict that this is the direction the current Court is headed. Application of the proposed requirements to the sequence of cases from *Gertz* to *Wolston*, where the meaning of public controversy was narrowed in each instance, shows that they predict each outcome perfectly. In many cases where lower courts have found public controversies, however, application of the suggested requirements would have decided the issues quite differently.[76]

In advancing these requirements, no criticism is implied of those who suggest alternative tests for determining public controversy as long as their arguments are couched in terms of how a particular state court decides a public controversy *should* be defined in that state. The Court in *Gertz* encouraged individual states to experiment by fashioning laws to arbitrate the tensions between press freedom and private rights as long as such experimentation did not violate first amendment requirements.[77]

A major cause of the confusion over the meaning of public controversy is in large measure ascribable to the reluctance of state authorities to clearly state that they don't know what the Supreme Court means by public controversy, but that they are willing to say what it means in their state. Most courts have not taken this path, perhaps because lower federal courts are understandably leery of suggesting innovative standards to courts in states where the

<hr />

75. Admittedly, this is in direct contradiction of the trend in some lower court decisions to extend *New York Times* protection [see for example Chuy v. Philadelphia Eagles Football Club, 595 F.2d 1265 (3rd Cir. 1979)]. At least tentative support for such a position appears in *Firestone*, where the Court was not reluctant to evaluate the legitimacy of the issue (and found it wanting). Professor Frederick Schauer, in what may prove a seminal article published after the Spring 1984 first amendment conference at the College of William and Mary, points the way to a theoretical basis for this position as well. Schauer, *Public Figures*, 25 WM. & MARY L. REV. 905 (1984). Schauer argues there are strong first amendment-based reasons for distinguishing between public figures such as Henry Kissinger or the president of General Motors and those persons of public interest who are not similarly situated in regard to their influence on public policy. It is reasonable to believe the Supreme Court may adopt a similar rationale for differentiating between important public policy debates and questions involving matters of lesser public importance. *Cf.* Dun & Bradstreet v. Greenmoss Builders, _____ U.S. _____ (June 27, 1985).
76. Likely examples include Rosanova v. Playboy Enterprises, Inc., 580 F.2d 859 (5th Cir. 1980) and Steaks Unlimited v. Deaner, 623 F.2d 264 (3rd Cir. 1980).
77. Gertz v. Robert Welch, Inc., 418 U.S. 323, 347 (1974).

definition of public controversy is unclear and state courts feel that the press protection side of the private rights-free speech equation is best left to the Supreme Court's first amendment interpretations.[78] Alternatively, it simply may be that the issue has not yet been presented to the appropriate state court.

For whatever reasons, the clear invitation of the Court in *Gertz* to seek creativity in the law of defamation at the state level has, for the most part, been ignored. Those state courts recognizing their option to fashion their own standards have generally done so only in deciding what fault standard applies.[79] Even in states adopting negligence, however, those representing defendants in defamation suits may be able to convince the court to extend additional protections to the free press interests that go beyond the rather limited guidelines set down by the Supreme Court. Certainly those who argue that the concept of public controversy should be read broadly or should be based on a theoretical perspective should make their case strongly at the state level, as the Court in *Gertz* plainly encourages them to do.

---

78. *See, e.g.,* Cahill v. Hawaiian Paradise Park Corp., 56 Haw. 522, 536, 543 P.2d 1356, 1366 (1975), where the Hawaiian Supreme Court refused to adopt a standard other than negligence, despite arguments in favor of a *Rosenbloom*-like test, in part because it would be "difficult to see in the Hawaii constitution [with wording identical to the first amendment] a purpose to afford more extensive privileges to the news media than have been found [by the Supreme Court of the United States] in the first amendment."
79. *See, e.g.,* Collins and Drushal, *The Reaction of the State Courts to* Gertz v. Robert Welch, Inc., 28 Case W. Res. 306 (Winter 1978).

ROBERT L. SPELLMAN

Avoiding the Chilling Effect: News Media Tort and First Amendment Insurance

Robert L. Spellman is an attorney and
faculty member in the School of Journalism, Southern Illinois University at
Carbondale.

As tort lawsuits against the news media and litigation over first amendment issues continue to increase, insurance is assuming more importance. By spreading risk and removing threats to survival, insurance can offset any chilling effect[1] on editorial policy resulting from tort lawsuits against journalists and their media employers. It can also encourage news media challenges to actions that threaten first amendment values.

This article describes the special types of insurance available to newspaper publishers and radio/television broadcasters and how insurance carriers assess risks. It also describes how coverages have expanded to include non-traditional tort risks. Further, it explores some of the legal issues inherent in the use of insurance, including public policy prohibitions against insurers' payment of some types of judgments against the media.[2]

The importance of insurance is spotlighted by both the rising volume of media tort lawsuits and the increase in dollar amounts of court awards. The average dollar award in media tort actions exceeds those in medial malprac-

1. The chilling effect is documented in Massing, Michael, *The Libel Chill: How Cold is it Out There?* COLUM. J. REV. 31 (May/June 1985).
2. Much of the material for this article comes from policy forms and rating plans filed with the Ohio Department of Insurance by CNA Media/Professional Insurance, Inc., Employers Reinsurance Corp., Fireman's Fund Insurance Cos., and Seaboard Surety Co. Outlines of tort and first amendment policies of Mutual Insurance Company, Ltd. were supplied by Arthur B. Hanson, Washington, DC. retired U.S. general counsel. Paul L. O'Brien, Washington, DC, current U.S. general counsel, supplied information on changes in the Mutual policy. Not much has been published on media insurance. Published sources include LANKENAU, MEDIA INSURANCE: PROTECTING

tice and product liability suits.[3] Mutual Insurance Company, Ltd., which underwrites tort insurance for more than forty percent of United States daily newspapers, paid out $26.9 million in losses during the twelve years ending in mid-1981.[4]

To underwrite the unique risks faced by journalists in gathering and reporting news, insurance companies have developed special media perils and first amendment policies.[5] Losses covered include legal expenses as well as court awards and settlements. The policies provide coverage in three areas. First, they cover losses stemming from traditional communications torts. Most losses are for libel or invasion of privacy, but coverage also includes those losses incurred in claims for physical trespass in the gathering of news, infringement of copyright, title or slogan, and plagiarism, piracy or misappropriation of ideas.

Second, coverage is provided for losses incurred for claims in such emerging litigation arenas as editorial products liability, negligent misstatement, infliction of emotional distress, infringement of civil rights, and violation of securities laws. So far, plaintiffs have seldom prevailed on such claims, but the news media incur substantial legal costs in defending themselves.

The third policy is first amendment coverage. This coverage reimburses publishers and broadcasters for legal expenses incurred in defending significant first amendment interests. It includes such actions as news media suits for access to courtrooms, and defenses against subpoenas for reporters' notes.

About eighty percent of losses paid by insurers under tort coverages are for legal expenses.[6] Of course, first amendment coverage is simply a specialized form of legal expenses insurance. It is relatively new but has spread rapidly (it is not available under regulations of the New York State Department of Insurance).[7]

Coverage of legal expenses is essential for news outlets. Costs are higher

---

AGAINST HIGH JUDGEMENTS, PUNITIVE DAMAGES AND DEFENSE COSTS (1983); Worral, *The Insurance Issue and Identifying Problem Areas of Libel Litigation, and* Galane, *Libel: Punitive Damages,* 622-45, in WINFIELD, LIBEL LITIGATION (1979); *and* Soloski & Dyer, *The Cost of Prior Restraint;* U.S. v. The Progressive 3, 16-19 COMMUNICATIONS AND THE LAW (April 1984); *and* Massing, *supra* note 1, at 33-34. These sources include some policy forms. Although the risks covered may differ somewhat, media perils policies are also written for magazine publishers, book publishers, wire services, syndicators, newspaper and magazine columnists, book authors, cable television networks and stations, advertising agencies, public relations agencies, and commercial printers. For a media conglomerate, an insurer will write one policy covering all its outlets.

3. Friendly, *Libel Awards Found Higher Than Two Other Categories,* New York Times, March 10, 1984, at 10.
4. *$26 Million Paid on Libel Policies,* EDITOR AND PUBLISHER, May 12, 1984, at 32.
5. In addition to the companies listed in note 2, media perils policies are written by Chubb/Pacific Insurance Co. and Lloyd's of London.
6. *Supra* note 3.
7. Fagerberg, *Libel Policy Deductibles and Limits,* in LANKENAU, *supra* note 2, at 364.

for the news media than many other business firms because of a peculiar pattern of lower court losses that are reversed on appeal. One study found that the news media lost seventy-seven percent of suits that went to trial; at the appellate level, the news media prevailed in seventy-eight percent of the cases.[8] Being forced to take cases to the appellate level results in substantially increased legal costs. Further, some news outlets follow a policy of never settling a libel case.[9] While this may reduce the cost of court awards and eliminate settlement costs, it increases legal expenses.

Another trend is for more libel cases to go to trial. Prior to 1978, the predominant view was that the first amendment compelled courts to make summary judgment the rule in libel cases.[10] That view was questioned by Chief Justice Burger in a footnote in the U.S. Supreme Court's *Hutchinson v. Proxmire* decision.[11] In part, the footnote said that a libel action often calls "a defendant's state of mind into question" and, thus, "does not readily lend itself to summary disposition."[12] Going to trial substantially increases expenses. It cost CBS $250,000 to produce "The Uncounted Enemy: A Vietnam Deception." Defending the resulting libel suit filed by General William C. Westmoreland, including expenses of a lengthy trial, cost the network more than ten times the cost of producing the show.[13]

First amendment insurance apparently was first written in 1980. Typical policy language says that the carrier will indemnify against legal expenses incurred

> in the prosecution or defense of any action, suit or proceeding which involves a significant infringement of the Insured's rights of freedom of speech or press guaranteed by the First Amendment of the Constitution of the United States. . .or the Con-

---

8. Franklin, *Suing Media for Libel: A Litigation Study,* No. 3 AMERICAN BAR FOUNDATION RESEARCH JOURNAL 795-831 (1981). *See also* Franklin, *Winners and Losers and Why: A Study of Defamation Litigation,* No. 3 AMERICAN BAR FOUNDATION RESEARCH JOURNAL 455-500 (1980).
9. Weinberg, *Libel: The Press Fights Back,* COLUM. J. REV. 66 (November/December 1983).
10. Washington Post Co. v. Keogh, 365 F.2d 965, 968 (D.C. Cir. 1966), *cert. denied,* 385 U.S. 1011 (1967).
11. Hutchinson v. Proxmire, 443 U.S. 111, 120 n.9 (1979).
12. *ID.*
13. There have been numerous news accounts on the legal expenses of the suit. *See* Farber, *Westmoreland Trial Provides Insights into Era of Vietnam War,* New York Times, Dec. 31, 1984, at 19. An excellent case study is Soloski & Dyer, *supra* note 2. the article includes information on legal expenses of several cases in addition to that on *The Progressive.* The increasing number of celebrity libel suits and the disposition of judges to permit them to go to trial in causing an increase in insurance premiums. Klrtz, *Celebrity Plaintiffs Raise Cost of Libel Insurance,* EDITOR AND PUBLISHER, Dec. 15, 1984, at 13.

stitution of any state in which the Insured is domiciled or doing business.[14]

Where an insured and its carrier disagree over whether a significant first amendment interest is involved, there is provision for arbitration.

Only legal expenses are covered. Excluded are such costs as court-imposed fines or *Snepp*-type[15] loss of profits. Also excluded are legal expenses of enforcement of any freedom of information or open meeting law, or of any antitrust action. Included are legal expenses of cases involving search of newsrooms, subpoenas of reporters' notes or broadcasters' outtakes, prior restraints on publication, closure of court proceedings, including pre-trial and post-trial hearings, and disclosure of confidential sources.

The key issue in tort policies is the definition of loss and whether it includes punitive damages. One insurer's policy form reads:

> "Loss" means the total sum, exclusive of criminal fines and criminal penalties and any defense costs resulting therefrom, which the insured becomes legally obligated to pay in settlement of claims or in satisfaction of judgments, including court costs and investigative discovery, adjustment and legal expenses, but the word "loss" does not include salaries paid to employees of the insured.[16]

Another carrier's policy form limits loss to "all sums which the Insured shall become legally obligated to pay as compensatory damages for injury. . . ."[17]

For the publisher or broadcaster who wants comprehensive coverage, the first provision is preferable because it includes punitive damages in jurisdictions where insurers may legally pay such damages. The second provision limits payment to compensatory damages.

Generally, media perils insurance is individually underwritten. Basic premium rates are filled with regulators, but the number and variety of subjective factors which can vary rates make the rates individual ones for practical purposes. In many situations, competition among carriers plays as important a role as risk in setting premiums.

For newspaper publishers, circulation is the key factor in setting base

14. Language is from Employers Reinsurance Corp. multimedia liability policy form.
15. Frank Snepp authored a book and refused to submit it to government review in violation of an agreement he had signed as a Central Intelligence Agency employee. In *Snepp v. United States* (444 U.S. 507 (1980)), the court ruled that profits on the book must be held in constructive trust for the U.S. government.
16. CNA Media/Porfessional media perils policy form for newspaper publisher coverage.
17. Firemen's Fund publishers liability policy form.

rates. For radio/television outlets, a multiple of advertising rates is used to establish base rates. Key factors for both media are the size of deductibles and limits on coverage. Deductibles can range from $1,000 to $250,000 and limits can be written on a per occurrence or aggregate basis. Increases in the limit do not produce proportional rises in premiums. One carrier's rating plan permits a rise in the limit from one to five million dollars for an eighty percent increase in premiums.[18]

The limit should exceed one million dollars even for small outlets. Illustrative of the prudence of a high limit is a libel suit lost by the Alton (Ill.) *Telegraph*. After a jury awarded the plaintiff $9.2 million, the *Telegraph* was forced to file for bankruptcy because its resources could not cover an appeal bond. Finally, the case was settled for $1.25 million, of which one million dollars came from the newspaper's insurer paying the policy limit.[19] Several multi-million dollar awards have been returned against small newspapers. For a newspaper group or television network, the prudent limit should be at least a high eight-figure amount.

A major factor in rate-setting is geography. The law in some states is more favorable to persons suing for libel damages or other media-related torts. Further, the dollar amount of court awards is higher in some states than others.[20] Generally, a media outlet serving a large metropolitan area will be penalized in underwriting because court awards tend to be higher in such areas. One insurer increases premiums fifty percent for California radio stations.[21] In underwriting first amendment coverage, however, the difference in legal climates among the states is not as significant a factor.

Among the other factors that can result in higher premiums for newspapers are: extensive investigative reporting, gossip columns, controversial style or format, restaurant and entertainment reviews, satire, general coverage of public affairs, and unfavorable claims experience. Some of the factors that can result in lower premiums are: heavy content of puzzles, games and articles on hobbies, diet and food preparation, garden, home repairs, lovelorn advice and religion; experienced management; law firm on retainer; and in-house educa-

18. CNA Media/Professional rating plan.
19. Green v. Alton Telegraph, 8 MED. L. REP. 1345 (Ill. App. 1982); Friendly, *Settlement Due in Alton Telegraph Case,* New York Times, April 15, 1982, 12.
20. CNA Media/Professional's rating plan has three geographic areas. The areas with the most favorable rate include: District of Columbia, Georgia, Idaho, Illinois, Indiana, Iowa, Kansas, Kentucky, Michigan, Minnesota, Mississippi, Missouri, Nebraska, New York, North Carolina, Oregon, Pennsylvania, South Dakota, Virginia, Washington, West Virginia, and Wisconsin. The middle group includes: Arizona, Arkansas, Colorado, Connecticut, Delaware, Louisiana, Maine, Maryland, Massachusetts, Montana, Nevada, New Jersey, New Mexico, North Dakota, Ohio, Rhode Island, Tennessee, Texas, Utah, Vermont, and Wyoming. The areas with the least favorable rate include: Alaska, Alabama, California, Florida, Hawaii, New Hampshire, Oklahoma, and South Carolina.
21. Employers Reinsurance rating plan.

tion of employees on potential legal exposure.

For radio/television outlets, in addition to most of the factors that apply to newspapers, controversial programming and call-in and talk shows can increase premiums. Innocuous programming or lack of significant local programming can reduce premiums.[22]

Mutual Insurance Company, Ltd., the largest media tort insurer for U.S. newspapers, has made a significant change in its underwriting policy. Previously, it had not rated newspapers on the basis of adverse experience. Now five-year experience of newspapers is being examined, and premium surcharges are being levied where outlets have adverse claims experiences. Mutual's U.S. general counsel says "the marketplace no longer permits" giving all newspapers the same risk rating.[23]

Due to rising costs, Mutual is making a major change in coverage of legal expenses on tort claims. Previously, the company paid all legal expenses after the deductible was satisfied; now it pays only eighty percent. The change was designed to encourage newspapers to better control legal expenses and to look at cost-effectiveness in considering whether to settle claims. Says Mutual's counsel, "Potential legal fees of $150,000 against an $8,000 settlement should result in more instances where the decision is made to opt for the settlement."[24]

Premiums for media tort insurance are increasing rapidly. Increases of two hundred percent or more have been reported by some outlets;[25] however, the increases are not due to a rise in the number of lawsuits. Officials of two major insurers report the volume of lawsuits appears to be stable.[26] Rather, the increases are attributable to larger—often huge—damage awards and rising legal expenses.[27] Legal expenses of an average libel suit have been estimated at $150,000; the cost is higher in major metropolitan areas.[28]

Rising premiums for libel insurance apparently led Mutual to withdraw from the first amendment insurance market. As libel premiums increased, many newspapers cut first amendment coverage. As a result, the number of papers carrying first amendment coverage with Mutual declined from almost 400 at the start of 1985 to less than 200 by mid-1985.

The increase in news media legal exposure through tort suits in such non-traditional areas as editorial product liability, negligent misstatement, inflic-

22. The factors are from the CNA Media/Professional and Employers Reinsurance rating plans.
23. Paul L. O'Brien, U.S. general counsel, Mutual Insurance Company, Ltd., speech to American Newspaper Publishers Association, Miami Beach, Florida, May 6–8, 1985, p. 10. Copy of speech was supplied by Mr. O'Brien.
24. *Id.* at 9. The coinsurance feature does not apply to Mutual's first amendment policies.
25. Newsom, C. *Special Report: Insurance,* PRESSTIME 16 (March 1985).
26. Massing, *supra* note 1, at 33, quoting Paul L. O'Brien and Lawrence Worrall, President, CNA Media/Professional Insurance, Inc.
27. *Supra* note 23, at 9–10; Kirtz, *supra* note 13.
28. *Supra* note 23, at 3.

tion of emotional distress, civil rights infringement and violation of security laws has produced broader insurance coverage. In some cases, the suits are creative efforts to skirt restrictions that courts have placed on libel and privacy actions. In other instances, recovery is sought for injuries not covered by tradi tional communications torts.

In *Gutter v. Dow Jones, Inc.,* [29] an Ohio appellate court reversed a grant of summary judgment to *The Wall Street Journal* after it was sued by a securities buyer for negligent misrepresentation. Phil Gutter purchased bonds incorrectly listed in the publication as trading with interest. Later, he sold the bonds at a loss of $1,693 and claimed the loss stemmed from a drop in the price of the bonds after the newspaper correctly reported the securities were trading without interest. Gutter alleged that he relied on the newspaper for bond prices and that the bond listing was published with the intent that investors would rely upon it. The court ruled that liability could be found against the financial journal if plaintiff could prove that the "information was published for the specific benefit and guidance of a limited group of subscribers with the knowledge or intention that it would influence and be relied upon by that limited class in making investments in bonds, that plaintiff was such a subscriber and investor who reasonably relied upon such informa- tion . . . and that plaintiff suffered economic injury as a result of his reliance."[30]

The court distinguished the bond buyer's claim from that of a securities trader in *Jaillet v. Cashman,* [31] the case publications have relied upon for more than sixty years to shield them from liability for publishing incorrect infor- mation on financial markets. In *Jaillet,* a trader had claimed losses resulting from decisions made on the basis of information transmitted over the Dow Jones & Co. brokerage house wire. Unlike allegations made by Gutter, the Ohio court said, the *Jaillet* plaintiff "was found to be a member of the general public in relation to the supplier of information, rather than a member of a limited class whose reliance upon the information was foreseen by the sup- plier of information."[32]

The court also took notice of *De Bardeleben Marine Corp. v. United States.* [33] Probably because the case arose in admiralty law, it has escaped notice in a media tort context. The case stemmed from an accident in a Tampa, Florida, harbor in which a tugboat's anchor hit a natural gas pipeline and caused an explosion. The tugboat's owner claimed the accident resulted from

---

29. Gutter v. Dow Jones, Inc., No. 84AP-1029, slip op. (10th District Ct. of Appeals, May 16, 1985).
30. *Id.* at 4.
31. Jaillet v. Cashman, 115 Misc. 383, 189 N.Y.S. 743 (Sup. Ct. 1921) *aff'd,* 235 N.Y. 511, 139 N.E. 714 (1923).
32. Gutter v. Dow Jones, Inc., *supra* note 29, at 6.
33. De Bardeleben Marine Corp. v. United States, 451 F.2d 140 (5th Cir. 1971).

the absence of the pipeline on charts published by the U.S. Coast and Geodetic Survey and sued for negligent misrepresentation. The court ruled against the tugboat owner only because the vessel's charts were outdated. Had the vessel's charts been current and the pipeline not been shown, the court said, it would have found the government liable. The court said the charts are the type of publication distributed to a class of users who rely upon them and the reliance is foreseeable.

The *De Bardeleben* court said the tugboat owner was in a different position than the average newspaper reader "absent some special relationship between writer and reader."[34] The usual newspaper publishers "lack the financial resources to compensate an indeterminate class who might read their work. Potential liability would have a staggering deterrent effect on potential purveyors of printed material."[35] The Ohio court seized on the words "absent some special relationship between writer and reader" and held the plaintiff should have an opportunity to prove such a relationship.

The Ohio plaintiff failed to make a scintilla of a showing that a special relationship with *The Wall Street Journal* existed. While a mere assertion might suffice in some situations to overcome summary judgment, it can only have a chilling effect in a media context. The legal expenses incurred in defending the suit far exceed the $1,693 in alleged damaged. Sensitivity to the first amendment suggests that there be at least some factual showing of a special relationship.[36] Otherwise, given the huge number of investors who obtain financial information from newspapers, the specter of staggering legal expenses arises.

One type of editorial product liability suit involves claims of injury due to incomplete information. A jury in Massachusetts returned verdicts totaling $825,000 for two students who alleged a Rand McNally & Co. junior high school science textbook was the proximate cause of an explosion in which they were injured.[37] Apparently, the jury found negligence in the proximity of instructions on two experiments which the students claimed led to the explosion. Rand McNally did not appeal.

Probably the most publicized editorial product liability suit was *Olivia N. v. National Broadcasting Co.*[38] The plaintiff claimed she was assaulted

34. *Id.* at 148.
35. *Id.*
36. *See* Yiamouyiannis v. Consumers Union, 619 F.2d 932, 940–42 (2d Cir. 1980), *cert. den.,* 449 U.S. 839 (1980).
37. Cited in Schlain, *Media Related Risks and Those Not Often Included in the Basic Libel Policy—Part I,* in Lankenau, *supra* note 2 at 435. *See also* Cardozo v. True, 342 So. 2d 1053 (Fla. App. 1977) (warrant applies only to physical condition of book and not to editorial content), *and* Libertelli v. Hoffman-LaRoche, Inc., 7 Med. L. Rep. 1734 (S.D. N.Y. 1981) (Physician's Desk Book does not warrant accuracy of information therein).
38. Olivia N. v. National Broadcasting Co., 126 Cal. App. 3d 488, 178 Cal. Rptr. 888 (1981), *cert. denied,* 458 U.S. 1108 (1982). *See also* Weirum v. RKO General, Inc., 15 Cal.

as a result of the assailant's viewing of *Born Innocent*, a television movie. A California appellate court ruled that, because the film did not encourage violence, the first amendment barred imposing liability for incitement.

In *Hyde v. City of Columbia*,[39] in which a reporter and two newspapers were among the defendants, a Missouri appellate court ruled the plaintiff was entitled to a trial on her claim of negligent infliction of injury. Police furnished and the newspapers printed the name and address of an abduction victim. She claimed the abductor obtained the information from the newspapers and this enabled him to terrorize her. Since the information published was truthful, as to the media defendants, the decision probably could not have withstood federal constitutional review by a higher court.[40]

Recovery for intentional infliction of emotional distress is available only if the conduct is "extreme and outrageous."[41] This makes recovery difficult in cases involving responsible members of the news media. It is more likely to occur in cases involving gossip and sex-oriented publications. The bar is likely to take claims of intentional infliction more seriously as a result of a $200,000 jury verdict for the Reverend Jerry Falwell in his suit against *Hustler* magazine. In that case, the jury found no liability under libel law, but held for the plaintiff on a claim of intentional infliction of emotional distress.[42] It is noteworthy that the claim was based on a sexual parody rather than a truthful news story.

A *prima facie* tort is similar to that of intentional infliction of emotional distress. Defined as the intentional infliction of harm—resulting in damages—through an act or acts otherwise legal, the tort appears to be confined to New York law.[43] In *Morrison v. National Broadcasting Co.*,[44] the court ruled a *prima facie* tort could be pleaded, but the statute of limitations on libel applied. A lower New York court held that editing of a television interview in such a manner as to convey a false impression could be a *prima facie* tort.[45]

3d 40, 123 Cal. Rptr. 468 (1975) (jury verdict affirmed against broadcaster in wrongful death action where contestants forced decedent's car off the highway in effort to win contest to locate traveling disc jockey); Walt Disney Productions, Inc. v. Shannon, 247 Ga. 402, 276 S.E.2d 580 (1981) (clear danger that injury would result from broadcast required under first amendment to impose liability).

39. Hyde v. City of Columbia, No. WD 32,706, slip op. (Mo. Ct. App. June 15, 1982).

40. The U.S. Supreme Court refused to impose liability for invasion of privacy for publication of a truthful report of a public record in Cox Broadcasting Corp. v. Cohn, 320 U.S. 467 (1975).

41. Yeager v. Local Union 20, 6 Ohio St. 3d 369, 453 N.E.2d 666 (1983).

42. The decision was widely publicized. *See, e.g., The Reverend vs. the Hustler*, NEWSWEEK, Dec. 17, 1984, at 101.

43. SACK, LIBEL, SLANDER AND RELATED PROBLEMS 471 (1980).

44. Morrison v. National Broadcasting Co., 19 N.Y.2d 453, 280 N.Y.S.2d 641, 227 N.E.2d 572 (1967).

45. Catalona v. Capital Cities Broadcasting Corp., 63 Misc.2d 595, 313 N.Y.S.2d 52 (Albany Co. 1970).

A New York court ruled against plaintiffs who had alleged negligent infliction of emotional distress against the *New York Daily News* and *New York Post* for publishing erroneous paid death notices. Apparently, a trickster had purchased obituaries and supplied false information. The court held that a newspaper owes no duty to the alleged decedent or his family to verify information supplied for paid obituaries.[46]

In *National Bar Association v. Capital Cities Broadcasting*,[47] a black Buffalo judge claimed that the *Buffalo News* and station WKBW-TV conspired with a state agency to have her removed from office. The conspiracy was alleged to have been the publication and telecast of adverse reports on her judicial performance to give the state agency a basis for investigation. The court, refusing to grant summary judgment, ruled that the allegation, if true, would support a finding that the media defendants acted under color of law and violated federal civil rights statutes. It held the plaintiffs were entitled to their opportunity to prove the conspiracy existed.

Plaintiffs alleged violation of fourth amendment constitutional rights in *Zerilli v. Evening News Association*.[48] The *Detroit News* published stories disclosing information that the Federal Bureau of Investigation had obtained illegally from wiretaps of the plaintiffs' telephone conversations. Since a tort suit for fourth amendment search and seizure violations under authority of *Bivens v. Six Unknown Named Agents of Federal Bureau of Narcotics*[49] requires state action, the plaintiffs alleged a conspiracy between the *Detroit News* and the FBI. In affirming a dismissal of the complaint, the court declined to rule that the news media could never be found liable under a *Bivens*-type action.

Violation of first amendment rights and a federal civil rights statute was alleged in *South Wind Motel v. Lashutka*[50] because a newspaper failed to print a story about an incident the plaintiff wanted publicized. While the claims were dismissed, the judge complimented the plaintiff's attorney on her creative pleading, and the newspaper incurred legal expenses in fighting the action.

In *Reliance Insurance Co. v. Barron's*,[51] an insurance company charged securities fraud and sought damages for an article that adversely commented on a stock offering. The court avoided ruling on whether a newspaper could ever be found liable for violation of federal securities laws for publishing an article on a securities offering. It held that Reliance's claim could not stand

46. Rubinstein v. New York Post Corp., 11 MED. L. REP. 1329 (Sup. Ct. N.Y. Co. 1985).
47. National Bar Association v. Capital Cities Broadcasting, 10 MED. L. REP. 2317 (W.D.N.Y. 1984). *But see* May v. Michigan, 10 MED. L. REP. 2454 (E.D. Mich. 1984).
48. Zerilli v. Evening News Association, 628 F.2d 217 (D.C. Cir. 1980).
49. Bivens v. Six Unknown Named Agents of Federal Bureau of Narcotics, 403 U.S. 388, 91 S. Ct. 1999, 29 L.Ed.2d 619 (1971).
50. Southwind Motel v. Lashutka, 9 MED. L. REP. 1661 (S.D. Ohio 1983).
51. Reliance Insurance Co. v. Barron's, 442 F. Supp. 1341, 3 MED. L. REP. 1641 (S.D. N.Y. 1977).

because it was an effort to avoid the more exacting standards of proof required in a libel action.

While plaintiffs seldom prevail, the review of some of the non-traditional tort claims being filed demonstrates that the news media face significant risk from such claims and are incurring substantial expenses defending themselves from them. It also illustrates the prudence of insuring against them. Some of the claims may be covered by the broad language of media perils policies. Most insurers will extend coverage by rider.[52]

Prudence dictates that publishers and broadcasters do not rely on general liability insurance policies for coverage of non-traditional communications torts. Some insurers have said such torts are not covered by general liability policies.[53] Further, general liability policies usually grant the insurer control of counsel selection and defense. This can lead to defense tactics insensitive to first amendment values. Generally, media perils policies place control in the hands of the insured.[54]

In *Gertz v. Robert Welch, Inc.*,[55] the U.S. Supreme Court held that actual malice must be proven in libel cases for punitive damages to be awarded. Actual malice is a term of art. It means the plaintiff knew what (s)he published was false or had serious doubts as to its truth or falsity.[56] The requirement is in addition to what state law may demand. States may continue to require proof of common law malice—that is, bad motives—or gross recklessness.[57] Five states prohibit award of punitive damages in libel cases.[58]

In most states,[59] when punitive damages are awarded because a publication or broadcast was intended to harm a person, public policy bars an insurance carrier from paying the punitive damages. The rationale is that the purpose of punitive damages—to deter such conduct in the future—would be defeated if reimbursement by an insurer were permitted. Generally, public policy also bars insurers from paying awards for compensatory damages where there was an intention to harm an individual.[60] The prohibition is based on

---

52. *See* Schlain, *supra* note 37.
53. *Id.*
54. *Id.*
55. Gertz v. Robert Welch, Inc., 418 U.S. 323 (1974).
56. New York Times Co. v. Sullivan, 376 U.S. 254 (1964); St. Amant v. Thompson, 390 U.S. 727 (1968).
57. Cantrell v. Forest City Publishing Co., 419 U.S. 469 (1975).
58. Louisiana, Massachusetts, Nebraska, Oregon and Washington. New Hampshire does not permit recovery of punitive damages, but a plaintiff may receive "enhanced" damages where actual or common law malice is proven. *See* Dougherty, *Punitive and Presumed Damages in Libel Actions,* in LANKENAU, *supra* note 2, at 110–11.
59. A survey of the states' laws on the issue of payment of damages by insurers is found in Lankenau, *Public Policy Limitations on the Insurability of Punitive and Actual Damages—Part I,* in LANKENAU, *supra* note 2, at 183–260. *See also* entries on punitive damages in Libel Defense Resource Center, *LDRC 50-State Survey 1983* (1984).
60. Public Service Mut. Ins. Co. v. Goldfarb, 53 N.Y.2d 392, 442 N.Y.S.2d 422, 426 N.E.2d 810 (1981).

the principle that a tortfeasor should not be allowed to benefit from an intentional act of injury.

Often punitive damages are awarded where there was no intent to harm a person, but the conduct was so reckless that the law finds deterrence is appropriate. In some cases, including New York and California, public policy does not permit an insurer to pay punitive damages awarded to punish such conduct.

In *Employers Reinsurance Corp. v. National Enquirer, Inc.*,[61] the insurance carrier asked a California court to rule that it did not have to pay punitive damages levied against the *National Enquirer* in a libel suit brought by actress Carol Burnett. The court held that both public policy and California's insurance code prohibited an insurer from paying any type of punitive damages. Because the case was decided in California, the court ruled the insurer had no obligation to pay damages in California or elsewhere, which barred the publication from seeking payment because the insurance contract was executed elsewhere.

Forum shopping is possible in libel actions. Kathy Keeton, an associate of the publisher of *Penthouse* magazine, brought a libel suit in Ohio against *Hustler* magazine. The suit was dismissed because Ohio's one-year statute of limitations had expired. Then Keeton filed an action in New Hampshire, which has a six-year statute of limitations. *Hustler* had a circulation of about 15,000 copies monthly in New Hampshire. In *Keeton v. Hustler Magazine, Inc.*,[62] the U.S. Supreme Court ruled that the magazine's contact with New Hampshire was sufficient for a suit to be maintained there. That decision permits a vindictive plaintiff to select a forum in a state where obstacles to punitive damages awards are low and where insurers are prohibited from paying punitive damages.

The Bermuda-based Mutual Insurance Company, Ltd. was established by the American Newspaper Publishers Association (ANPA) in 1961 and is the insurer for about 800 daily newspapers, which are members of the association. It maintains no offices in the United States and writes policies only on applications mailed to its offices in Bermuda. As an off-shore insurer, in the company's judgment, it is not subject to state public policy prohibitions and can pay all damages incurred by its media clients.[63]

Other insurers provide media policyholders with letters of intent stating they will pay punitive damages. They also execute insurance contracts in

61. Employers Reinsurance Corp. v. National Enquirer, Inc., Civ. No. C-387419, slip op. (Sup. Ct. Los Angeles Co. 1982).
62. Keeton v. Hustler Magazine, Inc., ____ U.S. ____, 104 S. Ct. 1473 (1984).
63. Mutual Insurance Company, Ltd., "Outline of Group Libel Policy." It will insure only ANPA member daily newspapers under its basic policy. It will insure broadcast outlets only if they are owned by an ANPA member that insures its newspapers with Mutual. The company has a separate policy for weekly newspapers.

favorable jurisdictions. While these insurers may pay all claims as a matter of good faith, courts will not enforce and may prohibit any payments where such payments violate public policy.[64]

If an insurance carrier is not obligated to pay all or part of an award of damages, its insured is entitled to independent counsel at the expense of the insurer. The rationale here is that a conflict of interest exists between the carrier and its insured. *Nike, Inc. v. Atlantic Mutual Insurance Company*[65] resulted from a California libel suit against Nike. The carrier informed Nike that it would defend against the action, but it reserved a right not to pay any judgment stemming from libelous statements made with malice. It suggested Nike retain independent counsel at its own expense. Nike employed its own counsel, and eventually, the claim was settled with neither Nike nor Atlantic Mutual paying any monetary damages. Nike sued its insurer for reimbursement of its expenses in retaining independent counsel.

The court ruled that Atlantic's reservation of a right not to pay damages stemming from malicious statements created a conflict of interest between the carrier and its insured. The court said the conflict "could potentially have affected the way in which counsel that had been appointed by Atlantic would conduct the defense."[66] Thus, it was held, "the interest of the insurer in controlling the defense must give way to the interest of the insured in being represented by independent counsel of its own choice."[67]

Generally, because of the doctrine of *respondeat superior*, a media employer's policy also covers its employees. The possibility exists that both compensatory and punitive damages will be awarded against an employee and only compensatory damages will be imputed to the employer. In such situations, under the reasoning of *Nike, Inc.*, the carrier would be obligated to pay the expense of independent counsel for an employee.

An insurer's duty to defend is broader than its duty to pay. As applied to a communications tort policy, this principle was tested in *Ruder & Finn, Inc. v. Seaboard Surety Company*.[68] Ruder & Finn, Inc., a public relations firm, was sued for libel and several other torts as a result of anti-aerosol press releases it prepared for the Natural Resources Defense Council. The firm tendered defense to Seaboard under its libel policy. The insurer refused to defend and maintained the suit sounded in product disparagement rather than defamation. After successfully defending against the suits, Ruder & Finn sued

64. Bender, J., *Public Policy Limitations on Insurability of Punitive and Actual Damages— Part II,* in LANKENAU, *supra* note 2, at 271–74.
65. Nike, Inc. v. Atlantic Mutual Insurance Company, 578 F. Supp. 948 (N.D. Cal. 1983). This case was brought to the author's attention by Arnold S. Graber, The Reporters Committee for Freedom of the Press.
66. *Id.* at 949.
67. *Id.*
68. Ruder & Finn, Inc. v. Seaboard Surety Company, 52 N.Y.2d 663, 439 N.Y.S.2d 858, 422 N.E.2d 518 (1981).

Seaboard for reimbursement of its expenses.

Noting that the tort complaint against Ruder & Finn spoke of false statements, the court ruled that this was sufficient to trigger Seaboard's duty to defend. The court said:

> The duty to defend arises whenever the allegations in the com-
> plaint fall within the risk covered by the policy. It therefore
> includes the defense of those actions in which alternative
> grounds are asserted, even if some are without the protection
> purchased. Further, a policy protects against poorly or in-
> completely pleaded cases as well as those artfully drafted. Thus
> the question is not whether the complaint can withstand a mo-
> tion to dismiss for failure to state a cause of action. Nor is
> the insured's ultimate liability a consideration. If, liberally con-
> strued, the claim is within the embrace of the policy, the in-
> surer must come forward to defend its insured no matter how
> groundless, false or baseless the suit may be.[69]

As to another suit against Ruder & Finn, in which the complaint did not allege false statements, the court held that Seaboard had no duty to defend.

Protection of journalists against libel and other communications tort liabili-ty might be expected to be a key issue in collective bargaining. It is not. Only the Vancouver-New Westminster local of The Newspaper Guild has contracts requiring publishers to indemnify editorial employees against libel awards and the legal expenses incurred in defending them.[70]

It is probably not an issue because newspapers and broadcasters find it advantageous to include employees in their insurance coverage. Generally, due to vicarious liability, an employer is equally responsible for any damages due to an employee's acts. An employer is likely to have deeper pockets and to be a plaintiff's target for payment of a judgment. Thus, it is in an employer's interest to include employees in his/her insurance coverage.

In summary, the scope of media tort liability and first amendment in-surance coverage is expanding. While tort insurance can offset any chilling effect on news gathering and reporting of the rising volume of litigation and the increasing dollar amounts of awards, its impact is abridged by public policy

---

69. *Id.* at 521 (citations omitted).
70. Richard J. Ramsey, Executive Secretary, Contracts Committee, The Newspaper Guild (personal communication, March 14, 1984). Generally, a book publisher requires an author to carry communications tort insurance and have the publisher named as an additional insured. There is a movement among authors to shift the cost burden on insurance for both authors and publishers to publishers. Insurers sell separate policies for columnists. It is possible that publishers assume the premium expense as part of contracts with columnists.

barriers to paying some types of damage awards. First amendment insurance is an encouraging development. It alleviates the financial burden on any single media outlet of defending first amendment interests.

KYU HO YOUM
HARRY W. STONECIPHER

"Innocent Construction" Rule Survives Challenge

Kyu Ho Youm is a faculty member of
Loras College in Dubuque, Iowa, and a
graduate of Southern Illinois University-
Carbondale with a doctorate in journalism. He also holds a master's degree
in journalism from SIU-C and a
bachelor's degree in English literature
from Konkuk University in Seoul, Korea.
Harry W. Stonecipher is professor
emeritus of journalism at SIU-C, where he
was a member of the faculty from 1971 to
1984. He earned a doctorate in journalism
from SIU-C. He received his bachelor's
and master's degrees from the School of
Journalism at the University of Missouri.

Justice Oliver Wendell Holmes once observed: "A word is not a crystal, transparent and unchanged, it is the skin of a living thought and may vary greatly in color and content according to the circumstances and the time in which it is used."[1] Whether or not a word or phrase is libelous, likewise, may require careful analysis and interpretation in terms of its milieu and its context within a given message. Several attempts have been made to provide guidance to journalists and others in distinguishing defamatory words from those which might be safely classed as nondefamatory, sometimes with compendiums of words which various courts have found to be defamatory.[2] But as one practicing media attorney has cautioned, lists of words may be misleading because the same word or expression may vary with context,

1. Towne v. Eisner, 245 U.S. 418, 425 (1918).
2. See, e.g., W. PROSSER, HANDBOOK OF THE LAW OF TORTS 739–41 (4th ed. 1971); 1 A. HANSON, LIBEL AND RELATED TORTS, §§ 20–24 (1969); P. ASHLEY, SAY IT SAFELY 19–25 (4th ed. 1969), 1 E. SEELMAN, THE LAW OF LIBEL AND SLANDER IN THE STATE OF NEW YORK 31–54 (1964); P. WITTENBERG, DANGER WORDS 282–308 (1947).

jurisdiction, and time.[3]

The determination of libelous expression becomes even more difficult when ambiguity of meaning, questions of identification, and hyperbolic language become involved. The judicial approach generally used is that the case must be submitted to the jury unless the court can say that the language precipitating the libel action is not reasonably capable of defamatory meaning. *Restatement (Second) of Torts* explains: "The jury determines whether a communication, capable of a defamatory meaning, was so understood by its recipient."[4] In Illinois and a few other states, however, the so-called innocent construction rule denies the jury such a role. In a 1962 case, *John v. Tribune Co.*,[5] for example, the Illinois Supreme Court held that an allegedly defamatory publication is to be read as a whole and the words are to be given their natural and obvious meaning. If such words are capable of being read innocently, they must be so read and declared nonactionable as a matter of law,[6] i.e., the judge makes the determination. California,[7] New Mexico,[8] Ohio,[9] and Oklahoma[10] have at one time or another applied similar innocent construction defenses as a matter of common law in libel litigation.[11]

Criticism has accompanied the innocent construction concept, however, even in Illinois, where it has been most extensively utilized. Robert Phelps and Douglas Hamilton have observed that "Sloppy reporters in Illinois are the beneficiaries of. . .the innocent construction."[12] Laurence Eldredge, professor of law at the University of California and an advisor for the American Law Institute, has argued that the rule is a step backward in defamation law, permitting newspapers in some states to destroy people's reputations without liability merely by phrasing a defamatory statement so that it is "capable of

3. R. SACK, LIBEL, SLANDER, AND RELATED PROBLEMS 74 (1980).
4. RESTATEMENT SECOND OF TORTS, § 614 (1977).
5. John v. Tribune Co., 24 Ill. 2d 437, 181 N.E.2d 105 (1962), *cert. denied,* 371 U.S. 877 (1962).
6. *Id.* at 442–43, 181 N.E.2d at 108.
7. *See, e.g.,* Peabody v. Barham, 52 Cal. App. 2d 581, 126 P.2d 668 (1942); Babcock v. McClatchy Newspapers, 82 Cal. App. 2d 528, 186 P.2d 727 (1947); MacLeod v. Tribune Publishing Co., 52 Cal. 2d 553, 343 P.2d 36 (1959).
8. *See, e.g.,* Reed v. Melnick, 81 N.M. 608, 471 P.2d 178 (1970); Monnin v. Wood, 86 N.M. 460, 525 P.2d 387 (1974).
9. *See, e.g.,* Becker v. Toulmin, 165 Ohio St. 549, 138 N.E.2d 391 (1956); England v. Automatic Canteen Co. of America, 349 F.2d 989 (6th Cir. 1965) (applying the Ohio rule); Smith v. Hunting Publishing Co., 410 F. Supp. 1270 (S.D. Ohio 1975) (applying the Ohio rule).
10. *See, e.g.,* Winters v. Morgan, 576 P.2d 1152 (Okla. 1978) (Lavender, V.C.J., dissenting).
11. For a discussion of the use of the innocent construction rule and its variations in states other than Illinois, *see* Kyu Ho Youm, " 'Innocent Construction' as a Libel Defense: Is It *Still* a 'Minority of One' Doctrine?" Paper presented at the 1983 convention of the Association for Education in Journalism and Mass Communication (AEJMC) in Corvallis, Oregon.
12. R. PHELPS & E. HAMILTON, LIBEL: RIGHTS, RISKS, RESPONSIBILITIES 20 (rev. ed. 1978).

an innocent interpretation."[13] And in a 1981 law review article criticizing the Illinois innocent construction rule, Michael Polelle of John Marshall Law School observed: "It was said of the Holy Roman Empire that it was neither holy, nor Roman, nor an empire. It could likewise be said that the innocent construction rule in Illinois defamation law is neither innocent, nor constructive, nor a rule."[14]

Despite frequent criticism, the innocent construction rule has been utilized extensively in Illinois since it was first recognized by the Illinois Supreme Court in *John v. Tribune Co.* in 1962. While its use has waned or been discontinued in most other states, it has grown in Illinois. Even the 1964 *New York Times* case (enunciating the "actual malice" defense)[15] and its progeny have had little impact upon the continued application of the innocent construction rule in Illinois.[16] Indeed, the first real threat to the continued use of innocent construction in Illinois came late in 1982, when it was challenged by an attorney libel plaintiff, Robert A. Chapski, in an appeal taken to the Illinois Supreme Court. The court took a critical look at how the lower courts had applied the *John* decision during the past twenty years and found that it was time for some modification.[17]

This article will reexamine the innocent construction rule as a common law libel defense, focusing upon its use in Illinois during the past twenty years. Three questions will be explored: what is the underlying legal rationale of the innocent construction rule as a common law libel defense?; how extensively and under what circumstances had the innocent construction rule been utilized as a libel defense in Illinois?; and how has the innocent construction rule been modified by *Chapski* and what is the likely effect of these modifications?

I. HISTORICAL DEVELOPMENT

It is generally understood that the innocent construction rule derives its origin from the doctrine of "mitior sensus" (literally, "milder or more lenient sense") adopted by the English courts in their administration of libel litigation in the late sixteenth century.[18] Indeed, the Illinois Appellate Court

---

13. Eldredge, *The Spurious Rule of Libel Per Quod,* 79 HARV. L. REV. 733, 742 (1966).
14. Polelle, *The Guilt of the "Innocent Construction Rule" in Illinois Defamation Law,* 1 N. ILL. L. REV. 181 (1981).
15. New York Times Co. v. Sullivan, 376 U.S. 254 (1964).
16. *See, e.g.,* Stonecipher & Trager, *The Impact of Gertz on the Law of Libel in Illinois,* 1979 S. ILL. L.J. 73, 85.
17. *See* Chapski v. Copley Press, 92 Ill. 2d 344, 442 N.E.2d 195 (1982).
18. *See, e.g.,* Eldredge, *supra* note 13, at 742; Comment, *Symposium: Libel and Slander in Illinois,* 43 CHI.[-] KENT L. REV. 2, 11 (1966); Comment, *The Illinois Doctrine of Innocent Construction: A Minority of One,* 30 U. CHI. L. REV. 524, 536 n.9 (1963) [hereinafter cited as *The Illinois Doctrine*].

in *Dauw v. Field Enterprises, Inc.*, did trace the pedigree of the innocent construction rule to the English "mitior sensus" doctrine.[19] The court stated:

> Originally adopted in England as the doctrine of "mitior sensus," the rule [of innocent construction] is that when the words which form the heart of a defamation suit can be given two or more meanings, one of which is favorable and not defamatory, the court will construe the words in the favorable sense.[20]

And finally, in the *Chapski* case, the Illinois Supreme Court explained the historical evolution of the innocent construction defense in connection with the English doctrine of "mitior sensus."[21]

A. The British "Mitior Sensus" Doctrine

The "mitior sensus" doctrine held that words complained of be interpreted, not in their natural sense, but, whenever possible, in "mitior sensu," and that the plaintiff negate any possibility of defamatory construction of the words in question.[22] As Eldredge pointed out in his law review article, this doctrine was devised by the English common law courts to restrain the sudden proliferation of defamation suits in the late sixteenth and early seventeenth centuries.[23]

The first English defamation action in which the "mitior sensus" doctrine appeared was *The Lord Cromwell's Case.*[24] The doctrine was not directly applied in this case, but it was utilized as dictum in ruling against the plaintiff. *Stanhope v. Blith*[25] is regarded as the first reported defamation case in England in which the doctrine of "mitior sensus" was applied as a rule of law.[26] While writing for the court in *Stanhope*, Chief Justice Wray clarified the purpose of the doctrine: to check the flow of slander actions. He said:

19. Dauw v. Field Enterprises, Inc., 78 Ill. App. 3d 67, 397 N.E.2d 41 (1979).
20. *Id.* at 71, 397 N.E.2d at 44, citing Case of the Lord Cromwell, 4 Co. Rep. 12b, 76 Eng. Rep 877 (1578–81).
21. Chapski v. Copley Press, 92 Ill. 2d, 344, 349–51, 442 N.E.2d, 195, 197–98.
22. *Id.* at 350, 442, N.E. 2d at 198, *citing* W. PROSSER, HANDBOOK OF THE LAW OF TORTS 747 (4th ed. 1971) and Holdsworth, *Defamation in the Sixteenth and Seventeenth Centuries,* 40 L.Q.R. 302, 405–8 (1924) [hereinafter cited as *Defamation*]. *See also* 8 W. HOLDSWORTH, A HISTORY OF ENGLISH LAW 355 (2d ed. 1937) [hereinafter cited as ENGLISH LAW].
23. Eldredge, *supra* note 13, at 742. *See also Defamation, supra* note 22, at 404, cited in *Chapski v. Copley Press* 92 Ill. 2d 344, 350, 442 N.E.2d at 198.
24. The Lord Cromwell's Case, 4 Co. Rep. 12b, 76 Eng. Rep 877 (1578–81).
25. Stanhope v. Blith, 4 Co. Rep. 15a, 76 Eng. Rep. 891 (1585).
26. Lovell, *The "Reception" of Defamation by the Common Law,* 15 VAN. L. REV. 1051, 1064 (1962).

"[A]ctions for scandals should not be maintained by any strained construction or argument, nor any favour given to support them, forasmuch as in these days they more abound than in times past, and the intemperance and malice of men increase."[27]

In the same year that *Stanhope* was decided, the English common law rule was again successfully invoked in holding nonactionable the expression, "B seeks my life."[28] To impute a mere intention to commit a crime or to accuse a man of an impossible crime was also declared nondefamatory on the basis of the "mitior sensus" rule.[29] As with the American innocent construction rule,[30] the English courts, in applying the "mitior sensus" doctrine, also flatly rejected innuendo in interpreting the defamatory meaning of words.[31]

For the first time since its birth some thirty years earlier, the "mitior sensus" rule failed to prevail in a 1607 case, *Morison v. Cade*.[32] The court refused the adoption of the rule in the construction of the words, "I have had the use of her body." The court, in rejecting the rule, signaled a change in the "mitior sensus" doctrine by emphasizing the "usual and common sense" of the words complained of.[33] Despite the apparent modification in the English doctrine in *Morison*, its use and vitality was maintained in dealing with defamation cases.[34]

Holt v. Astgrigg, a 1608 slander case,[35] indicates the extreme to which the "mitior sensus" doctrine was to go. The case resulted from the statement: "Sir Thomas struck his cook on the head with a cleaver, and cleaved his head; the one part lay on the one shoulder, and another part on the other." The words were apparently referring to a homicidal act, but the court held: "[S]lander ought to be direct, against which there may not be any intendment: but here, notwithstanding such wounding, the party may yet be living; and it is then but trespass. Wherefore it was adjudged for the defendant."[36]

Even though the "mitior sensus" rule was still being applied as late as 1835,[37] it is generally agreed that the doctrine had ceased being an effective

27. Stanhope v. Blith, 4 Co. Rep. at 15b, 76 Eng. Rep. at 892.
28. Hext v. Yeomans, 4 Co. Rep. 15b, 76 Eng. Rep. 893 (1585). *See also* Snag v. Gee, 4 Co. Rep. 16a, 76 Eng. Rep. 896 (1597).(The court held that if a man said of another, "He killed my wife," there was no liability for the defamer when she is alive.)
29. *See, e.g.,* Eaton v. Allen, 4 Co. Rep. 16b, 76 Eng. Rep. 896 (1598); Crofts v. Brown, 3 Bulst. 167, 81 Eng. Rep 181 (1607); Jackson v. Adams, 2 Bing. N.C. 402, 132 Eng. Rep. 158 (1835).
30. *See* text accompanying *infra* note 67.
31. *See, e.g.,* James v. Rultech, 4 Co. Rep. 17a, 76 Eng. Rep. 900 (1599); Barham v. Nethersal, 4 Co. Rep. 20a, 76 Eng. Rep. 908 (1602).
32. Morison v. Cade, Cro. Jac. 162, 79 Eng. Rep. 142 (1607).
33. *Id.*
34. *See, e.g.,* Robins v. Hildredon, Cro. Jac. 65, 79 Eng. Rep. 55 (1608); Powell v. Hutchinsons, Cro. Jac. 205, 79 Eng. Rep. 179 (1609).
35. Cro. Jac. 185, 79 Eng. Rep. 161 (1608).
36. *Id.*
37. *See, e.g.,* Jackson v. Adams, 2 Bing. N.C. 402, 132 Eng. Rep. 158 (1835).

judicial weapon in the administration of defamation cases by the early 1800s.[38]

As noted earlier, the *Morison* case strongly implied a modification in the "mitior sensus" doctrine, which was positively reaffirmed in *Somers v. House* in 1694.[39] Indeed, the *Somers* court went even further than *Morison* in drawing the boundary for application of the English doctrine. The court said the doctrine should be limited to situations "where the words in their natural import are doubtful, and equally to be understood in the one sense as in the other."[40] And in 1714, the court in *Harrison v. Thornborough*[41] attempted to provide an alternative to the "mitior sensus" doctrine, holding:

> [W]hen the words were capable of two constructions, the Court always took them mitiori sensu. But latterly these actions have been more discountenanced. . . . *The rule therefore that has now prevailed is, that words are to be taken in that sense that is most natural and obvious, and in which those to whom they are spoken will be sure to understand them.*[42]

Several reasons for the decease of the "mitior sensus" doctrine may be cited in connection with problems inherent in the rule. First, the rule was created principally for the effective administration of defamation cases, which were inundating the English common law courts in the late sixteenth century, not for protection of the plaintiff's reputation or good name. Second, the rule had become too far expanded to be a judicially sound doctrine. Third, judges were focusing too much on the act of the plaintiff, which had prompted the allegedly defamatory statement, rather than upon the damages arising from the defendant's publication or statement.

B. Early Development in the United States

The United States apparently has been much less hospitable toward the "mitior sensus" doctrine than had been Great Britain.[43] Although the English "mitior sensus" doctrine was never utilized by the American courts in toto, with some modification, it resulted in the American version of the doctrine,

38. *See, e.g.,* Chapski v. Copley Press, 92 Ill. 2d, 344, 350, 442 N.E.2d, 195, 198, *citing* Roberts v. Camden, 9 East 93, 103 Eng. Rep 508 (1807); Eldredge, *supra* note 13 at 735; J. BAKER, AN INTRODUCTION TO ENGLISH LEGAL HISTORY 371 (2d ed. (1979). *But see* ENGLISH LAW, *supra* note 22, at 356.
39. Somers v. House, Holt, K.B. 39, 90 Eng. Rep. 919 (1694).
40. *Id.*
41. Harrison v. Thornborough, 10 Mod. Rep. 196, 88 Eng. Rep. 691 (1714).
42. *Id.* at 197–98, 88 Eng. Rep. at 691–92 (emphasis added). *See also* Baker v. Pierce, 6 Mod. Rep. 23, 87 Eng. Rep. 787 (1704) (Holt, C.J., dissenting).
43. *See, e.g.,* Clifford v. Cochrane, 10 Ill. App. 570 (1882); Kamp v. U.S., 176 F.2d 618 (D.C. Cir. 1948); Riley v. Dun & Bradstreet, Inc., 172 F.2d 303 (6th Cir. 1949).

i.e., the so-called innocent construction rule.

The first case involving the innocent construction rule was *Young v. Richardson*, an 1879 Illinois appellate court case.[44] The *Young* court stated that "words alleged to be libelous will receive an innocent construction if they are fairly susceptible of it."[45] The invocation of the rule, according to Polelle, was a judicial device by the courts to mitigate the assumption of strict liability for allegedly libelous per se words on the part of libel defendants.[46]

Between 1900 and the time the Illinois Supreme Court established the definition of the common law rule in *John v. Tribune Co.* in 1962, more than fifteen reported defamation cases[47] were decided by either state appellate courts or federal courts in Illinois, at least in part, on the basis of the innocent construction rule. In a 1928 libel action, *Fulrath v. Wolfe*,[48] for example, the Illinois Appellate Court took judicial notice of the innocent construction rule, saying: "The words of an alleged libel where susceptible of it, will receive an innocent construction by interpretation."[49] *Fulrath* is distinguished from *Young* in that the word "fairly" was omitted from the former.

During the 1950s, the innocent construction rule was relied upon by the federal courts in Illinois in at least three diversity cases.[50] The Seventh Circuit's application of the innocent construction rule in its decision in *Crosby v. Time, Inc.*[51] is noteworthy in that the common law rule was successfully employed as a defense in a group libel case.

II. THE INNOCENT CONSTRUCTION RULE IN ILLINOIS

As the definition of "innocent construction" indicates, the rule is clearly

44. Young v. Richardson, 4 Ill. App. 364 (1879).
45. *Id.* at 374.
46. Polelle, *supra* note 14, at 192. *See also The Illinois Doctrine, supra* note 18, at 531.
47. *See, e.g.,* Brewer v. Hearst Publishing Co. 185 F.2d 846 (7th Cir. 1951); LaGrange Press v. Citizen Publishing Co., 252 Ill. App. 482 (1929); Eick v. Perk Dog Food Co., 347 Ill. App. 293, 106 N.E.2d 742 (1952); Tiernan v. East Shore Newspapers, Inc., 1 Ill. App. 2d 150, 116 N.E.2d 896 (1953); Eapton v. Vail, 2 Ill. App. 2d 287, 119 N.E.2d 410 (1954); Fulrath v. Wolfe, 250 Ill. App. 130 (1928); Davis v. Ferguson, 246 Ill. App. 318 (1927); Dilling v. Illinois Publishing and Printing Co., 340 Ill. App. 303, 91 N.E.2d 635 (1950); Parmelee v. Hearst Publishing Co., 341 Ill. App. 339, 93 N.E.2d 512 (1950); Gogerty v. Covins, 5 Ill. App. 2d 74, 124 N.E.2d 602 (1955); Piancenti v. Williams Press, Inc., 347 Ill. App. 440, 107 N.E.2d 45 (1952); Sullivan v. Illinois Publishing Co., 186 Ill. App. 268 (1914); Crosby v. Time, Inc., 254 F.2d 927 (7th Cir. 1958); Schy v. Hearst Publishing Co., 205 F.2d 750 (7th Cir. 1953); Creitz v. Bennett, 273 Ill. App. 88 (1933).
48. Fulrath v. Wolfe, 250 Ill. App. 130 (1928).
49. *Id.* at 135, *citing* Young v. Richardson, 4 Ill. App. 364 (1879) *and* Isabella Harkness v. Chicago Daily News Co., 102 Ill. App. 162 (1902).
50. *See, e.g.,* Brewer v. Hearst Publishing Co., 185 F.2d 846 (7th Cir. 1951); Crosby v. Time, Inc., 254 F.2d 927 (7th Cir. 1958); Schy v. Hearst Publishing Co., 205 F.2d 760 (7th Cir. 1953).
51. Crosby v. Time, Inc., 254 F.2d 927 (7th Cir. 1958).

designed to deal with defamatory expression capable of being interpreted innocently. The courts, in applying the innocent construction rule to determine the meaning of ambiguous language, try not to isolate the defamatory words from the context in which they are communicated.

The innocent construction rule, however, is not limited to cases involving ambiguous expression. The rule may also be employed as a defense in libel and slander actions in which the identification of the plaintiff has not been reasonably established. The *John* case[52] illustrates a situation in which the common law rule was applied to address the issue of the missing colloquium, i.e., proof that the words complained of were spoken "of and concerning" the plaintiff.

The innocent construction rule is also frequently relied upon to handle those cases in which name-calling, inadvertent hyperbole and jokes of a defamatory nature are involved. The application of the rule in such actions apparently follows the principle that the meaning of a statement should be gathered not only from the words singled out, but from the context of the publication at issue.

A. Ambiguity: Questions of Meaning

The Illinois courts, in applying the innocent construction rule in cases where ambiguous expression is involved, frequently consult the definition of words in authoritative dictionaries. The choice of dictionary meanings is qualified by the *John* court's holding that the words be given their "natural and obvious meaning."[53]

Under the innocent construction rule, the Illinois appellate courts have held unactionable such phrases as "fix" in regard to parking tickets,[54] "rip-off speculators,"[55] and "slumlord" or "slum landlord."[56] However, the word "fag," which was used to describe a night club singer, was declared to be incapable of an innocent construction.[57] The court stated that "the sole occasion upon which the word 'fag' is commonly used in the United States, in the form of a noun and to connote an adult human being, is with reference to a homosexual."[58]

In other cases, ambiguity arises not from individual words but as the result of the structure of an allegedly defamatory phrase or clause within a

---

52. For a discussion of the *John* case, *see* text accompanying *infra* note 68.
53. *See, e.g.,* Watson v. Southwest Messenger Press, 12 Ill. App. 3d 968, 299 N.E.2d 409 (1973); Moricoli v. Schwartz, 46 Ill. App. 3d 481, 361 N.E.2d 74 (1977).
54. Watson v. Southwest Messenger Press, 12 Ill. App. 3d 968, 299 N.E.2d 409 (1973).
55. Bruck v. Cincotta, 56 Ill. App. 3d 260, 371 N.E.2d 874 (1977).
56. Rasky v. Columbia Broadcasting System, 103 Ill. App. 3d 577, 451 N.E.2d 1055 (1981).
57. Moricoli v. Schwartz, 46 Ill. App. 3d 481, 361 N.E.2d 74 (1977).
58. *Id.* at 483, 361 N.E.2d at 76.

statement. Thus, the rule was prevalent where the expressions, such as "alleged racial steering"[59] and "It could have been. . .crime,"[60] were at issue. In *Jacobs v. Gasoline Retailers' Association*,[61] the Illinois Appellate Court found nondefamatory a magazine picture with the words, "Wanted! from Robert (Bobby) Jacobs $4,435.24!", notwithstanding the plaintiff's argument that he was portrayed as a wanted criminal. The court stated: "[T]here is only a general similarity between the picture on the cover of the magazine and a criminal-wanted poster. The cover says 'wanted! from,' not 'wanted for.' It states that the plaintiff is wanted for a sum of money, not for a crime."[62]

The courts, however, have not confined application of the innocent construction rule to ambiguity resulting from the meaning of the words or phrases in the context in which they are used. When the words or phrases at issue are not ambiguous in terms of their import or context, they may still be construed by the parties involved to be capable of both a defamatory and nondefamatory interpretation. When the courts deal with this problem, they generally consider the circumstance under which the communication took place.[63]

Lack of personal knowledge of the allegedly defamatory publication on the part of those at whom it is directed can be the basis for invocation of the innocent construction rule. In *Vee See Construction Co., Inc. v. Jensen & Halstead, Ltd.*,[64] the plaintiff argued that the language of the letter in question conveyed the idea that the plaintiff was cheating the board of education by instructing the painters to apply only two coats of paint where three were required. The court, in rejecting the argument, reasoned: "Keeping in mind that all of the persons who received copies of the letter may not have had personal knowledge of the contract specifications, we still fail to see how the letter conveys a defamatory meaning."[65]

B. Colloquium: Questions of Identification

The intended purpose of the innocent construction rule is to mitigate the impact of strict liability on the libel defendants by declaring a publication non-actionable as a matter of law if it is capable of an innocent construction. However, the rule has also been expanded by applying it to cases where identification is at issue.

59. Homestead Realty Co. v. Stack, 57 Ill. App. 3d 575, 373 N.E.2d 429 (1978).
60. Makis v. Area Publications Corp., 77 Ill. App. 3d 452, 395 N.E.2d 1185 (1979).
61. Jacob v. Gasoline Retailers' Association, 28 Ill. App. 3d 7, 328 N.E.2d 187 (1975).
62. *Id.* at 10, 328 N.E.2d at 189.
63. *See, e.g.,* Levinson v. Time, Inc., 89 Ill. App. 3d 338, 41 N.E.2d 1118 (1980).
64. Vee See Construction Co., Inc. v. Jensen & Halstead, Ltd., 79 Ill. App. 3d 1084, 399 N.E.2d 278 (1979).
65. *Id.* at 1088, 399 N.E.2d at 281.

To establish the connection of the defamatory words or phrases to the plaintiff is not an easy task. Indeed, the "colloquium" problem cannot stand alone in establishing the defamatory nature of a publication. It is frequently complemented by inducement and innuendo.[66] But while the three may work together to prove that a publication or statement defames the plaintiff, inducement and innuendo cannot be used to upset use of the innocent construction rule where colloquium is at issue.[67] The court's approach toward innuendo and inducement is that when the allegedly defamatory but ambiguous expression can be construed innocently, the aid of extrinsic facts through innuendo or inducement cannot transform the innocent meaning into a defamatory one.

The problem of proving that the defamatory words are "of and concerning" the plaintiff, however, is not always concerned with identifying a specific person in an allegedly defamatory publication or statement. The problem of colloquium may also turn upon: whether or not a group, or groups, is defamed; the use of fictitious names; or the use of an alias which incidentally identifies some other innocent person. The Illinois landmark case, *John v. Tribune Co.*, serves as a good example of a "colloquium" issue that resulted from usage of aliases.

The *John* case concerned newspaper articles about a police raid on a Chicago house of prostitution. The articles identified the arrested proprietor of the house as Dorothy Clark, also known as "Dolores Reising, 57, alias Eve Spiro and Eve John." By sheer coincidence, the plaintiff in this case, whose maiden name was Eve Spiro, and whose name at the time of the raid was Eve John, was living in the basement of the building in question.

The Illinois Supreme Court, examining the nature of the alias, observed:

> A name or names reported as the "aliases," or also-known, are the names that have been assumed by the subject identified by the name preceding the alias...the alias names do not change the subject of the publication...but simply disclose the subject's false name or names. The alias names therefor

---

66. One authority explains "inducement" and "innuendo" as follows:

> [W]hen the defamatory meaning of the communication or its applicability to the plaintiff depended upon extrinsic circumstances, the pleader averred their existence in a prefatory statement called the "inducement"....The communication he set forth verbatim and in the "innuendo" explained the meaning of the words. The function of the innuendo was explanation; it could only explain or apply them in the light of the other averments in the declaration.

RESTATEMENT (SECOND) OF TORTS § 563 comment f (1977).

67. *See, e.g.,* Springer v. Harwig, 94 Ill. App. 3d 281, 481 N.E.2d 870 (1981); Van Tuil v. Carroll, 3 Ill. App. 3d 869, 279 N.E.2d 361 (1972); Zeinfeld v. Hayes Freight Lines, Inc., 41 Ill. 2d 345, 243 N.E.2d 217 (1968).

[sic], necessarily cannot be read as identifying the "of and concerning" or "target" name of the publication.[68]

Ambiguous or unspecific pronouns or nouns, e.g., "they," "some," "any," "dozens," have provided grounds for the application of the innocent construction rule because of the unclear identification of the defamed person.[69] In connection with the application of the rule, group libel actions may be expected to cause even more difficulty in establishing colloquium.[70]

C. Hyperbole: Questions of Style

In dealing with hyperbole, epithets, or name-calling, the courts clearly place more emphasis upon the context of the precipitating circumstances in which they are communicated than upon their common import as generally understood by the public. Moreover, the effect of those expressions has more to do with emotional feelings than with the actual meanings of the words. In light of the nature of vituperative or opprobrious expression, jurisdictions applying the innocent construction rule utilize the doctrine to deal with statements that frequently are no more than either idle comments or the venting of the speaker's or writer's emotions. Even though the language used may imply some defamatory representations on the part of those at which the language is directed, those who read or hear the language do not necessarily understand it as libelous to the reputation of the "target" person or persons.

In *Sloan v. Hatton*,[71] for example, the Illinois Appellate Court held nonactionable as a matter of law the defendant's letter criticizing the plaintiff's business. Characterizing the defendant's words as a "verbal jab" prompted by the frustration over the plaintiff's making trouble for him, the court said that the "unguarded statement made in the heat of a business or commercial dispute, if it contains words affecting fitness for the business ability of complainant" does not qualify in all cases as libel per se.[72]

The Illinois Appellate Court in *Angelo v. Brenner*[73] focused upon the circumstances under which the defendant's statement was made. The defendant psychiatrist said the plaintiff, a police officer, was "unfit to be a policeman." Noting that the statement was "an angry comment by the indignant husband

---

68. John v. Tribune Co., 24 Ill. 2d 437, 442, 181 N.E.2d 105, 108 (1962).
69. *See, e.g.,* Belmonte v. Rubin, 68 Ill. App. 3d 700, 386 N.E.2d 904 (1979); Bravo Realty v. Columbia Broadcasting System, 84 Ill. App. 3d 862, 406 N.E.2d 61 (1980); Chapski v. Copley Press, 100 Ill. App. 3d 1012, 427 N.E.2d 638 (1981), *rev'd,* 92 Ill. 2d 344, 442 N.E.2d 195 (1982); Lepman v. Everett, 333 F.2d 154 (7th Cir. 1964).
70. *See, e.g.,* Crosby v. Time, Inc., 254 F.2d 927 (7th Cir. 1958).
71. Sloan v. Hatton, 66 Ill. App. 3d 41, 383 N.E.2d 259 (1978).
72. *Id.* at 44, 383 N.E.2d at 262.
73. Angelo v. Brenner, 84 Ill. App. 3d 594, 406 N.E.2d 38 (1980).

of a woman who had violated traffic law," the court held:

> [T]he statement was made before only three other police of-
> ficers who were assumedly aware of the reason for defendant's
> presence at the police station and assumedly accustomed to
> the not uncommon response of a motorist or other interested
> party upon receiving a traffic citation. In light of all of these
> circumstances, we believe that an innocent construction should
> be placed on defendant's statement.[74]

III. THE CHALLENGE OF *CHAPSKI*

The innocent construction rule has been subjected to criticism from within the courts in Illinois as well as outside. Indeed, the rule has been seriously challenged as to its judicial soundness as a defamation defense on at least four occasions.[75] However, the Illinois appellate courts have refused to question the rationale behind the rule, and made it clear that the Illinois Supreme Court should be the proper judicial forum for bringing about a modification in the rule.

Since the innocent construction rule was first recognized in 1962 by the Illinois Supreme Court in *John*, prior to the *Chapski* case the doctrine had been applied by the Illinois high court in only three defamation cases.[76] While in two of the three cases the rulings favored the defendants, in the latest of the three cases the court, while recognizing its earlier *John* holding, rejected the defendant's innocent construction argument without discussing the pros and cons of the rule.[77] The innocent construction rule, however, faced its most serious challenge in the 1982 libel case, *Chapski v. Copley Press*.

A. *Chapski v. Copley Press*

This case resulted from a series of articles published by the defendant's newspaper, the *Elgin Daily Courier-News*. The newspaper articles concerned the juvenile and divorce proceedings in which the plaintiff was involved as an attorney. Chapski contended that the stories in question damaged his reputa-

---

74. *Id.* at 599, 406 N.E.2d at 42. *See also* Delis v. Sepsis, 9 Ill. App. 3d 217, 292 N.E.2d 138 (1972).
75. *See, e.g.,* Levinson v. Time, Inc., 89 Ill. App. 3d 338, 41 N.E.2d 1118 (1980); Kakuris v. Klein, 88 Ill. App. 3d 597, 410 N.E.2d 984 (1980); Vee See Construction Co. v. Jensen & Halstead, Ltd., 79 Ill. App. 3d 1084, 399 N.E.2d 278 (1979); Makis v. Area Publications Corp., 77 Ill. App. 3d 452, 395 N.E. 2d 1185 (1979).
76. *See, e.g.,* Zeinfeld v. Hayes Freight Lines, Inc., 41 Ill. 2d 345, 243 N.E.2d 217 (1969); Valentine v. North American Co. for Life and Health Insurance, 60 Ill. 2d 168, 328 N.E.2d 265 (1974); Catalano v. Pechous, 83 Ill. 2d 146, 419 N.E.2d 350 (1980).
77. Catalano v. Pechous, 83 Ill. 2d 146, 158, 419 N.E.2d 350, 356.

tion as a lawyer. But the newspaper defendant claimed that it carried the articles only for the purpose of questioning a court procedure as a whole involving the plaintiff, not the plaintiff himself. Therefore, the defendant argued, they were not libelous as to the plaintiff, as asserted, because of a failure to establish colloquium.

The case was decided for the defendant by the Illinois Appellate Court, Second District, when it affirmed the trial court's judgment.[78] The appellate court held that the defendant's articles complained of were susceptible of an innocent construction. The court reasoned that the publication at issue criticized the judicial system's handling of the proceedings involving the plaintiff, not the plaintiff as an attorney, where the innocent construction rule was prevalent as a matter of law. The plaintiff then appealed the appellate court's decision in *Chapski* to the Illinois Supreme Court.

Before the court, the defense counsel argued that, "whatever the final merits were determined to be with respect to Chapski's libel suit, it was not the proper case on which to put on trial the innocent construction rule, since the plaintiff had not urged abolishing the rule in lower courts."[79] In addition, the defense contended that the privilege of reporting of official court records did not constitute defamation, whether it was agreeable to the person involved or not. On the other hand, Chapski said that he was " 'a victim' of the state's libel law under the innocent construction rule," adding that "we have to look at it from the standpoint of an average reader, not a Rhodes Scholar."[80]

The Illinois Supreme Court in *Chapski*, for the first time, devoted a considerable portion of its opinion to a discussion of the rationale behind the innocent construction rule, both legal and historical. To begin with, the court took notice of the inconsistent application of the rule in defamation cases, citing as examples eleven cases decided by the Illinois appellate courts and by the federal courts sitting in Illinois.[81]

Second, the court noted four appellate court cases in which the rule was vigorously questioned from the perspective of its judicial appropriateness as "a fair statement of the law."[82]

Third, the court dealt with the question of how the rule has been applied and in what situations: (1) the rule has been applied in slander as well as in libel cases, (2) the rule has been utilized to determine whether the words or phrases in question are actionable per se, and (3) the rule has been employed where the missing colloquium issue arises.[83]

---

78. Chapski v. Copley Press, 100 Ill. App. 3d, 1013, 427 N.E.2d at 638.
79. Cheryl Frank, unpublished news story on the oral arguments in Chapski v. Copley Press, 92 Ill. 2d 344, 442 N.E.2d 195 (1982).
80. *Id.*
81. Chapski v. Copley Press, 92 Ill. 2d, 344, 348, 442 N.E.2d, 195, 196–97.
82. *Id.,* 442 N.E.2d at 197.
83. *Id.* at 348–49, 442 N.E.2d at 197.

Fourth, in the course of discussing the critical treatment accorded to the innocent construction rule by legal scholars, the court called attention to the connection between the rule and the English "mitior sensus" doctrine, citing Eldredge's *The Law of Defamation*. [84] Given the fact that the Illinois Supreme Court had *never* discussed the common law rule as an outgrowth of the English doctrine until *Chapski*, it is surprising that the court would do so twenty years after *John*.

And finally, in justifying the innocent construction rule, the court explicitly accepted the rationale of the Illinois Appellate Court in *Dauw v. Field Enterprises, Inc.* in 1979.[85] The court, citing *Dauw*, said: "Perhaps the strongest reason advanced in support of the rule is that it comports with the constitutional interests of free speech and free press and encourages the robust discussion of daily affairs."[86]

After treating the innocent construction rule to an unusually critical dissection, the court, in a unanimous decision written by Justice Underwood, noted that a modification in the common law rule would better protect the individual's good name at stake in a libel suit, and at the same time, encourage the first amendment principle of the "robust discussion of daily affairs." The court then held that:

> [A] written or oral statement is to be considered in context, with the words and the implications therefrom given their natural and obvious meaning; *if, as so construed, the statement may reasonably be innocently interpreted or reasonably be interpreted as referring to someone other than the plaintiff it cannot be actionable per se.* This preliminary determination is properly a question of law to be resolved by the court in the first instance: whether the publication was in fact understood to be defamatory or to refer to the plaintiff is a question for the jury should the initial determination be resolved in favor of the plaintiff.[87]

The court rejected the defense's argument against application of such a modified rule in the present case and reversed the rulings of the appellate court. *Chapski* represents the first effort of the Illinois Supreme Court to modify the innocent construction defense since its formal adoption by the court in *John* in 1962.

---

84. *Id.* at 349, 442 N.E.2d at 197.
85. Dauw v. Field Enterprises, Inc., 78 Ill. App. 3d 67, 397 N.E.2d 41 (1979).
86. Chapski v. Copley Press, 92 Ill. 2d, 344, 350, 442 N.E.2d, 195, 198.
87. *Id.* at 352, 442 N.E.2d at 199 (emphasis added).

B. Survival Through Modification

The *Chapski* decision is clearly a pivotal case in regard to the future of the innocent construction rule as a libel defense in Illinois. In the face of growing criticism and judicial challenges, the Illinois Supreme Court was virtually forced to review the twenty-year history of the rule in Illinois. Even though the rule had admittedly been applied by the lower courts "in something less than a completely uniform fashion,"[88] the court also noted that attempts to eliminate use of the rule had likewise been consistently rejected in the past. The principal criticism of the rule, according to *Chapski*, was that the lower courts too often strained to find unnatural but possibly innocent meanings of words where such a construction was clearly unreasonable and a defamatory meaning was far more probable.[89]

But rather than reject the rule enunciated in *John* in 1962, the *Chapski* court chose instead to remedy such "unreasonable" construction, which the court noted was clearly incompatible with the *John* requirement that words must be given their "natural and obvious meaning." The court noted that this inherent conflict contained in the definition itself had been resolved by a number of lower courts, though perhaps unwittingly, "by construing the words innocently as a matter of law only where the words are *reasonably* susceptible of such a construction or the allegedly defamatory language is ambiguous."[90] It was this latter approach, applying the test of reasonableness, that the court took in *Chapski*. Given the inconsistencies, inequities, and confusion that were apparent in the court's review of the twenty-year history of innocent construction, modification was inevitable.

From the journalist's point of view, modification of the innocent construction rule was clearly preferable to rejection of the rule, an action sought by some critics. Indeed, modification of the rule may help to ensure its survival in Illinois. The court had noted that the original "mitior sensus" doctrine in Great Britain, upon which the innocent construction rule was based, was abandoned after a series of cases in which the rule went through a period of "artificial and strained application" resulting in some "remarkable judicial acrobatics."[91] The modified approach set out in *Chapski* should help to prevent a similar end in the case of the innocent construction rule.

Indeed, modification of the rule also may help to ensure the future use of innocent construction in Illinois because of the link which the court saw between this common law libel defense and the *New York Times* "actual malice" rule based on the first amendment. As pointed out above, the court noted

88. *Id.* at 348, 442 N.E.2d at 197.
89. *Id.* at 350, 442 N.E.2d at 198.
90. *Id.* at 351, 442 N.E.2d at 198 (emphasis in original).
91. *Id.* at 350, 442 N.E.2d at 198, *citing* Lovell, *supra* note 26, at 1064–65.

that "the strongest reason advanced in support of the rule is that it comports with the constitutional interests of free speech and free press and encourages the robust discussion of daily affairs."[92] While allowing the first amendment guarantees the "breathing space" essential to their "fruitful exercise," the innocent construction modification was still viewed by the *Chapski* court as continuing "to protect the individual's interest in vindicating his good name and reputation."[93] The Illinois Supreme Court, in other words, saw their modifications as having a salutary effect on the continued application of the rule in Illinois libel cases.[94]

IV. CONCLUSION

In 1962, the Illinois Supreme Court in *John v. Tribune Co.* established the innocent construction rule, which has provided libel defendants, including scores of media defendants, with an effective common law defense. The *John* opinion required that the allegedly defamatory language be read as a whole and the words given their natural and obvious meaning. Words allegedly libelous that are capable of an innocent construction must be read and declared nonactionable as a matter of law, i.e., the judge shall make the determination. From the libel defendant's point of view, the innocent construction rule provides a speedy and usually less costly method of settling a libel action

92. *Id.,* 442 N.E.2d at 198.
93. *Id.* at 351–52, 442 N.E.2d at 198–99.
94. Since the Illinois Supreme Court modified the innocent construction rule in *Chapski* in October 1982, the state courts and federal courts in Illinois have applied the "reasonable" concept of the common law defense in twenty defamation cases as of May 1985. Of these, the rule prevailed in fourteen and failed in six. For cases in which the courts employed the *Chapski* version of the innocent construction rule *for* defendants, *see* Owen v. Carr, No. 4-84-0417, slip op. (App. Ct. Ill. filed May 14, 1985); Grisanzio v. Rockford Newspapers, Inc., 132 Ill. App. 3d 914, ___ N.E.2d ___ (1985); Dauw v. Kennedy & Kennedy, Inc., 130 Ill. App. 3d 163, 474 N.E.2d 380 (1984); Meyer v. Allen, 127 Ill. App. 3d 163, 468 N.E.2d 198 (1984); Renard v. CBS, 126 Ill. App. 3d 563, 467 N.E.2d 1090 (1984); Sivulich v. Howard Publications, Inc., 126 Ill. App. 3d 129, 466 N.E.2d 1218 (1984); Matchett v. Chicago Bar Ass'n, 125 Ill. App. 3d 1004, 467 N.E.2d 271 (1984), *cert. denied,* 105 S. Ct. 2115 (1985); Audition Div. Ltd. v. Better Bus. Bureau, 120 Ill. App. 3d 254, 458 N.E.2d 115 (1983); Antonelli v. Field Enterprises Inc., 115 Ill. App. 3d 432, 450 N.E.2d 876 (1983); Cartwright v. Garrison, 113 Ill. App. 3d 536, 447 N.E.2d 446 (1983); Pruitt v. Chow, 747 F.2d 1104 (7th Cir. 1984) (applying the Illinois rule); Paul v. Premier Ele. Const. Co., 581 F. Supp. 721 (N.D. Ill. 1984) (applying the Illinois rule); Spelson v. CBS, 581 F. Supp. 1195 (N.D. Ill. 1984) (applying the Illinois rule); and Heying v. Simonaitis, 126 Ill. App. 3d 157, 466 N.E.2d 1137 (1984). For cases in which the courts utilized the *Chapski* rule of innocent construction *against* defendants, *see* Resudek v. Sberna, 132 Ill. App. 3d 783, ___ N.E.2d ___ (1985); Fried v. Jacobson, 99 Ill. 2d 24, 457 N.E.2d 392 (1983); Erickson v. Aetna Life & Ca. Co., 127 Ill. App. 3d 753, 469 N.E.2d 679 (1984); Am. Int'l Hospital v. Chicago Tribune Co., 120 Ill. App. 3d 435, 458 N.E.2d 1305 (1983); Crinkley v. Dow Jones & Co., 119 Ill. App. 3d 147, 456 N.E.2d 138 (1983); Costello v. Capital Cities Media, Inc., 111 Ill. App. 3d 1009, 445 N.E.2d 13 (1982).

because a jury trial is generally avoided.

During the past twenty years since *John*, the state courts and the federal courts in Illinois have utilized the innocent construction rule in more than sixty reported cases. Such cases deal primarily with actions resulting from publications that contained ambiguous language where questions of meaning were raised. But the innocent construction rule has also been employed in at least two other areas: where the publication left questions concerning identification of the plaintiff, the so-called colloquium issue, and where questions concerning style (e.g., use of hyperbole, epithets, or name-calling) were involved.

While the innocent construction rule proved an expeditious method of settling some libel actions, the Illinois courts have not always been consistent in dealing with the requirements set out in *John*. Growing criticism, both outside and inside the court, focused upon various inconsistencies in application of the rule. Some critics called for revisions in this rule to curb its "mischievous spread" and to bring Illinois back into "the mainstream of common law defamation development."[95] In the face of such criticism, the Illinois Supreme Court sought to modify the rule in *Chapski*, in a unanimous opinion announced in October of 1982. The primary change was the addition of a requirement that the innocent interpretation arrived at must be *reasonable*. Or, as the court put it, "if, as so construed, the statement may reasonably be innocently interpreted, or reasonably be interpreted as referring to someone other than the plaintiff it cannot be actionable *per se*." *Chapski* dealt with the issue of colloquium, therefore, the second part of the statement was most pertinent to the case at hand.

While the *Chapski* court modified the rule itself, it refused to make innocent construction a jury issue as suggested by some critics. The court said: "This preliminary determination is properly a question of law to be resolved by the court in the first instance." Only if the initial determination, the question of whether or not the publication is capable of an innocent construction, is resolved in favor of the plaintiff would the case go to the jury to determine if the publication was, in fact, understood to be defamatory or to refer to the plaintiff. This portion of the *Chapski* holding is important, for it safeguards the primary advantage of the innocent construction rule—retention of the speedy economical aspects of such a defense.

The effect of the requirement of reasonableness in future libel litigation is more difficult to assess. The court itself viewed the modification as one which was needed to resolve the inherent conflict in the rule's requirement that the words be given their "natural and obvious meaning." This, like the doctrine of "mitior sensus," had led courts to strain to find unnatural but

95. Polelle, *supra* note 14, at 181.

possibly innocent meanings of words where such a construction was clearly unreasonable and a defamatory meaning was far more probable. The *Chapski* court noted that, in some cases, the lower courts had required that before the words could be construed innocently, they must, as a matter of law, be reasonably susceptible to such a construction. On the other hand, if *Chapski* is interpreted too stringently by the lower courts, what have been law questions under *John* may result in questions for the jury to determine, destroying the essence of the economic value of the rule.

Finally, it is clear that the Illinois Supreme Court in *Chapski* has taken issue with the *application* of the innocent construction rule, not with the *judicial propriety* of the rule itself. The modifications, therefore, should not discourage the continued use of the rule. By requiring that the words in question be *reasonably* capable of an innocent construction, the *Chapski* opinion should work to perpetuate future use of the rule by reducing the possibility of its overexpansion and eventual demise.

KYU HO YOUM

"Single Instance" Rule as a Libel Defense

Kyu Ho Youm is assistant professor of journalism at Loras College in Dubuque, Iowa. He holds an M.A. and Ph.D. in journalism, both from Southern Illinois University-Carbondale.

"To err is human, to forgive divine," as Alexander Pope stated in 1711.[1] In a similar vein, English political philosopher John Locke observed: "All men are liable to error, and most men are in many points, by passion or interest, under temptation to it."[2] Likewise, the law of defamation, which largely deals with "relational interests" of individuals,[3] responds to these common-sense comments on the imperfection of human beings. As one New York appellate court declared: "[I]nfallibility is not a human trait and even the most skillful may make a mistake on a single occasion. . . ."[4]

Considering that defamation is often explained in terms of the tendency of words to injure reputation,[5] any comment that injures a person's ability to conduct a business or to perform one's profession or occupation successfully

1. A. POPE, 1 AN ESSAY ON CRITICISM 558 (1711).
2. J. LOCKE, 2 AN ESSAY CONCERNING HUMAN UNDERSTANDING 457 (Dover ed. 1959).
3. Noting that individuals have a right to protect their "general social relations" with others, one legal scholar has characterized defamation as an injury to the individual's "relational interests," which are distinctive from family relations, trade relations, professional relations and political relations. See Green, *Relational Interests,* 31 ILL. L. REV. 35 (1936).
4. Twiggar v. Ossining Printing & Pub. Co., 161 A.D. 718, 146 N.Y.S. 529 (2d Dep't. 1914), *appeal dismissed,* 220 N.Y. 716, 116 N.E. 1080 (1917), *quoted in* Craig v. Moore, 4 MEDIA L. REP. 1402, 1405 (Fla. Cir. Ct. 1978).
5. One authority explains: "A communication is defamatory if it tends so to harm the reputation of another as to lower him in the estimation of the community or to deter third persons from associating or dealing with him." RESTATEMENT (SECOND) OF TORTS § 559(1977) [hereinafter cited as RESTATEMENT]. *See also* PROSSER AND KEETON ON THE LAW OF TORTS 773 (W. Keeton ed. 5th ed. 1984) [hereinafter cited as PROSSER & KEETON ON TORTS] ("Defamation is rather that which tends to injure 'reputation' in the popular sense; to diminish the esteem, respect, good-will or confidence in which the plaintiff is held, or to excite adverse, derogatory or unpleasant feelings or opinions against him.").

can be considered defamatory.[6] When it comes to the New York appellate court's note of human beings' fallibility, however, there is a legally recognized exception to the English judicial premise that "[T]he law [of libel] has always been very tender of the reputation of tradesmen, and therefore words spoken of them in the way of their trade will bear an action, that will not be actionable in the case of another person."[7]

This judicial limitation to the legalistic tenderness for those in business, a trade, or a profession is the so-called "single instance rule," as it is widely referred to in the state of New York.[8] The defamation rule, which David Anderson of the University of Texas School of Law has dismissed as a judicial "artifice,"[9] is basically premised on the notion that everyone probably makes mistakes of one kind or another, and therefore "[L]anguage charging a professional person with ignorance or error on a single occasion but which does not accuse him or her of general incompetence, ignorance or lack of skill is not defamatory, per se, unless special damages are pleaded."[10] This common law libel doctrine has served libel defendants, both media and nonmedia, as an additional protection from liability for their allegedly defamatory statements in jurisdictions adopting the rule.

Notwithstanding its significance, both historical and judicial, analysis of the single instance rule has been surprisingly limited. Most scholarly discussion of the rule has been largely cursory or superficial, failing to put the rule into a proper perspective.[11] Indeed, some of the major mass communications law textbooks do not even mention the rule in their examination of libel

---

6. RESTATEMENT (SECOND) OF TORTS states:

> One who publishes a slander that ascribes to another conduct, characteristics or a condition that would adversely affect his fitness for the proper conduct of his lawful business, trade or profession, or of his public or private office, whether honorary or for profit, is subject to liability without proof of special harm.

RESTATEMENT § 573 (1977).
7. Harman v. Delany, 2 Strange 898, 899, 93 Eng. Rep. 925, 926 (1731). See generally Lawson, The Slander of a Person in His Calling, 15 AM. L. REV. 573 (1881).
8. The single instance rule is also known by "single-mistake" rule. See, e.g., D. PEMBER, MASS MEDIA LAW 118 (3d ed. 1984); R. PHELPS & E. HAMILTON, LIBEL: RIGHTS, RISKS, RESPONSIBILITIES 76 (rev. ed. 1978).
9. Anderson, Presumed Harm: An Item for the Unfinished Agenda of Times v. Sullivan, 62 JOURNALISM Q. 26 (1985).
10. Brower v. New Republic, 7 MEDIA L. REP. 1605, 1610 (N.Y. Sup. Ct. 1981).
11. See, e.g., D. GILLMOR & J. BARRON, MASS COMMUNICATION LAW 197 (4th ed. 1984); H. NELSON & D. TEETER, JR., LAW OF MASS COMMUNICATIONS 79–80 (5th ed. 1986); PEMBER, supra note 8, at 118–19; PHELPS & HAMILTON, supra note 8, at 76–78; R. SACK, LIBEL, SLANDER, AND RELATED PROBLEMS 70–71 (1980); B. Sanford, LIBEL AND PRIVACY 89–90 (1985).

law.[12] This scarcity of analysis and scholarly treatment of the single instance rule may explain in part why the rule has sometimes been confused with the "single publication rule."[13]

This study will reexamine the single instance rule as a libel defense, focusing upon its use in those jurisdictions adopting the rule. Three questions will be explored:

(1) How has the single instance rule evolved as a common law libel defense in the United States?
(2) What is the underlying legal rationale of the single instance rule as a libel defense?
(3) How extensively and under what circumstances has the single instance rule been utilized as a libel defense?

I. HISTORICAL DEVELOPMENT

It is generally understood that the single instance rule has evolved from *Foot v. Brown*,[14] an 1811 slander case in New York.[15] The *Foot* case resulted from a statement concerning an attorney: "Foot will lead his client to ruin, because he knows nothing about his cause."[16] This disparaging comment related to the plaintiff's legal counselling service in an ejectment suit.[17] The

---

12. *See, e.g.,* T. CARTER, M. FRANKLIN & J. WRIGHT, THE FIRST AMENDMENT AND THE FOURTH ESTATE (3d ed. 1985); W. FRANCOIS, MASS MEDIA LAW AND REGULATION (3d ed. 1982).
13. *See, e.g.,* Brower v. New Republic, 7 MEDIA L. REP. 1605, 1610 (N.Y. Sup. Ct. 1981). Under the single publication rule as adopted by the Uniform Single Publication Act:

> No person shall have more than one cause of action for damages for libel or slander or invasion of privacy or any other tort founded upon any single publication or exhibition or utterance, such as any one edition of a newspaper or book or magazine or any one presentation to an audience or any one broadcast over radio or television or any one exhibition of a motion picture. Recovery in any action shall include all damages for any such tort suffered by the plaintiff in all jurisdictions.

14 U.L.A. 351 (1980).
14. 8 Johns. 64 (N.Y. 1811).
15. *See, e.g.,* Brower v. New Republic, 7 MEDIA L. REP. 1605, 1609–10 (N.Y. Sup. Ct. 1981); Cohn v. Am-Law, 5 MEDIA L. REP. 2362, 2368 (N.Y. Sup. Ct. 1980); Handelman v. Hustler Magazine, Inc., 469 F. Supp. 1048, 1052 (S.D.N.Y. 1978) (applying the New York law); Bordoni v. New York Times Co., 400 F. Supp. 1223, 1228 (S.D.N.Y. 1975) (applying the New York rule).
16. Foot v. Brown, 8 Johns. 64, 65 (N.Y. 1811).
17. One authority defines "ejectment" as "an action to restore possession of property to the person entitled to it." BLACK'S LAW DICTIONARY 464 (rev. 5th ed. 1979).

plaintiff claimed that the statement was defamatory of his fairness, skill, and integrity in his profession as an attorney, and he won a jury verdict against the defendant.[18]

The defendant then filed a motion in arrest of judgment on the jury verdict. Before the court, the defense argued that the ignorance imputed by the statement at issue did not relate to the plaintiff's general qualifications as an attorney. It focused instead on his professional skill as shown in a particular case—i.e., the ejectment proceedings, in which the plaintiff was involved as an attorney.[19] Refuting the "old" rule that "all words which tend to disparage a man in his trade or profession are actionable," the defendant characterized the rule as "too vague" and "not correct" in that "all comparisons between professional men would be actionable."[20] In connection with his attack on the old libel rule, the defense counsel contended that words are not actionable "which charge a person with ignorance or want of professional knowledge or skill in a particular case."[21]

The defense made a distinction between the nonactionable words and the actionable words, which fall into three classes of libel cases, such as:

> 1. Where the words charge the person with a want of fidelity or integrity in his trade or profession generally. . . . 2. Where the words charge a person with dishonesty, corruption, or want of integrity, in a particular case. 3. Where the words impute ignorance or want of skill in general terms.[22]

The defense, citing an English defamation case, *Poe v. Mondford*[23] as controlling, explained that the court should distinguish expression about a person *generally* in his or her trade or profession from expression charging him or her with ignorance or want of skill *in a particular instance*.[24] The defense also noted that while words spoken charging a person with want of ability in a particular case are not actionable, "to charge a man with want of *integrity*, in a particular instance, is actionable."[25] It was observed:

18. Foot v. Brown, 8 Johns. 64 (N.Y. 1811).
19. *Id.* at 65.
20. *Id.* at 66.
21. *Id.*
22. *Id.* (citations omitted)
23. Cro. Eliz. 620, 78 Eng. Rep. 861 (1598).
24. Foot v. Brown, 8 Johns. 64, 66–67 (N.Y. 1811). The defense cited five more English and American cases in support of its "single instance" argument. The cases are: Townsend v. Hughes, 1 Freeman 217, 89 Eng. Rep. 155 (1676); Redman v. Payne, 1 Mod. 19, 86 Eng. Rep. 698 (1681); Lancaster v. French, 2 Strange 797, 93 Eng. Rep. 855 (1727); Harman v. Delany, 2 Strange 898, 93 Eng. Rep. 925 (1731); and Backus v. Richardson, 5 Johns. 476 (1809).
25. *Id.* at 67. (emphasis in original)

> The charge of dishonesty or want of integrity in any case must
> be injurious. Dishonesty is a violation of the oath taken by
> attorney, as well as a breach of moral duty. But if a man acts
> honestly, to the best of his knowledge or ability, in the case
> intrusted to him, the charge of want of skill or ability, in a
> single instance, is neither disgraceful nor injurious.[26]

The plaintiff responded that "Any words spoken of a man in his profession which are calculated to destroy the confidence of those who employ him, are actionable, and the law implies damage from the nature and tendency of the words spoken."[27] In reply, the defendant's counsel asserted that unless special damage could be shown on the part of the plaintiff, the charge of ignorance which is not general as to his profession nor impeaching his integrity should not be actionable.[28]

In its *per curiam* opinion,[29] the New York Supreme Court in *Foot*[30] generally agreed with the arguments of the defense. To begin with, the court took note of the fact that the words at issue in the case were to charge the plaintiff with ignorance in the "particular" ejectment suit involving him.[31] Since the allegedly libelous charge "does not affect the party generally in his profession," the New York high court ruled, "the law will not give a remedy" for the plaintiff who did not plead special damages for the complained of expression.[32]

Secondly, the court, relying on the *Poe* case as an authoritative precedent, emphatically stated that words affecting an individual's credit in his or her profession in pointing to ignorance or want of skill in general, or a want of integrity either in general or in particular, are defamatory enough to be subject to liability.[33]

26. *Id.*
27. *Id.*
28. *Id.* at 67–68.
29. The *per curiam* opinion of the *Foot* case was apparently written by Chancellor Kent, then Chief Justice of New York. *See* W. KENT, MEMOIRS AND LETTERS OF JAMES KENT 118 (1898) ("I [James Kent, better known as Chancellor Kent] remember that in eighth Johnson [Johnson's Reports] all the opinions for one term are '*per curiam*.' The fact is I wrote them all and proposed that course to avoid exciting jealousy, and many a *per curiam* opinion was so inserted for that reason.").
30. The Supreme Court of New York at the time of the *Foot* decision was the highest court in the state of New York. Since 1846, when the new Constitution of New York provided for a Court of Appeals as the state's highest appellate court, it has been a court of general and original jurisdiction, possessing also some appellate jurisdiction. *See* N.Y. CONST. of 1846, art. VI, §§ 2–3. For the text of the New York Constitution of 1846, see 5 THE FEDERAL AND STATE CONSTITUTIONS 2563–92 (F. Thorpe comp. & ed. 1909).
31. Foot v. Brown, 8 Johns. 64, 68 (N.Y. 1811).
32. *Id.*
33. *Id.*

Thirdly, noting that there had been no cases reported that ruled culpable the words charging a professional person with ignorance in a *particular* case, the court declared: "To carry the right of action so far would be unnecessary for the protection of any profession, and would be an *unreasonable check upon the freedom of discussion.*"[34]

Finally, the New York court analytically examined the allegedly libelous words at issue and held that they did not charge the plaintiff with ignorance in general in his legal profession. The court observed: "The additional words . . . that 'the plaintiff would lead the party on to ruin,' were consequence of his ignorance of that particular case, and a deduction from that assumed fact."[35]

The reasoning of the *Foot* court in reversing the judgment against the defendant was adopted by the Supreme Court of Connecticut in 1854. In *Camp v. Martin,*[36] the court found nondefamatory the comment of the defendant on the plaintiff, a physician: "If Dr. C[amp]. had continued to treat her, she would have been in her grave before this time; his treatment of her was rascally."[37] In the opinion written by Justice Storrs, the court, quoting verbatim from the New York decision in *Foot,*[38] ruled that to charge a physician with mismanagement in the treatment of a particular case is nonactionable.[39] In connection with the adoption by the Connecticut Supreme Court of the single instance rule, it is noteworthy that the *Camp* court rejected the argument of the plaintiff that the libel defense was seriously questioned in *Sumner v. Utley,*[40] an 1828 slander case in Connecticut.[41] The court held:

> [T]he court, in that case [*Sumner v. Utley*], so far from varying the [single instance] rule, as we have given it, clearly intended to sanction it; and that that case was decided for the plaintiff, not on the ground, that the words charged imputed to him merely ignorance or a want of skill, in the particular case respecting which they were spoken, but that by a fair construction of them, they amounted to an imputation upon him, of a want of general professional knowledge and skill.[42]

In the same year that Connecticut embraced the single instance rule, the New York Supreme Court, now an intermediate court in the state of New York under the 1846 Constitution,[43] refused to accept the common law defense

34. *Id.* (emphasis added)
35. *Id.* at 68–69.
36. 23 Conn. 86 (1854).
37. *Id.* at 87.
38. *Id.* at 89–90.
39. *Id.* at 89.
40. 7 Conn. 257 (1828).
41. Camp v. Martin, 23 Conn. 86, 90 (1854).
42. *Id.*
43. *See supra* note 30.

on the ground that *Foot v. Brown*[44] was not a "sound" case to be followed as a precedent.[45] In *Secor v. Harris*[46] the court, which one legal scholar erroneously concluded "expressly repudiated" the single instance rule,[47] held: "The case of *Poe v. Mendford* [sic], and of *Foot v. Brown* were reviewed by the supreme court of Connecticut, in the case of *Sumner v. Utley* . . . with most distinguished ability, and the doctrine of those repudiated."[48] The present case originated from the statement of the defendant concerning the plaintiff: "Doctor Secor killed my children. He gave them tea-spoonful doses of calomel, and they died. . . . They did not live long after they took it. They died right off—the same day."[49] Justice Mason wrote for the court: when a physician is charged with gross ignorance and a total want of skill in his profession, in a single instance, the words are actionable of themselves in that the charge implies gross ignorance and unskillfulness in the profession of the physician.[50]

With regard to the ruling of the New York court in *Secor,* one commentator termed the court's interpretation of the Connecticut case of *Sumner v. Utley* "remarkable" in that the court evidently misunderstood the judicial parameters of the *Sumner* ruling.[51] Noting that the primary legal question in the Connecticut case was whether the allegedly defamatory statement of the defendant charged the physician plaintiff with mere ignorance in a particular case, or with a want of general professional knowledge and skill, he observed: "It was the application of a legal rule, and not its existence or propriety, that was determined in *Sumner v. Utley.*"[52]

In a 1914 case, *Twiggar v. Ossining Printing & Pub. Co.,*[53] the New York appellate court still adhered to the single instance rule as established in *Foot.* Under the common law libel defense, the court reversed the lower court's libel ruling against the defendant.[54] Justice P. J. Jenks, who wrote the opinion for the *Twiggar* court, obviously ignored the *Secor* decision.[55] Laurence Eldredge, professor of law at the University of California Hastings College of the Law, characterized the failure of the *Twiggar* court to consider *Secor* as "hard to understand" and "incredible"[56]

---

44. 8 Johns. 64 (N.Y. 1811).
45. *See* Secor v. Harris, 18 Barb. 425 (N.Y. 1854).
46. *Id.*
47. L. ELDREDGE, THE LAW OF DEFAMATION 41 n.97 (1978).
48. Secor v. Harris, 18 Barb. 425, 427 (N.Y. 1854).
49. *Id.* at 425.
50. *Id.* at 426.
51. Lawson, *supra* note 7, at 596.
52. *Id.*
53. 161 A.D. 718, 146 N.Y.S. 529 (2d Dep't. 1914), *appeal dismissed,* 220 N.Y. 716, 116 N.E. 1080 (1917).
54. 146 N.Y.S. 529, 530 (2d Dep't. 1914).
55. For a discussion of the *Secor* case, see text accompanying notes 45–50, *supra.*
56. ELDREDGE, *supra* note 47, at 141.

In connection with the historical development of the single instance rule in New York, it is no less surprising than the *Secor* court's unconvincing refutation of the rule[57] that the New York Supreme Court in *Vosbury v. Utica Daily Press Co.*[58] declared:

> The [single instance] principle enunciated in *Foot v. Brown* has not . . . received the sanction of our court of last resort. Now, it is the unquestionable rule that all words are actionable *per se* which tend to injure a person in his trade, occupation, profession or business.[59]

In 1963, the New York Court of Appeals, the state's high court,[60] citing *Foot v. Brown* and *Twiggar v. Ossining Printing & Pub. Co.*, recognized the single instance rule with approval. The Court in *November v. Time*[61] held:

> [T]he [single instance] rule . . . holds that language charging a professional man with ignorance or mistake on a single occasion only and not accusing him of general ignorance or lack of skill cannot be considered defamatory on its face and so is not actionable unless special damages are pleaded.[62]

Since the New York Court of Appeals affirmed the single instance rule in 1963, the libel defense has been increasingly applied by state and federal courts in New York as well as in various jurisdictions in other states. The application of the rule, however, varies from jurisdiction to jurisdiction.

II. APPLICATION OF THE "SINGLE INSTANCE" RULE

A. New York Cases

According to the *Restatement (Second) of Torts,* a charge in the form of libel of a single act of misconduct in the plaintiff's business, trade, profession, or office may be sufficient to support an action for libel without allegation or proof of special damages, even though the charge does not imply a habitual course of conduct or lack of the qualities or skill that the public is reasonably entitled to expect of persons engaged in such calling.[63] The single instance rule, therefore, as defined by the New York Court of Appeals in *November v. Time,*[64] contradicts the general law as stated by the American

---

57. For a discussion of the *Secor* case, see text accompanying notes 45–50, *supra.*
58. 183 A.D. 769 (3d div. 1918).
59. *Id.* at 771–72.
60. *See supra* note 30.
61. 13 N.Y.2d 175 (1963).
62. *Id.* at 178. (citations omitted)
63. RESTATEMENT §569 comment e (1977).
64. 13 N.Y.2d 175, 178 (1963).

Law Institute in the *Restatement*. The rule requires, for example, that special damages be pleaded and proved for libelous comments on ignorance or mistake of a professional on a single occasion to subject the defendant to liability.

A 1975 federal libel case involving the *New York Times* demonstrates how the single instance rule prevails where no special damages are pleaded. In *Bordoni v. New York Times Co.*,[65] the plaintiff claimed that the defendant newspaper injured his right to reputation with a news story concerning his resignation as a director of a banking corporation. The plaintiff charged that the *Times* article at issue defamed him in his business reputation, professional competence, and standing as an expert in international financial affairs, among other things.[66] The defendant moved to dismiss the complaint, in part on the basis of the New York single instance rule, arguing that the complaint was deficient because of its failure to plead special damages.[67] The U.S. District Court, Southern District of New York, agreeing with the defense, stated: "[T]he article does not defame the plaintiff in his calling, and even if it did call into question his business judgment in advocating the foreign-exchange policy, the 'single-instance' rule would bar recovery" of damages in that the plaintiff's advice on foreign-exchange trading was "single advice or advocacy of a single policy of investment to management" of his bank.[68]

The single instance rule was stated as a dictum in *Brower v. New Republic*.[69] This libel case involved an allegedly defamatory article published in *New Republic* magazine about the plaintiff, an attorney involved in the campaign to exonerate the Rosenbergs. The New York appellate court ruled the publication in question nonactionable in that it was "pure, as distinct from mixed, opinion . . . absolutely protected as free speech under the First Amendment."[70] The court further noted that even if the magazine article was found to be defamatory, it still could not be actionable because of the plaintiff's failure to plead special damages under the single instance rule of

---

65. 400 F. Supp. 1223 (S.D.N.Y. 1975).
66. *Id.* at 1227.
67. *Id.* at 1225.
68. *Id.* at 1229 (applying the New York law). *See also* Twiggar v. Ossining Printing & Pub. Co., 161 A.D. 718, 146 N.Y.S. 529 (2d Dep't 1919) (charging dentist with unskillful work on a patient held not to state a claim in the absence of an allegation of special damage); Brower v. New Republic, 7 MEDIA L. REP. 1605 (N.Y. Sup. Ct. 1981) (allegedly false publication concerning an attorney's involvement in the Rosenberg espionage case held nonactionable because of the plaintiff's failure to plead special damages); Shaw v. Consolidated Rail Corp., 74 A.D.2d 984 (1979) (allegedly defamatory letter ruled not culpable because no special damages are pleaded).
69. 7 MEDIA L. REP. 1605 (N.Y. Sup. Ct. 1981).
70. *Id.* at 1610–11.

New York.[71] The court also observed that the rule required the allegedly defamatory publication be understood in the context of the "ongoing" controversy between those involved.[72]

In another New York libel case, *Tracy v. New York Magazine*,[73] it was ruled on the basis of the single instance rule that the defendant's magazine article about the plaintiff, then the campaign manager for a New York City mayoral candidate, was protected expression. The allegedly libelous article described the plaintiff as "a retired mounted policeman whose only distinction in a long career came when he fell asleep in a boxcar in the West Side freightyards and woke up the next day with his horse in Schenectady."[74] Noting that the subject of the published article dealt with a "single mistake" on the part of the plaintiff, the court held that the defendant was not subject to liability for the publication at issue.[75] What is particularly noteworthy about the application of the single instance rule in *Tracy* is that the common law libel defense was successfully utilized even where an allegedly defamatory falsehood was involved.[76]

B. Other Jurisdictions

One Florida jurisdiction explicitly adopted the single instance rule in 1978, when the Florida Circuit Court in *Craig v. Moore*[77] ruled: "Nor is it libelous to charge an individual with a single mistake or of acting foolishly on a single occasion."[78] This Florida case arose from a radio editorial caustically questioning whether the plaintiff was fit to be reelected as mayor of Jacksonville Beach, Florida.[79] The court granted the defendant's motion for summary judgment primarily on the ground that the complained of statement was an expression of opinion. From the perspective of the court's adoption of the single instance rule, the opinion was not as clear as it might have been in regard to what constituted the "single mistake" of the plaintiff.

71. *Id.* at 1609–10.
72. *Id.* at 1609. In *New Republic* magazine, it was stated that the plaintiff allegedly revealed to the authors of the magazine article certain facts concerning the Rosenberg espionage case. *Id.* at 1606–1607.
73. 3 MEDIA L. REP. 2294 (N.Y. Sup. Ct. 1978).
74. *Id.*
75. *Id.* at 2295.
76. *See id.* at 2294.
77. 4 MEDIA L. REP. 1402 (Fla. Cir. Ct. 1978).
78. *Id.* at 1405, citing *Twiggar v. Ossining Printing & Pub. Co.* and four other New York cases.
79. *Id.* at 1403. The complained of article was part of defendant's news broadcast at 6 A.M. on September 28, 1977 from Radio Station WAPE-690. It stated in part: "Well, what else can we expect from Mayor Guy Craig? This deceptive individual who quite often misleads, if not blatantly lies to reporters from this radio station. What often [sic] could you expect from him? Can you believe people elected him to begin with? Can you believe people will probably reelect him?" *Id.*

Although Illinois has not adopted the single instance rule *in toto,* the judicial concept of the rule, however, has been utilized in several defamation decisions involving the Illinois "innocent construction rule."[80] *Halpern v. News-Sun Broadcasting Co.,*[81] for example, is one of the several Illinois libel cases illustrating application of the single instance rule by way of the state's concept of innocent construction.

The defendant in *Halpern* was sued for publishing an allegedly libelous statement concerning the death of a mentally retarded patient in a nursing home operated by the plaintiff. The article stated that the death of the patient resulted from pneumonia and malnutrition, not from food poisoning "as the death certificate indicated."[82] The plaintiff contended that the article charged him with the crime of falsifying the death certificate. The Illinois appellate court held:

> [T]he crime to which plaintiffs are apparently referring, requires that the false statements be made wilfully and knowingly. The article as published, may reasonably be interpreted to mean that the death certificate was erroneous. This error, however, could easily be the result of a *simple mistake* and need not necessarily have been deliberately made.[83]

The court then ruled that the article was not libelous.

In a 1981 Illinois case, *Britton v. Winfield Public Library,*[84] the court noted that the allegedly defamatory words on the plaintiff's conduct concerned "one incident" and not a character attack in general upon the plaintiff. On grounds of the innocent construction rule, but obviously utilizing the New York single instance rule, the article was held nondefamatory.[85]

80. The innocent construction rule, as most expansively applied by Illinois courts to defamation cases as a libel defense, has been defined by the Illinois Supreme Court as follows:

> [A] written or oral statement is to be considered in context, with the words and the implications therefrom given their natural and obvious meaning; if, as so construed, the statement may reasonably be innocently interpreted or reasonably be interpreted as referring to someone other than the plaintiff it cannot be actionable per se.

    Chapski v. Copley Press, 92 Ill. 2d 344, 350, 442 N.E.2d 195, 198 (1982).
81. 53 Ill. App.3d 644, 368 N.E.2d 1062 (1977).
82. *Id.* at 647, 368 N.E. at 1064.
83. *Id.* at 649, 368 N.E.2d at 1066, citing Ill. Rev. Stat. ch. 111½, para. 73–27(1)(a) (emphasis added).
84. 101 Ill. App.3d 546, 428 N.E.2d 650 (1981).
85. The publication challenged to be libelous in the *Britton* case was a letter written by the defendant and published in newspapers. In the letter, the defendant stated that the plaintiff, then village administrator, used "dirty tricks" as part of his "cheap and dishonest government." *Id.* at 547, 428 N.E.2d at 651.

The U.S. Court of Appeals, Seventh Circuit, also borrowed the concept of the single instance rule in *Fleck Bros. Co v. Sullivan*[86] in applying the Illinois common law libel rule of innocent construction. The alleged libel at issue in the federal court was in a letter stating that the defendant had handled and collected a certain amount of money from the plaintiff corporation for a service fee. The Seventh Circuit observed that the statement in the letter merely indicated "a single instance in which plaintiff failed to pay an obligation in the ordinary course of business," and further added that a single such instance could result from mistake or a good faith dispute over liability.[87] The court's decision, however, was based upon the innocent construction rule, noting that "the publication was not actionable without proof of special damage."[88]

At least one Georgia jurisdiction has also adopted the single instance rule. In *Holder Const. Co. v. Ed Smith & Sons*,[89] a Georgia appellate court ruled that the defendant's letter, alleged by the plaintiff to be defamatory of him, came under the rule.[90] Applying the single instance rule, for which the court declared that New York had been "the primary authority,"[91] it was held that the statement in the letter was not libelous in that it imputed mere negligence on the plaintiff as to a single transaction.[92] Before the *Holder Const. Co.* case, the Georgia Supreme Court, as well as the appellate courts, had taken note of the principle of single instance as a libel defense.[93]

The Massachusetts Supreme Court also recognized the single instance rule in 1887 as a libel defense. That is, in *Dooling v. Budget Pub. Co.*,[94] the court employed the rule in affirming judgment for the defendant, who published an allegedly libelous statement concerning the plaintiff, a caterer. The complained of publication stated that a dinner served by the plaintiff

---

86. 385 F.2d 223 (7th Cir. 1967).
87. *Id.* at 224.
88. *Id.* at 225 (applying the Illinois law) (emphasis added).
89. 124 Ga. App. 89 (1971).
90. In the letter at issue, the defendant stated that the plaintiff, a dynamite subcontractor, came on the job to do the blasting and failed to inquire about the hazards of blasting at the construction and that, therefore, the plaintiff was responsible for the damage caused to a water line which was under the blast area. *Id.* at 90.
91. *Id.* at 91, citing Mason v. Sullivan, 271 N.Y.S.2d 314 (1966); Smith v. Staten Island Advance Co., 259 N.Y.S.2d 188 (1950); Amelkin v. Commercial Trading Co., 259 N.Y.S.2d 396 (1966); Blende v. Hearst Publications, Inc., 200 Wash. 426, 93 P.2d 733 (1939).
92. *Id.* at 92. *See also* Cowan v. Time, 245 N.Y.S.2d 723 (1963) (*Life* magazine article which depicts the plaintiff as careless in allowing too many people on his small boat held nondefamatory since it charges him with "a single act of carelessness").
93. *See, e.g.,* Van Epps v. Jones, 50 Ga. 238 (1873); Aiken v. Constitution Pub. Co., 72 Ga. App. 250 (1945).
94. 144 Mass. 258 (1887).

was "wretched" and that "even hungry barbarians might justly object" to the way it was served.[95] Answering the question whether the language used imported any personal reflection upon the plaintiff in his business, or whether it was merely disparaging the dinner that he provided, the Massachusetts court held:

> [T]here was no libel on the plaintiff in the way of his business. Though the language used was somewhat strong, it amounts only to a condemnation of the dinner, and its accompaniments. . . . [T]he charge was, in effect, simply that the plaintiff, being a caterer, on a single occasion provided a very poor dinner, vile cigars, and bad wine. Such a charge is not actionable without proof of a special damage.[96]

The Colorado Supreme Court ruled that the single instance rule was applicable to the words "crooks" and "deadbeat" used by the defendant in *Cinquanta v. Burdett*[97] in referring to the plaintiff. The court held that the allegedly defamatory remark at issue did not impute insolvency or mercantile dishonesty to the plaintiff. Instead, when viewed in the context of the surrounding circumstances precipitating the harsh words of the defendant, the court noted, the defendant was referring to the particular bill the plaintiff owed to him over his work on the plaintiff's restaurant.[98]

C. Judicial Limitation on the "Single Instance" Rule

The single instance rule often prevails where plaintiffs are allegedly defamed for their "single" mistakes in their professions or trades. As the New York court in *Twiggar* observed, however, the rule is "subject to the limitation that words, although directed to a single case, may, in themselves, imply general unskillfulness or general ignorance in the calling."[99] This judicial limitation upon the application of the single instance rule is, in part, explained by the fact that a statement can be made relating a particular instance that may be of such character that it imputes general incompetence. This is well illustrated by the Connecticut Supreme Court ruling in *Sumner v. Utley*, as noted earlier.[100] The court said: "[I]t is undisputably clear, that a calum-

---

95. *Id.*
96. *Id.* at 259–60.
97. 154 Colo. 37 (1963).
98. *Id.* at 40–41.
99. 146 N.Y.S. 529, 530 (2d Dep't. 1914).
100. For a discussion of the *Sumner* case, see text accompanying notes 40–42, *supra.*

nious report concerning a physician in a particular case, may imply gross ignorance and unskillfulness, and do him irreparable damage."[101]

In a pivotal, single instance rule case, *November v. Time,*[102] the New York Court of Appeals ruled against the defendant on the basis of the *Twiggar* limitation on the single instance rule. In the libel case, the defendant published in *Sports Illustrated* an article which the plaintiff, an attorney, argued accused him of deliberately giving erroneous legal advice to his client.[103] Agreeing with the plaintiff's charge that the article was defamatory, the New York high court commented: "[T]here is a great deal more in addition to that quoted paragraph and a reading of the whole of it may well have left a sophisticated and sports-conscious reader of the magazine with the impression that plaintiff had indulged in highly unprofessional conduct."[104] The court then reversed the lower court's judgment for the defendant.

More recently, the New York single instance rule did not carry the day when a federal district court in New York rejected defense arguments in *Handelman v. Hustler Magazine, Inc.*[105] that the common law libel defense should preclude the magazine from liability for its allegedly defamatory article. In the libel action, the plaintiff, a lawyer who represented the Loeb estate, complained that he was libeled by one sentence published in *Hustler* magazine, which read: "Loeb . . . fought the will for about six years, letting high-priced New York lawyers eat up over $800,000 before withdrawing his complaint, leaving his daughter to pay taxes on the rest."[106] The court ruled that "the single instance rule is inapplicable here because '[i]gnorance or mistakes are not involved.'"[107] The federal court added that the New York libel rule would not apply if a jury found that the complained of article showed that the plaintiff acted "in total disregard of professional ethics."[108]

Similarly, the New York appellate court refused to apply the single instance rule to a case involving a magazine article allegedly defamatory of an attorney. In *Cohn v. Am-Law,* a 1980 libel case,[109] the plaintiff argued that the article published in the defendant's newspaper was libelous per se

101. Sumner v. Utley, 7 Conn. 257, 260 (1828). The defendant said of the plaintiff, a physician: "He has killed three, and ought to be hung. . . . They all died through his mismanagement." These words were spoken with reference to the plaintiff's treatment of a woman and her twin children, one of whom was dead at birth, the other died two days later; the mother died some days later. *Id.* at 258. The court affirmed the lower court's ruling for the plaintiff.
102. 13 N.Y.2d 175 (1963).
103. *Id.* at 177.
104. *Id.* at 178. *But cf.* Beinin v. Berk, 88 A.D.2d (1981) (statement that the plaintiff is "no good as a lawyer" and "is not putting . . . much effort into it [a trust transaction]" held dismissable on the ground that it focuses on a particular occasion involving the plaintiff as an attorney).
105. 469 F. Supp. 1048 (S.D.N.Y. 1978).
106. *Id.* at 1049.
107. *Id.* at 1052, *quoting* Plaintiff's Memo, p. 5.
108. *Id.* (applying the New York law).
109. 5 MEDIA L. REP. 2367 (N.Y. Sup. Ct. 1980).

in that it tended to disparage his character as a lawyer.[110] The court, focusing on the distinction made by *November* between when the single instance rule prevails and when it does not,[111] held that the charge as published by the defendant newspaper as to the plaintiff was far from the charge of "ignorance or mistake on a single occasion" where the rule was applicable. Rather, the court noted:

> Such a charge goes well beyond a mistake of judgment or a lack of knowledge or even a lack of skill. . . . In effect, an attorney who fails to prepare himself for the task entrusted to him, is as guilty of so fundamental a breach of his professional obligation as if he were dishonest and without integrity. It is accordingly concluded that the single instance exception is not applicable in this case.[112]

III. SUMMARY AND CONCLUSIONS

In the law of defamation, which some authorities have noted "makes no sense,"[113] the single instance rule epitomizes how some aspects of libel law can but be explained by "historical accident and survival."[114] Furthermore, in terms of its application, the single instance rule may be characterized as a "well-defined" exception to libel law "that is easy to state but not so easy to apply."[115]

Nevertheless, this common law libel rule has been employed as a libel defense on a continuing basis in an increasing number of jurisdictions through the years. This is primarily related to its underlying *raison d'etre* as explicitly stated by courts: the premise that human beings tend to err, and to state that even a businessman or professional person has made a mistake in a particular instance should not presumptively cause damage to that person in his business or profession, because such a statement would imply no more than that the person was human.

There is no doubt that the origin of the single instance rule could be traced to *Foot v. Brown,* as frequently noted by courts applying the rule. A note of caution is in order, however, in accepting as irrefutable the widely held view that the 1811 New York libel case provided an unchallenged legal precedent, establishing the single instance rule in New York and other jurisdic-

---

110. *Id.* The article at issue in the case stated that the plaintiff as an attorney was unprepared for the sentencing of his client and did not know how to file for a stay of execution.
111. *See* November v. Time, 13 N.Y.2d 175, 178 (1963).
112. Cohn v. Am-Law, 5 MEDIA L. REP. 2367, 2368 (N.Y. Sup. Ct. 1980).
113. PROSSER & KEETON ON TORTS, *supra* note 5, at 771.
114. *Id.* at 772.
115. PHELPS & HAMILSON, *supra* note 8, at 76.

tions applying the common law libel defense. Indeed, the *Foot* case was judicially "repudiated" for its unsound reasoning in at least one subsequent case.[116] But as a judicial example of "historical accident," the rule was noted with approval by the *Twiggar* court in 1914.[117]

From a historical perspective, *November v. Time* contributed considerably to establishing the rule as a libel defense. This is true even though the 1963 case was not decided on the basis of the rule. The New York Court of Appeals affirmed the judicial rationale behind the rule.[118] In a way, while the *Foot* case provided a conceptual framework for the single instance rule, it remained for the *November* ruling to provide a solid framework. This in part explains why the rule has been utilized more frequently as a libel defense in the post-*November* period.

It is clear that the single instance rule has been most often applied by the New York courts. This has led some legal scholars to conclude that the rule is unique in terms of its jurisdictional application. But New York is far from the only state applying the libel defense. State appellate courts in Colorado, Connecticut, Florida, Georgia, and Illinois also have adopted or recognized the New York-enunciated rule and its variations in libel cases.[119] This expansive trend of the rule obviously refutes the view that the single instance rule is something of an anomaly in the United States.

When it comes to the scope of the rule's application, the single instance rule has been successfully applied in cases involving a single act of misconduct so long as the allegedly defamatory comments on the act are not so sweeping as to apply to the defamed person in general. On the other hand, the rule has been rejected where the complained of words, although dealing with a particular case, imply general unskillfulness or general ignorance in the trade, profession, or calling of the plaintiff. Among the cases in which the rule has failed to prevail as a libel defense are those involving physicians, attorneys, and others whose single act of misconduct the courts have ruled may be one that seriously reflects on their professional competence in general.

IV. APPENDIX

Foot v. Brown, 8 Johns. 64 (N.Y. 1811).
Secor v. Harris, 18 Barb. 425 (N.Y. 1825).
Sumner v. Utley, 7 Conn. 257 (1828).
Camp v. Martin, 23 Conn. 86 (1854).
Van Epps v. Jones, 50 Ga. 238 (1873).
Gunning v. Appleton, 58 N.Y. Prac. Rep. 471 (1880).

116. *See* text accompanying notes 45–50, *supra.*
117. *See* text accompanying notes 53–56, *supra.*
118. *See* text accompanying notes 61–62, *supra.*
119. For a list of cases in which the "single instance" rule was utilized as a common law libel defense, see Appendix.

Dooling v. Budget Pub. Co., 144 Mass. 258, 10 N.E. 809 (1887).

Battersby v. Collier, 34 A.D. 347, 54 N.Y.S. 363 (1898).

Outcault v. New York Herald Co., 117 A.D. 534 (1907).

Twiggar v. Ossining Printing & Pub. Co., 146 N.Y.S. 529 (2d Dep't. 1914), *appeal dismissed,* 220 N.Y. 716, 116 N.E. 1080 (1970).

Vosbury v. Utica Daily Press Co., 183 A.D. 769, 171 N.Y.S. 827 (1918).

Blende v. Hearst Publications, Inc., 200 Wash. 426 (1939).

Aiken v. Constitution Pub. Co., 72 Ga. App. 250 (1945).

Smith v. Staten Island Advance Co., 276 A.D. 978, 95 N.Y.S. 2d 188 (1950).

Hogan v. New York Times Co., 211 F. Supp. 99 (D.C. Conn. 1962), *affirmed,* 313 F.2d 354 (2d Cir. 1962).

Cinquanta v. Burdett, 154 Colo. 37, 388 P.2d 779 (1963).

November v. Time, Inc., 13 N.Y.2D 175, 194 N.E.2D 126 (1963).

Cowan v. Time, Inc., 245 N.Y.S.2d 723 (1963).

Amelkin v. Commercial Trading Co., 23 A.D.2d 830, 259 N.Y.S.2d 396, *affirmed,* 17 N.Y.2d 500, 214 N.E.2d 379 (1966).

Mason v. Sullivan, 26 A.D.2d 115, 271 N.Y.S.2d 314 (1966).

Fleck Bros. Co. v. Sullivan, 385 F.2d 223 (7th Cir. 1967).

Arnold Bernhard & Co. v. Finance Pub. Corp., 32 A.D.2d 516, 298 N.Y.S.2d 740, *affirmed,* 25 N.Y.2d 712 (1969).

Holder Const. Co. v. Ed Smith & Sons, Inc., 124 Ga. App. 89, 182 S.E.2d 919 (1971).

Halpern v. News-Sun Broadcasting Co., 53 Ill. App. 3d 644, 368 N.E.2d 1062 (1972).

Bordoni v. New York Times Co., 400 F. Supp. 1223 (S.D.N.Y. 1975).

Craig v. Moore, 4 MEDIA L. REP. 1402 (Fla. Cir. Ct. 1978).

Handelman v. Hustler Magazine, Inc., 469 F. Supp. 1048 (S.D.N.Y. 1978).

Tracy v. New York Magazine, 3 MEDIA L. REP. 2294 (N.Y. Sup. Ct. 1978).

Wexler v. Chicago Tribune Co., 69 Ill. App.3d 610, 387 N.E.2d 892 (1979).

Cohn v. Am-Law, 5 MEDIA L. REP. 2367 (N.Y. Sup. Ct. 1980).

Sadowy v. Sony Corp. of America, 496 F. Supp. 1071 (S.D.N.Y. 1980).

Shaw v. Consolidated Rail Corp., 74 A.D.2d 985 (3d Dep't. 1980).

Lyons v. New American Library, Inc., 78 A.D.2d 723 (3d Dep't. 1980).

Brower v. New Republic, 7 MEDIA L. REP. 1605 (N.Y. Sup. Ct., 1981).

Sprovero v. Miller, 404 So.2d 793 (Fla. App. 1981).

Briton v. Winfield Public Library, 101 Ill. App.3d 546, 428 N.E.2d 650 (1981).

Beinin v. Berk, 88 A.D.2d 884, 452 N.Y.S.2d 601 (1982).

Williams v. Burns, 540 F. Supp. 1243 (D.C. Colo. 1982).

Tanner & Gilbert v. Verno, 92 A.D.2d 802 (1st Dep't. 1983).

JEREMY COHEN
ALBERT C. GUNTHER

Libel as Communication Phenomena

Jeremy Cohen is an assistant professor of communication at Stanford University. Albert C. Gunther is an assistant professor of communication at the University of Minnesota.

The authors wish to acknowledge the useful insights provided by John McManus of Santa Clara University and Deborah Shannon of Associated Press.

> I believe with Thomas Jefferson that it is time enough for government to step in to regulate people when they do something, not when they say something, and I do not believe myself that there is any halfway ground if you enforce the protections of the First Amendment.
>
> Justice Hugo Black, 1962[1]

Assumptions about defamation and reputation within the disciplines of law and communication once were very similar. Calling a man a thief or questioning a woman's morals in the newspaper was thought to damage reputation— so much so that under the libel tort an individual could sue for substantial financial reparations.[2] We believed that mass media could sway public opinion in a powerful and uniform manner. But now, communication theory and jurisprudence have diverged. While communication science no longer accepts a simple cause/effect model in which a reputation is damaged in the instant

---

1. Cahn, *Interview with Justice Hugo Black,* 37 N.Y.U.L. REV. 549, 558 (June 1962).
2. *See generally,* R.D. SACK, LIBEL, SLANDER AND RELATED PROBLEMS (1980).

of a televised news bulletin, legal models continue to linger about just such assumptions.

The theory of libel per se, for example, assumes damage without proof that reputation actually is harmed.[3] Certain words are thought to carry an inherent effect on viewers and listeners, and this notion recently has supported interesting judicial conclusions. When *Time* magazine reported that an individual's name "appeared several times" in Federal Bureau of Investigation reports about the disappearance of Jimmy Hoffa, the trial court said the reference to FBI files was libel per se. The U.S. District Court framed the issue of libel per se as whether an article "is not reasonably susceptible of nondefamatory interpretation."[4] In fact, libel per se today may be the exception rather than the rule, but this does not mean a libel plaintiff must present empirical proof that his or her reputation was harmed. The theory of defamation rests on the belief that "[W]here there has been publication of defamatory matter to the general public, it is rational to presume or assume that there has been some harm to reputation, and the jury should be allowed to decide what the harm is with such evidence as may be made available on the matter."[5]

The question of harm to reputation, then, is one of degree rather than existence, and the burden of proof is on the defendant to convince a jury that defamatory speech has not damaged the plaintiff's reputation. That may not be an easy task for the defendant. Plaintiffs lacking direct evidence of reputational loss have argued successfully that "harm to reputation could reasonably be inferred."[6] As Professor William Prosser points out, "Normally, the publication of false and defamatory matter about the plaintiff is circumstantial evidence in and of itself that there was some impairment to reputation."[7] And the theory of libel appears to encompass more than reputation. A plaintiff who offers no proof of loss of reputation still may prevail. Successful plaintiffs have argued that the published defamation "caused mental anguish or humiliation."[8]

Does defamatory speech actually cause, as common sense surely suggests, a loss of reputation? There probably are instances when the answer

---

3. *See* PROSSER AND KEETON ON TORTS 795–96, 843 (W. Page Keeton 5th ed. 1984); SACK *supra* note 2, at 96–100.
4. Schiavone Construction v. Time, 619 F. Supp. 684, 695 (D.C.N.J. 1985).
5. PROSSER AND KEETON, *supra* note 3, at 796.
6. *Id.* at 797.
7. *Id.* at 843.
8. *Id.* at 844. Justice Powell pointed out in Gertz v. Welch, 418 U.S. 323, 350 (1974), "actual harm inflicted by defamatory falsehood include[s] impairment of reputation in the community, personal humiliation, and mental anguish and suffering."

is an unqualified yes.[9] But research in communication and in other behavioral sciences no longer supports the legal model of libel that has endured for centuries. Communication theory has come to reject the paradigm of powerful, uniform effects generated by mass media.[10]

The purpose of this article is to examine what we believe and what we know about libel where defamation intersects the fields of law and communication, and to question the legal assumptions where the views of these two fields have diverged. The natural place to begin is with the legal model of libel.

I. LIBEL LAW

In an earlier time, libel trials were a means to prevent violence. They provided an avenue for the state to monitor and to intercede. The state had an implicit interest, after all, when its citizens defamed each other because there was little question about the effect of defamatory speech. It led quite directly to duels and blood feuds—often enough, apparently, that through the eighteenth century England acted against political libels under the doctrine, "the greater the truth, the greater the evil."[11] Four categories of criminal libel were established in England; blasphemous libel, obscene libel, private libel, and of course, seditious libel.[12] Historians trace the first codified sanctions against libel to a 1275 statute enacted by Parliament against "any slanderous news ... or false news or tales whereby discord or occasion of discord or slander may grow between the king and his people or the great men of the Realm...."[13] The clear assumption was that defamatory speech had a powerful effect. In 1663, William Twyn came face to face with the British Crown's fear of that powerful effect when he printed a book containing the seditious libel of endorsing a right of revolution. Seditious language was treason, and fears of the effects of such language brought no small penalty. Offenders such as Twyn were hanged, cut down while still alive, emasculated, disemboweled, quartered, and finally beheaded.[14]

---

9. University of Iowa law professor Randall P. Bezanson concluded as part of a five-year libel study that the current model of libel "assumes that people's reputations can be seriously injured by published statements, as indeed they can...." 71 Iowa L. Rev. 1, at 226 (Oct. 1985). Our discussion recognizes that a false statement printed in a newspaper that someone has committed a criminal act may indeed affect the individual's reputation with family, friends, and employer. Our goal is not to suggest reputations cannot be harmed, but to explore the manner in which communications may contribute to such harm.
10. Schramm, *The Nature of Communication Between Humans,* in THE PROCESS AND EFFECTS OF MASS COMMUNICATION 8 (W. Schramm & D. F. Roberts eds. 1977).
11. E. EMERY & M. EMERY, THE PRESS IN AMERICA: AN INTERPRETIVE HISTORY OF THE MASS MEDIA. 58 (1984).
12. W. LEVY, EMERGENCE OF A FREE PRESS 8 (1985).
13. *Id.* at 6.
14. *Id.* at 9.

Lord Campbell's Act in 1843[15] made truth an acceptable defense in an English criminal libel suit, as it already was in civil libel actions, and the basic value system inherent in the modern libel tort was secure. That is not to suggest libel law has remained static, but rather that current libel law is based on certain values. For example, truth as a complete defense in common law carries the recognition that society places a higher value on the availability of truth than it does upon the desire to protect individual reputation.[16] Similarly, common law and constitutional interpretations have protected defamatory speech presented as opinion rather than fact,[17] and false defamations presented as fact that pertain to public persons involved in issues of public importance.[18] The actual damage to the reputation of an individual is seen as less than the damage to society that would be caused by either silencing or punishing defamatory speech.

When we consider libel law today, essentially we consider a litigation model that contains four elements:

Publication—Identification—Defamation—Fault

The first three elements relate directly to the notion that a reputation is damaged. The fault element relates to a value judgment placed on speech.

Each element serves a function, and all four must be proven in a suit against a mass media defendant before the plaintiff may prevail. Briefly, the publication element requires the plaintiff to prove that one person other than himself and the defendant saw or heard the defamatory communication. The logic is simply that reputation cannot be harmed unless others are aware of the damaging material. Identification also relates to reputation. This element requires that it be clear to the reader or the viewer to whom the information referred. Finally, the defamation element requires that the communication in question be of a defamatory nature—that is, that the information causes or

---

15. 687 Vict. Ch. 96, Section 6 (1843).
16. The Supreme Court recognizes the tension between freedom of expression and the need to protect individual reputation as a situation in which the Constitution requires balancing. *See Gertz, supra* note 8, at 341. Three useful discussions of reputation are presented in *Symposium: New Perspectives in the Law of Defamation,* 3 (74) CALIF. L. REV.: *The Sociological Foundations of Defamation Law: Reputation and the Constitution,* by Robert C. Post, 691–742; *The Meaning of Reputation in American Society,* by Robert N. Bellah, 743–752; *Reputation and the Modern Journalistic Imperatives,* by James Reston, 753–760.
17. *Supra* note 5, at 1640.
18. See Curtis Publishing Co. v. Butts, 380 U.S. 130 (1967).

tends to cause a representative minority of the community to form a negative opinion about the defamed individual.[19]

The defamation element of the libel tort raises important questions within the communication science context. Does the law require a communication-generated event—"event" meaning a change in attitude or at least the likelihood that there will be a change in the public's attitude about the plaintiff caused by a specific communication? The law recognizes more than one answer, and the substantive differences between these answers highlight major conceptual differences between "types" of libel. Two types of libel are identifiable. The first type includes libel per se and places the weight of damning evidence upon the communication per se rather than upon the audience, who may or may not receive and judge the message. Certain communications, such as our libel per se report that a man's name was in an FBI file, are considered inherently damaging and require no further proof of harm to reputation. The second type of libel is one that requires proof that reputation was harmed, although the proof need not be empirical. The emphasis is shifted from the communication itself to an examination of the audience's response to the message in question—or at least the plaintiff's argument as to how readers or viewers are likely to react.

While the first three elements of the libel tort— identification, defamation, and publication—deal specifically with the question of reputational harm, the fault element serves a different function. Appearing first in common law and then provided the status of first amendment doctrine in 1964,[20] the fault element creates a set of national standards that weight the free speech/individual reputation balance.

Public officials and public figures must prove the media guilty of actual malice—knowledge of falsity or reckless disregard of whether something was false or not—to prevail in a libel suit.[21] Proof of defamatory falsehoods is not sufficient. Even private persons suing mass media must reach a minimum threshold—proof of simple negligence.[22] The fault element does not relate in any way to the damage done to the defamed individual. Fault simply establishes the degree of culpability of the defendant within a framework of societal values. Recognizing the distinction between the libel tort elements relating to reputational damage and those that foster the value of freedom of expression, the four-element litigation model actually consists of two functionally distinct segments.

---

19. No single definition of defamation exists. Commonly cited is the Second Restatement of Torts, which states that a communication is defamatory if it tends so to harm the reputation of another as to lower him in the estimation of the community or to deter third persons from associating or dealing with him.
20. New York Times v. Sullivan, 376 U.S. 254 (1964).
21. Gertz, supra note 8.
22. Id.

JEREMY COHEN and ALBERT C. GUNTHER

Two-Segment Litigation Model

INDIVIDUAL'S REPUTATIONAL INTERESTS	SOCIETAL INTEREST
Publication-Identification-Defamation	Fault

Whether the fault requirement actually accomplishes its inherent societal goals of balancing open debate in a free marketplace of ideas with individual reputation is open to question and is beyond the scope of this discussion.[23] As yet, there is a dearth of material that goes beyond anecdotal evidence when commentators turn to discussions of balancing individual reputation with free expression.[24]

The publication-identification-defamation side of the model appears to receive less attention in the literature than does the discussion of fault. Some articles do address the application of these tort elements, but rarely do they confront the conceptual foundation of the elements. Nonetheless, addressing the defamation element, University of Texas libel scholar David Anderson has raised basic questions about the relation between libel awards and the amount of damage to reputation actually suffered by plaintiffs.[25]

More often, however, commentators simply rely on the 1974 landmark *Gertz v. Welch* (418 U.S. 323 (1974)) decision when questioning the rationality of the libel tort. The *Gertz* case expanded the constitutional protection of the *New York Times* rule to include public figures as well as public officials, and it announced a minimum, constitutionally mandated threshold of fault in suits against the media brought by private person plaintiffs. Justice Powell wrote for the Court, "[T]he common law of defamation is an oddity of tort law, for it allows recovery of purportedly compensatory damages without evidence

---

23. University of Iowa researcher John Soloski refers to the libel tort as "a system that disserves plaintiffs, defendants and the public...." *The Study and the Libel Plaintiff: Who Sues for Libel?* 71 IOWA L. REV. 217 (Oct. 1985). And Bruce E. Fein has called the reasoning behind the actual malice fault requirement, "profoundly flawed." NEW YORK TIMES V. SULLIVAN: AN OBSTACLE TO ENLIGHTENED PUBLIC DISCOURSE AND GOVERNMENT RESPONSIVENESS TO THE PEOPLE 3 (American Legal Foundation 1984). Nonetheless, Justice Brennan's *Sullivan, supra* note 20, opinion remains a strong and oft-quoted defense of the freedom of expression/individual reputation balance found in the actual malice fault requirement.
24. But see the systematic studies conducted by Bezanson, Cranberg, and Soloski, *Libel Law and the Press: Setting the Record Straight,* 71 IOWA L. REV. 215 (Oct. 1985); Franklin, *Winners and Losers and Why: A Study of Defamation Litigation,* 3 AMERICAN BAR FOUNDATION RESEARCH J. 797 (1980); Franklin, *Suing Media for Libel: A Litigation Study,* 3 AMERICAN BAR FOUNDATION RESEARCH J. 455–500 (1981); Silver and Bow, *Effects of* Herbert v. Landow *on the News Process,* 57 JOURNALISM Q. 115–118 (Spring 1980).
25. *See generally,* Anderson, *Reputation, Compensation and Proof,* 25 WILLIAM AND MARY L. REV. 747 (Sept. 1984).

of actual loss."[26] No one has measured empirically which receives more attention at a libel trial—proving the publication-identification-defamation elements, or arguing the fault element. Informal observation suggests the heaviest concentration is on questions of fault.

A journalist currently citing a libel suit may be representative in her opinion of the issue."What we wrote was negative and we just assumed that we defamed the plaintiff. We spent our time trying to prove there was no actual malice."[27] What may sound like an admission of malice wasn't really. Rather, it was a statement that the reporter believed the negative story she wrote about the defendant to be true and assumed her reader would as well. This simple, if common line of reasoning is complicated by the not uncommon experience of another journalist. After publishing a major story on environmental pollution, a reporter for a major newspaper in the northwest attended a party at a friend's home. He expected to find kudos and serious discussion of the ramifications of his article, which had run that morning. The discussion, the reporter said, ranged from "Dallas" and J.R. to inexpensive white wines that taste good, "but if anyone read anything I wrote you would never know it," the reporter added.[27a]

Two substantive conclusions become apparent. First, there is an important distinction in the litigation model between elements related to the harm done to reputation and the fault element that relates to wider societal values.

Second, it is clear that the publication-identification-defamation litigation model is based upon certain assumptions about the process and effects of communication. It is important to identify those assumptions. A useful means for doing so is to place the litigation model elements within the context of a basic, if primitive, communication model. For example, a well-known model posits that there is communication when there is a sender, a message, and a receiver:

Sender—Message—Receiver

In the litigation model, the sender is the defendant. The message contains *defamatory* words about an *indentifiable* plaintiff. The defamation meets the publication requirement when it is received by a person other than the defendent or the plaintiff so that *publication* involves both the sender and the receiver. The *fault* element is an attribute of the sender.

---

26. PROSSER AND KEETON, *supra* note 3.
27. Personal interview with the author, who asked that neither she nor her case be identified, since the case currently is under appeal.
27a. Personal conversation with David Morrissey, June 1984.

JEREMY COHEN and ALBERT C. GUNTHER

Overlap of Communication and Libel Litigation Models

SENDER	MESSAGE	RECEIVER
Media transmit a message.	The message is about an identifiable person and has the power to influence viewers/readers/listeners.	Audience receives message and is influenced.
PUBLICATION & FAULT	IDENTIFICATION & DEFAMATION	PUBLICATION & DEFAMATION

Even a model as simple as this one suggests important questions and some divergence between legal and communication approaches. The law makes assumptions about the process and effects of communication. Certain words, symbols, and pictures are thought to trigger uniformly negative responses in audiences towards the subject of those messages. Reputation is diminished. Communication research, on the other hand, offers little support for such a direct-effects hypothesis. The litigation model suggests defamation may be seen as existing inherently in the communication itself without regard to the audience; as a phenomenon that occurs upon impact of a defamatory communication with an audience; and as a phenomenon that is an audience behavior where defamation occurs as the audience hardens its opinions or forms a new opinion as a direct result of the suspect communication.

Communication research suggests that all three conclusions are simplistic. Further discussion of the communication/law dichotomy, however, requires first a brief review of the history of communication theory and then an exploration of communication theory applied directly to the issue.

II. COMMUNICATION RESEARCH

Along with the legal model, intuition tells us that false information, or misinformation, can do harm. Report falsely that a politician associates with organized crime figures and his reputation will suffer. The idea makes so much common sense it deserves to be true.

But social scientists have grown wary of intuition and common sense. The phenomenon called the third-person effect provides an ironic example.

In looking through literature shortly after World War II, a Columbia researcher, W. Phillips Davison, found an account of Japanese planes dropping propaganda leaflets on black soldiers stationed on Iwo Jima island. The leaflets urged the black soldiers not to risk their lives in "the white man's war against the Japanese." They advised the soldiers to give up or desert, claiming they (the Japanese) "had no quarrel with colored people." Davison found no evidence that the leaflets had any effect on the morale of the black troopers. But the white officers of this unit, apparently fearing that the attitudes of the black GIs would be swayed by this literature, withdrew their troops. Empirical examples of this third-person effect—that people feel media messages will have more influence on others than on themselves—have been demonstrated by Davison and others.[28]

In his discussion, Davison considers our exaggerated expectations about the effects of communications on others in a context closer to the topic of this article—fears about defamation and sedition:

> Throughout history, heretical doctrines and political dissidence have aroused concern, sometimes terror, among priests and potentates. How much of this apprehension and the resulting repression was due to the third-person effect? It certainly must have played a role, and probably has accounted for a grisly percentage of the world's suffering and horror. Exaggerated expectations about the effects of dissident communications have caused countless people to be incarcerated, tortured and killed.[29]

The third-person phenomenon is ironic because it implies more than just the fact that juries may be prone to overestimate the effects of a defamatory statement. It is a clue to why some of our earliest thinking about communications was likely to systematically overrate the power and influence of the mass media. It explains the intuitions of communication scholars that led to the powerful effects paradigm. And it explains the seemingly common-sense assumption of libel per se by legal scholars.

Historians of the communication research field agree that we began with the common sense assumption of powerful effects of mediated messages. The early conception was of largely undifferentiated effects as direct as a hypodermic injection.[30] Such a model of powerful effects, though not the basis for much empirical research, was widely accepted among the scholarly community as well as in the broader ranks of the educated in the United States and Europe

28. Davison, *The Third-Person Effect in Communication,* 47 Public Opinion Q. 1–15 (1983). *See also* Cohen, Mutz, Price, and Gunther, "Perceived Impact of Defamation: An Experiment in Third Person Effects." Paper presented to International Communication Association, Montreal, Canada, 1987; Mutz, "Perceptions of Others in the Public Opinion Process: The Third Person Effect and the Spiral of Silence." Paper presented to International Communication Association, Montreal, Canada, 1987.
29. Davison, *supra* note 28, at 14.
30. H. D. Lasswell, World Politics and Personal Insecurity (1935).

during the period from 1900 to World War II.[31] Direct and uniform effects of mass media seemed a logical way to make sense of events during that period when quantitative methods of testing empirical questions were new and not widely understood.

There are three other major reasons for the acceptance of this simple model. First, nineteenth century social philosophers had described a "mass" society of isolated individuals whose lives were no longer structured by the social controls of the agrarian village. People, therefore, were thought to be more susceptible to new information than before. Second, the emerging and technologically unfamiliar mass media when applied to state propaganda purposes (the vision of such popular books as *Brave New World* and *1984*) appeared capable of controlling what individuals thought. Third, the social upheavals of the early twentieth century—the two world wars, the Great Depression, Nazism, communism—created a climate of fear and instability in which mass-mediated messages could have unusual impact.

III. ANTECEDENTS TO THE POWERFUL EFFECTS ERA: THE MASS SOCIETY

Auguste Comte began a tradition of thought that developed into the early twentieth century conception of the "mass society." It was Comte, the father of modern sociology, writing during the 1830s and 1840s—the early years of the Industrial Revolution in France—who first suggested that specialization served to connect individuals in a common social purpose, but that overspecialization alienated individuals, separating them into isolated niches.[32] He argued that the more individuals were unlike one another in their social position and function, the greater would be their misunderstanding of other people.

---

31. Schramm's discussion (*supra* note 10) neatly summarizes this aspect of communication research history. However, it should be noted that other scholars have challenged the validity of what they call "received history." Chaffee and Hochheimer argue that the powerful-effects hypothesis was never seriously proposed by researchers; rather it appeared as a straw man conveniently constructed for attack during the limited-effects era. No one, they suggest, who sat down and thought for a morning about how communication works would advance such a simplistic model. *See The Beginnings of Political Communication Research in the United State: Origins of the "Limited Effects" Model*, in MASS COMMUNICATION IN THE UNITED STATES AND WESTERN EUROPE (E. M. ROGERS & F. BALLE eds. 1986). But the fact remains that, even as an artifact of historical prefaces, the notion of "a universal, massive pattern of media impact" seems to have an intuitive appeal that, in retrospect, has gained wide acceptance. Chaffee & Hochheimer, *The Beginning of Political Communication Research in the U.S.: Origins of the "Limited Effects" Model*, in 2 MASS COMMUNICATION IN THE UNITED STATES AND WESTERN EUROPE 31 (E. M. ROGERS & F. BALLE eds. 1985).
32. Comte, *The Positive Philosophy*, as cited in M. L. DEFLEUR & S. BALL-ROKEACH, THEORIES OF MASS COMMUNICATION (4th ed. 1982).

Herbert Spencer, writing from 1860 to 1900 in industrial Britain, picked up the theme and gave it the force of biological evolution as propounded by Charles Darwin.[33] A contemporary, Karl Marx, predicted social breakdown and revolution by the alienated industrial masses.[34] Ferdinand Tonnies, writing in Germany during the last decade of the nineteenth century, enunciated his distinction between *Gemeinschaft*—the reciprocal community bonds of kinship and village, and *Gesellschaft*—the impersonal, legalized, and formal contracts of a larger and anonymous industrial society.[35] The former he saw fading, replaced by the latter, creating a condition of isolation and tension, a volatile society. Another nineteenth century thinker making a contribution to the idea of a mass, atomized society was Emile Durkheim. He argued that as the division of labor in society increases, the psychological bonds among individuals are strained or severed.[36] He called the result *anomie*, or social disharmony.

The thinking of the most influential social theorists of the nineteenth century profoundly influenced the educated classes, the social philosophers, and the first communication theorists of the new century. But even without that intellectual inheritance, the idea of an increasingly disjoint "mass" society seemed evident in what sociologists Shearon Lowery and Melvin L. DeFleur call the "master trends" of turn-of-the-century Western society.[37] The first was industrialization. The second trend, urbanization, occurred as the workplace moved from farm to factory. People crowded into cities and towns perhaps only a few miles from the farms or villages where they grew up, but far removed from the traditions and other social controls of rural life. In the cities, they came into contact—and sometimes conflict—with individuals from remote parts of the country. In the United States, for example, immigrants lived and worked alongside people from foreign nations who shared neither language nor culture. The third master trend was modernization. Industrial society ran by the clock, rather than the rising of the sun, or the turning of the season. People became separated from the soil and the rhythms of nature. They were thrust into a man-made world of mortar, machines, and smokestack climates.

Thus early thinking about media and communication assumed an audience removed from its traditional interpersonal communication channels and more vulnerable to new media of enormous power. As psychologists David O. Sears and R. E. Whitney have noted, social scientists of the 1930s and 1940s expected

---

33. Spencer, *The Principles of Sociology*, as cited in DeFleur & Ball-Rokeach, *supra* note 32, at 149.
34. DeFleur & Ball-Rokeach, *supra* note 32, at 19.
35. Tonnies, *Gemeinschaft and Gesellschaft*, as cited in DeFleur & Ball-Rokeach, *supra* note 32, at 152.
36. Durkheim, *The Division of Labor in Society*, as cited in DeFleur & Ball-Rokeach, *supra* note 32, at 155.
37. S. Lowery & M. L. DeFleur, Milestones in Mass Communication Research 4–10 (1983).

"a totally gullible audience....For them the audience was monolithic and effects could be assumed...."[38]

World events—particularly the World War I and the communist revolution in Russia—and manipulation of new machines of communication that permitted rapid printing of tracts, telegraphy, and telephonic amplification of the human voice over unheard-of distances, set the stage for early twentieth century social scientists to propose powerful and direct media effects. Wilbur Schramm, who pioneered the organization of the communication research field, put it this way:

> [O]ne must recall how frightening World War I propaganda, and later Communist and Nazi propaganda, were to many people. At that time, the audience was typically thought of as a sitting target: if a communicator could hit it, he would affect it. This became especially frightening because of the reach of the new mass media. The unsophisticated viewpoint was that if a person could be reached by the insidious forces of propaganda carried by the mighty power of the mass media, he could be changed and converted and controlled. So propaganda became a hateword, the media came to be regarded fearfully, and laws were passed and actions taken to protect "defenseless" people against "irresistible" communications.[39]

This view was reinforced by war-time propagandists and newspaper editors who played up stories of enemy atrocities and brutality, but later acknowledged their manipulation of the media and discussed the possible undesirable outcomes from misuse of such powerful instruments.[40]

Harold D. Lasswell, whom Schramm names as one of the fathers of the social science of communication, incorporated some of this thinking when he compared propaganda to a "hypodermic needle" injecting a message into isolated individuals who had been stripped of their social supports and restraints by modern, urban, industrial society.[41] The direct effects model was prevalent in other social sciences as well. Most pre-1940 models of human behavior in psychology, for example, were built on the stimulus-response paradigm,[42] which generally fails to include thought as an intervening process between human perception and human behavior.

---

38. Sears, D. O. and Whitney, R. E., cited in Becker, McCombs and McLeod, *The Development of Political Cognitions*, in POLITICAL COMMUNICATION 23 (Steven H. Chaffee ed. 1975).
39. Schramm and Roberts, *supra* note 10, at 8.
40. DeFLEUR & BALL-ROKEACH, *supra* note 32, at 158–160.
41. LASSWELL, *supra* note 30.
42. Schramm and Roberts, *supra* note 10, at 7.

Other events of the period also suggested powerful media effects. On the night before Halloween, 1938, Orson Welles's radio broadcast, "War of the Worlds," created a general panic.[43] Subsequent surveys indicated that a third of the six million plus listeners thought the "Martian invasion" real, and of those, 70 percent admitted to being frightened or disturbed.

Lowery and DeFleur summarize the theory of direct and uniform media influence in four principles.[44]

1. The media present message to members of mass society who perceive them more or less the same way.
2. These messages are stimuli that influence the individual powerfully.
3. Members of mass society react to these messages in uniform ways.
4. Because persons are not bound by strong social controls imposed by family or tradition in mass society, they are defenseless against mediated messages.

IV. THE DEMISE OF DIRECT AND UNIFORM EFFECTS THEORY

In what way have communication scholars come to think differently? They now think the audience is rather independent, not easily persuaded by the media, *obstinate* in the words of one researcher.[45] Mediated messages have been shown to affect some persons but not others, and then in some circumstances, but not others.[46] Media consumers may avoid discordant information, or fail to "see" views that conflict with their preconceptions.[47] The audience is active. They *use* the media to seek certain gratifications.[48] The modern view, informed by decades of empirical research, supports an understanding antithetical to the assumption of direct and uniform effects.

Even during the height of the period we now call the powerful effects era, those assumptions were being questioned. A new methodology that subjected common sense notions to empirical tests had begun to be developed during the 1920s. The first of these quantitative studies of media effects were beginning to demonstrate that mass mediated messages influenced different people to different degrees. And these effects were indirect, conditional upon other influences and predispositions. These empirical studies provided a closer

43. LOWERY & DEFLEUR, *supra* note 37, at 66.
44. *Id.* at 23.
45. Bauer, *The Obstinate Audience: The Influence Process from the Point of View of Social Communication,* in Schramm and Roberts, *supra* note 10, at 326–346.
46. G. S. COMSTOCK, S. H. CHAFFEE, et al., TELEVISION AND HUMAN BEHAVIOR (1978).
47. McGuire, *Theoretical Foundation of Campaigns,* in PUBLIC COMMUNICATION CAMPAIGNS 44–45 (R. E. Rice and W. J. Paisley eds. 1981).
48. See generally, THE USES OF MASS COMMUNICATION: CURRENT PERSPECTIVES ON GRATIFICATIONS RESEARCH (J. Blumber and E. Katz eds. 1974).

analysis that belied the intuitive speculation of earlier scholars and the general public.

The first large-scale, quantitative analyses of media effects in the United States were the Payne Fund studies, examining the impact of the then-new technology of moving pictures on children and adolescents. These thirteen investigations were conducted over a three-year period, 1929–1932, and published in ten volumes in response to the great concern aroused in the public and scholarly community by the direct and uniform effects theory then in vogue.[49]

For the most part, the Payne studies questioned the "hypodermic needle" model. "Some of the major conclusions of the reports—for example, that the same message would affect children differently depending on the child's age, sex, predispositions, perceptions, and parental influence—are identical to summaries of the most recent studies on children and television," wrote Reeves and Baughman in a review of the original Payne reports by W. W. Charters.[50] Note that there are six distinct variables affecting outcomes in the statement above—a far cry from a direct and uniform effect for each child.

Even a second look at Lasswell's 1935 book, *World Politics and Personal Insecurity*, which introduced the "hypodermic needle" model, reveals no simple statement of direct effects as the syringe metaphor implies. The book lists contingencies that modify media effects. The first—and one widely found in the inter-war period of depression and the rise of threatening ideologies such as facism and communism—is social insecurity. The second is popular attention. But these alone are insufficient, as Lasswell himself pointed out: "That a particular group will be successful in capturing attention and guiding mass insecurities as desired *depends upon a variety of attending circumstances* (emphasis added)."[51]

The study that effectively repudiated the uniform and direct effects model, at least in the field of communication research, was Lazarsfeld, Berelson, and Gaudet's *The People's Choice*, published in 1944. Direct media influences on voter choices during the presidential election of 1940 in Erie County, Ohio, were exposed as minimal and contingent upon a much more complex array of historical and cognitive variables than had previously been imagined. Personal influences—what one's more expert friends thought about the issue and communicated first-hand—were discovered to be critical to opinion formation.[52]

49. LOWERY & DEFLEUR, *supra* note 37, at 32.
50. Reeves and Baughman, *"Fraught with Such Great Possibilities": The Historical Relationship of Communication Research to Mass Media Regulation*, in PROCEEDINGS OF THE TENTH ANNUAL TELECOMMUNICATIONS POLICY RESEARCH CONFERENCE 22 (O. Gandy et al. eds. 1983).
51. LASSWELL, *supra* note 30, at 8.
52. P. F. LAZARSFELD, B. BERELSON & H. GAUDET, THE PEOPLE'S CHOICE xx-xxv, 150–157 (1944).

Other empirical studies disconfirming uniform and direct effects were published during the same period. Perception of the media's impact was growing more complicated as quantitative methods broke down the simple assumptions of the early model. In one of these, Eunice Cooper and Marie Jahoda demonstrated that individuals will evade or misperceive mediated messages that conflict with strongly held beliefs or values.[53] Individuals exposed to a series of satiric cartoons depicting the prejudices of a "Mr. Biggot," repeatedly missed the point when the message targeted their own prejudice. Or subjects found confirmation for their prejudice by selecting only those parts of messages consonant with their prior beliefs.

V. CURRENT TRENDS VS. THE CLASSICAL MODEL

A useful way to view our still-evolving notions about mass media effects is to look at relatively current (1950–1985) research on attitude change—the attitude change in an audience that is linked to our assumptions about the effects of defamation.

Fears about the persuasive and potentially insidious effects of propaganda led to a series of experiments on source credibility in the early 1950s. Carl Hovland and others found that people discount information from "untrustworthy" sources. For example, subjects read an article arguing about the practicability of building an atomic-powered submarine. Of those who thought the article was authored by a highly credible source—prominent American scientist Robert J. Oppenheimer—more than one-third were persuaded by the information. For those who were told *Pravda* was the source of the article, no attitude change occurred.[54]

Studying a related phenomenon, Osgood and Tannenbaum found that information or arguments only somewhat divergent from those of audience members will result in attitude changes. But with a more widely discrepant message, subjects will maintain their point of view and discount the credibility of the source instead.[55]

Thus the damage resulting from a defamation may vary substantially with varying credibility, or ascribed credibility, of the source. Such findings suggest differential effects of a message when it appears in *The New York Times* versus supermarket tabloids. *Harper's* editor Lewis Lapham raised this ques-

53. Cooper and Johoda, *The Evasion of Propaganda: How Prejudiced People Respond to Anti-prejudice Propaganda,* in Schramm and Roberts, *supra* note 10, at 287–300.
54. *See* Hovland and Weiss, *The Influence of Source Credibility on Communicator Effectiveness,* 15 PUBLIC OPINION Q. 635–650 (1951). The credibility factor in these studies has often been called the sleeper effect, since the differences washed out after some weeks, unless subjects were reminded of the source.
55. Osgood and Tannenbaum, *The Principle of Congruity In the Prediction of Attitude Change,* 62 PSYCHOLOGICAL REV. 42–55 (1955).

tion when he expressed his surprise over the jury's decision in the widely publicized Carol Burnett suit in 1981: "The [*National*] *Enquirer* regularly publishes claims of sightings of UFO's and conversations with Elvis Presley from beyond the grave. To sue that kind of paper for libel—and to win...."[56]

Much research on the changing of attitudes has built on the framework of contingent conditions. For example, an audience seems to discriminate in its yielding to a message according to how the world around it seems to be reacting. Subjects appear to be less persuaded by a message when they "overhear" the rest of the audience disapproving of the message, so that the context of public opinion may outweigh the context of the message itself in its real impact on audience members.[57]

As another example, research has found that a person's involvement in the subject matter seems to be an important factor in the effect on his or her attitude. Attitude change is greater for highly involved subjects when they get more persuasive argumentation. But if subjects aren't especially interested in or concerned with a topic (probably the more general case), then peripheral qualities like source likability, source prestige, or simple message repetition will make the difference in how much people will believe defamatory information.[58]

Many believe that any media exposure, positive or negative, can be beneficial in some respects. This notion is characterized by the stereotypical politician who tells reporters, "I don't care what you say about me, just spell my name right." Social scientists have given us some evidence that mere exposure to an object enhances liking of that object,[59] and, more specifically, that up to a point, positive feeling about a political candidate increases simply with increased exposure to the candidate's name.[60] The researchers found a ceiling effect in this relationship, but it can be argued that in some situations, any publicity is good publicity.

Iowa's performing Cherry Sisters are the classic example, a trio of untalented farm girls who made a substantial reputation for themselves in the 1890s by capering about the stage, singing badly and dodging vegetables flung from the audience. They were the constant objects of scornful review, such as the comment by a *New York Tribune* critic: "Miss Jessie narrowly escaped being pretty, but her sisters never were in any such danger." The sisters applied

56. Lapham, *Can the Press Tell the Truth?* HARPER'S 51 (January 1985).
57. Landy, *The Effects of an Overheard Audience's Reaction and Attractiveness on Opinion Change,* 8 J. EXPERIMENTAL SOCIAL PSYCHOLOGY 276–288 (1972).
58. Chaiken, *Heuristic vs. Systematic Information Processing and the Use of Source vs. Message Cues in Persuasion,* 59 J. PERSONALITY AND SOC. PSYCHOLOGY 752–766 (1980).
59. Zajonc, *Attitudinal Effects of Mere Exposure,* J. PERSONALITY AND SOC. PSYCHOLOGY 9, Monograph 1-29 (1968).
60. Becker and Doolittle, *How Repetition Affects Evaluations of and Information Seeking about Candidates,* 52 JOURNALISM Q. 611–617 (1975).

this any-publicity-is-good-publicity hypothesis as they sued various newspapers for allegedly libelous reviews of their burlesque performance. In one such case, the court examined a particularly unkind review—which described the plaintiffs with such phrases as "stringhalt," "spavined," and "capering monstrosity"—printed in *The Des Moines Leader*. To be fair to all parties, the judge requested a performance of selections from the Cherry Sisters' act. When the show was over, the judge threw out the charge of libel.

Whatever the outcome, the sisters generally performed to packed houses after such suits.[61]

Another line of communication research has looked at the difference between one-sided and two-sided messages and a subject's resulting persuasibility. The evidence suggests what has come to be called the inoculation effect. As expected, subjects who had "heard both sides" on an issue were significantly less affected by subsequent messages.[62] Thus the effects of defamatory messages are likely to differ depending on what other information or argument has been aired on the subject.

Communication research has produced a large body of work on the selectivity of message receivers. Yale scholar William McGuire, as one example, formulated a hierarchy of response steps mediating persuasion, such as exposure, attention, interest, comprehension, learning, yielding, remembering, retrieving, decision-making, and behaving. In McGuire's model, attitude change at each step depends crucially on the effect at antecedent steps, and thus persuasion becomes a chancy outcome in many message situations.[63] Selectivity functions appear inconsistently, but they are widely documented in research,[64] and have been a major argument in the case against our early assumptions that the mass media have uniform and widespread effects on audience attitudes.

Though research on the conditional nature of effects on attitudes is central to the arguments in this article, other lines of inquiry have produced other evidence that the true process of communication violates many of our original common-sense assumptions about it. A structural factor with growing impact on the question of message effects is information overload. As the media increasingly saturate communication channels with information, one postulated outcome is narcotizing dysfunction—the phenomenon of an audience of spectators who take no action, an audience that mistakes *knowing* about issues for *doing* something about issues.[65]

61. Fuller, *The Cherry Sisters,* 60 THE PALIMPSEST 121–129 (1979).
62. R.E. PETTY & J.T. CACIOPPO, ATTITUDES AND PERSUASION: CLASSIC AND CONTEMPORARY APPROACHES (1981).
63. McGuire, *supra* note 47.
64. Sears and Freedman, *Selective Exposure to Information: A Critical Review,* in Schramm and Roberts, *supra* note 10.
65. Lazarsfeld and Merton, *Mass Communication, Popular Taste, and Organized Social Action,* in THE COMMUNICATION OF IDEAS (L. Bryson ed. 1948).

Media researchers now think that in the face of such a flood of messages, audiences exhibit an ever greater selectivity of attention, so that fewer messages reach each individual in the great "atomized mass" (almost certainly not atomized at all) we once envisioned. The concept of broadcasting, for example, has been supplemented with "narrowcasting," programming directed at relatively smaller, selective audiences, as an important strategy in commercial communication. As a result, the extent of diffusion of any particular message, including those for which the mass media are regularly sued, grows increasingly uncertain.

Though these last two models argue that the media do have some types of broad effects, they are not built on the conditions that usually attend defamation cases—single-shot news stories with particular, allegedly libelous, information. Rather they depend on long-term and more generalized socialization effects, such as cultivation or desensitization.

Agenda-setting is another prominent vein of research raising questions about our oversimplified model of the effects of particular messages. The hypothesis claims, to paraphrase a popular quotation, that the media "tell us not what to think, but what to think about."[66] Shaw and McCombs argued that our classic view of powerful media effects caused us to look in the wrong place. We were looking for attitude and opinion change when the effects were more likely to be found in a change in the public agenda. The researchers found support for their argument by analyzing media content while logging the public opinion agenda that appears to follow from that content.[67] Their findings suggest that media may affect the salience, or relative importance, of issues and events in our minds more than the opinions and attitudes we maintain.

Media scholars now consider that long-term messages probably eclipse the impact of information that appears once or only a few times. This accretionary effect Wilbur Schramm described as less dramatic but probably more potent—"not the gross anti-social effects, but the gradual building up of pictures of the world from what the mass media choose to report of it."[68]

The weight of this and much more accumulated research has tilted the scale of opinion about media effects—we now accept that there are major effects from messages, but they are not the simple and direct effects that intuition, and defamation judgments, appear to presume.

66. B. COHEN, THE PRESS AND FOREIGN POLICY 120 (1963).
67. McCombs and Shaw, *The Agenda-Setting Function of Mass Media,* 36 PUBLIC OPINION Q. 176–187 (1972).
68. Schramm, *The Nature of Communication Between Humans,* in Schramm and Roberts, *supra* note 10, at 52–3.

VI. CONCLUSION

The legal concept of defamation invests the power to create among others a negative attitude about an individual through a single exposure to words, pictures, or other symbols that possess shared meaning. At the very least, defamatory statements are conceptualized in law as trigger mechanisms that cause people to form certain beliefs or attitudes. An actionable defamation either harms an individual's reputation, as might be the case for a well-known official or entertainer, or it creates a negative reputation for a person who had no previous reputation to speak of outside an immediate circle of friends and perhaps co-workers. In either case, the legal concept views defamatory communication as an agent that is both necessary *and* sufficient in and of itself to alter the opinions of reasonable people. In law, defamatory communications are causal and their effects are direct. A negative communication is transmitted; it is received by others; and the recipients form an attitude or belief, or change an attitude or belief in a negative direction. The law conceptualizes the communication model of libel as:

DEFAMATION—RECEPTION—ATTITUDE FORMATION

Based on our discussion of some of the findings in communication science, a very different concept is suggested. Rather than viewing a defamatory communication as an isolated act that triggers a specific and predictable phenomenon, researchers view communication as a process containing a series of steps within complex interactions among people. Normally, people neither receive, nor act on, communication in a void. People process messages. Within that process they consider, sometimes consciously, sometimes unconsciously, the credibility of the source of the message, the credibility of who the message is about, and the credibility of the content of the message itself. People processing information consider past experience and past knowledge. And at times upon receiving new information, people go through a checking process before acting upon it. Reading or hearing that a politician is suspected of campaign law violations, the citizen may turn to other sources if interest is sufficient.

A communication science-generated model of the process involved in actually defaming an individual through the mass media—that is, in causing a representative minority of a community to think less of the person or shun that person—is complex. It must account for the sending and receiving of information and identify changes in psychological or physical behavior that occurs, if not directly, then at least in part from the defamatory message. In short, communication science would view the defamatory elements publication-identification-defamation as necessary, but not necessarily sufficient, conditions to alter the opinions of reasonable people. A summary of the applicable communication research discussed above can be graphically presented.

Figure 1. Summary of Some Mediating Variables in the Defamatory Communication Process

WHO	SAYS WHAT	IN WHAT CHANNEL
audience[69] ┃ credibility[71] context ┃ ┃ incredulity[70] ┃ diversity of[72] ┃ sources ┃ ┃ volume of[73] ┃ information	involvement[74] ┃ one-sided[79] ┃ two-sided ┃ selectivity[75] ┃ repetition[80] (McGuire's ┃ hierarchy) ┃ ┃ message[76] ┃ earlier discrepancy ┃ competing[81] ┃ prior[77] ┃ earlier opinion ┃ conflicting[82] ┃ credibility[78] ┃ agenda ┃ setting[83]	incredulity[84] ┃ mere ┃ exposure[88] ┃ perceived[85] ┃ channel[89] audience ┃ diversity context ┃ ┃ involvement[86] ┃ channel[90] ┃ prestige ┃ selectivity[87] ┃ accretion[91] ┃ effect

TO WHOM

WITH WHAT EFFECT?

69. See supra note 57.
70. See supra note 55.
71. See supra notes 54 and 56.
72. See supra note 65.
73. See supra notes 65 and 68.
74. See supra note 58.
75. See supra note 63.
76. See supra note 55.
77. See supra notes 55 and 62.
78. See supra note 56.
79. See supra note 62.
80. See supra notes 60 and 68.
81. See supra note 62.
82. See supra note 62.
83. See supra note 67.
84. See supra note 55.
85. See supra note 28.
86. See supra note 58.
87. See supra notes 63 and 64.
88. See supra note 59.
89. See supra note 68.
90. See supra notes 54 and 56.
91. See supra note 68.

Obviously, the legal process takes little of this summary into account. Nor could a trial situation reasonably be expected to accommodate the intricacies of such a model. Nonetheless, the divergence between communication science and tort law raises questions that need not frustrate those who acknowledge problems with the basic structure of current libel law. We need to begin by asking basic questions.

Is communication research relevant to libel law? Yes. The contrast between the simplistic approach to communication in the legal model and the process approach in the communication science model demonstrates both the potential contribution of social science to law and the immediate difficulty of ensuring an appropriate and useful interaction. It is the study of communication science that makes it clear that the legal concept of reputation is inadequate. It is vague. It requires assumptions about the ways people make decisions that are unsupported. The legal construction of the process of defamation is, in fact, challenged by the weight of scientific evidence.

In and of itself, law and legal inquiry are simply not well equipped to deal with the complexity of concepts such as reputation. This finding may explain why legal commentators concentrate on the fault element rather than on the defamation element. Because the legal concept of defamation is ill defined, its construction lacks qualitative standards that can be applied consistently. One consequence of the legal system's inattention to communication research is the acceptance as proof of damage evidence that is at best circumstantial or that relies on nothing beyond the visceral. At its worst, the legal concept of defamation is a tautology as long as we accept as proof of harm the mere presence of a defamatory statement.[92]

If libel law is intended to protect reputation or to ensure reparation for damaged reputation, it is doomed to inconsistency and failure until a satisfactory definition of reputation is developed. In contrast, the fault element is constructed upon a foundation of case law that establishes by example the normative values that set the limits of liability for journalists and others involved in communication. Standards of care within concepts such as actual malice and reasonable care can be carefully crafted and applied with reasonable consistency. This is the kind of thing law does best. Identifying changes in attitude is not.

More than a half century beyond the notion of powerful uniform effects generated by communication, researchers are well equipped to begin to work with jurists and others interested in defamation. Communication can provide important considerations for those who determine the law through legislation and through jurisprudence. It is not necessary to accept Justice Black's

---

92. Abraham Kaplan has written, "[A] tautological statement...tells us nothing whatever about the world for it remains true no matter what is the case in the world." THE CONDUCT OF INQUIRY 100 (1964).

absolutist views on the meaning of the first amendment to appreciate his contention that the government should "regulate people when they *do* something, not when they *say* something."[93]

Communication research does not suggest that an individual's reputation cannot be harmed by falsehoods generated to the public through various channels of the mass media. Rather, research in communication brings us to a point at which we may begin to operate with more precision to identify what we mean by damage to reputation, and to identify the circumstances under which a communication may be reliably held to account for damage to reputation.

Behavorial science has not yet been called on to provide and probably cannot yet provide a simple and useful formula for defamation. But that cannot be in and of itself a sufficient excuse for the law to act in this area without knowledge. And without knowledge of the relation between communication and reputation, law and adherence to law must operate contingent upon authority that may well be arbitrary. In terms of libel, law has had to concoct a theory of behavior without help from science. It has been almost ninety years since Oliver Wendell Holmes wrote, "[W]hat have we better than a blind guess to show that the...law in its present form does more good than harm?"[94] Holmes might well have been speaking of libel law in 1987.

93. Cahn, *supra* note 1.
94. Holmes, *The Path of the Law,* 10 HARVARD L. REV. 457, 470 (1897).

ROBERT L. SPELLMAN

Fact or Opinion: Where to Draw the Line

Robert L. Spellman is an attorney and
head of the News-Editorial Sequence,
School of Journalism, Southern Illinois
University at Carbondale.

When Bertell Ollman applied for a position as chairman of the political science department at the University of Maryland, he did more than set off a controversy about whether an avowed Marxist should hold such a position at a public university. He triggered a legal dispute about what is opinion and what is a false statement of fact. Such disputes hold high stakes for journalists. Opinion is immune under the first amendment from recovery of damages for libel; false statements of fact are not. As the U.S. Supreme Court said in *Gertz v. Robert Welch, Inc.*:

> Under the First Amendment there is no such thing as a false idea. However pernicious an opinion may seem, we depend for its correction not on the conscience of judges and juries but on the competition of other ideas. But there is no constitutional value in false statements of fact.[1]

1. 418 U.S. 323, 339–340 (1974). For second thoughts of Justices Rehnquist and White, see their dissent to the denial of certiorari, Miskovsky v. Oklahoma Publishing Co., 459 U.S. 923 (1982).

   The *Gertz* language was *dictum*. Nevertheless, most of the federal circuits have followed the *dictum*. McBride v. Merrell Dow and Pharmaceuticals, Inc., 717 F. 2d 1460 (D.C. Cir. 1983); Bose Corp. v. Consumers Union, Inc., 692 F.2d 189 (1st Cir. 1982), *aff'd on other grounds*, 466 U.S. 485 (1984); Cianci v. New Times Publishing Company, 639 F. 2d 54 (2d Cir. 1980); Avins v. White, 627 F.2d 637 (3d Cir.), *cert. den.*, 449 U.S. 982 (1980); Church of Scientology v. Cazares, 638 F.2d 1272 (5th Cir. 1981); Orr v. Argus–Press Co., 586 F.2d 1108 (6th Cir.), *cert. den.*, 440 U.S. 960 (1979); Action Repair, Inc. v. American Broadcasting Companies, Inc., 776 F.2d 143 (7th Cir. 1985); Lauderback v. American Broadcasting Companies, 741 F. 2d 193 (8th Cir. 1984), *cert den.*, 469 U.S. 190 (1985); Lewis v. Time, Inc., 710 F.2d 549 (9th Cir. 1983); Rinsley v. Brandt, 700 F. 2d 1304 (10th Cir. 1983); Keller v. Miami Herald Publishing Co.,

Those words in the 1974 *Gertz* decision swept away the common law rule that libel suits could be maintained for defamatory opinion.[2] Under the common law rule, those sued for libelous opinion could assert a privilege of fair comment. Generally, that privilege was available only if the opinion was about a public matter, was the honest opinion of the author, was uttered without malice, and was based on fully disclosed facts.[3] If the comment questioned the character or other aspects of an individual's personality, it had to be fair. A jury determined fairness.[4] Only the requirement for full disclosure of facts has survived under the constitutional opinion privilege enunciated in *Gertz*.[5]

Journalists conceive of opinion as editorials, writings of columnists, fine and popular arts reviews, and analysis of issues and events. The constitutional privilege encompasses more. It includes the opinions of sources—frequently found in what journalists consider objective news stories—and reporter's conclusory statements, often found in investigative journalism. Journalists have fared well when they have claimed the opinion privilege in libel suits on news stories.[6] Generally, they have prevailed in suits based on traditional journalistic

---

778F.2d 711 (11th Cir. 1985). *See also* National Foundation for Cancer Research, Inc. v. Council of Better Business Bureaus, Inc., 705 F.2d 98 (4th Cir.), *cert den.*, 464 U.S. 830 (1983) (opinion privilege adopted on authority other than *Gertz*). Among the state decisions following the *dictum* in *Gertz* are Gregory v. McDonnell Douglas Corp., 17 Cal. 3d 596, 131 Cal. Rptr. 641 (1976); Rinaldi v. Holt, Rinehart & Winston, Inc., 42 N.Y. 2d 369, 397 N.Y.S.2d 943 (1976), *cert den.*, 434 U.S. 969 (1977); Myers v. Boston Magazine, 403 N.E.2d 376 (Mass. 1980); Burns v. McGraw-Hill, Inc., 659 P. 2d 1351 (Colo. 1983); Henry v. Halliburton, 11 Media L. Rep. 2185 (Mo. 1985); Scott v. News-Herald, 25 Ohio St. 3d 243 (1986).

    Justice Lewis Powell wrote the opinion in *Gertz*. It is doubtful that he expected the far-reaching interpretation that has been given to the *dictum*. Powell dissented in Old Dominion Branch No. 496, National Association of Letter Carriers, AFL-CIO, v. Austin, 418 U.S. 264 (1974), a decision handed down the same day as *Gertz*. Courts have cited *Old Dominion* as an underpinning for a broad interpretation of the opinion privilege. See discussion, *infra*.

2. Restatement (Second) of Torts § 556 (1977).
3. Note, *Fact and Opinion After Robert Welch, Inc.: The Evolution of a Privilege,* 34 Rutgers L. Rev. 82, 85–87 102 (1981).
4. *Id* at 87.
5. Restatement, *supra* note 2.
6. Orr v. Argus-Press Co., *supra* note 1; Burns v. Denver Post, 606 P.2d 1310 (Colo. App. 1979); Belo Corporation v. Rayzor, 644 S.W.2d 71 (Tex. App. 1982); Cole v. Westinghouse Broadcasting Company, Inc., 435 N.E.2d 1021 (Mass. 1982); Goodrich v. Waterbury Republican-American, Inc., 386 Mass. 303, 448 A.2d 1317, *cert den.*, 459 U.S. 1037 (1982); Belli v. Berryhill, 11 Media L. Rep. 1221 (Cal. App. 1984); Deluca v. New York News, Inc., 438 N.Y.S.2d (N.Y. Sup. Ct. 1981).

opinion such as editorials,[7] columns,[8] cartoons[9] and reviews.[10] Nevertheless, a number of cases have arisen where courts have held traditional opinion to contain libelous statements of fact.[11]

Often when the constitutional opinion privilege has been claimed, courts have been faced with the difficulty of distinguishing between fact and opinion.[12] Much of the development of the law since *Gertz* on the difference between fact and opinion came to a head after Ollman sued Rowland Evans and Robert Novak, the syndicated columnists. Ollman asserted that a Novak and Evans column misrepresented his political philosophy, his teaching practices, and his status as a political scientist, and therefore was libelous. The 1985 decision[13] by the District of Columbia Court of Appeals produced the most comprehensive tests yet for distinguishing between fact and opinion.

This article discusses the background of *Ollman v. Evans,* sets forth and analyzes the two tests[14] contained in the decision, and then focuses on *Janklow v. Newsweek, Inc.*,[15] an effort by the Eighth Circuit Court of Appeals to reconcile the two tests in *Ollman.* The *Janklow* decision is significant because it provides strong guidance in applying the opinion privilege to stories that many journalists would consider factual news accounts. Moreover, it gives protection to journalists against undue judicial intrusion into editorial decision making.

I. BACKGROUND ON OPINION PRIVILEGE

Libel was a strict liability tort at common law. In 1964, in *New York Times Co. v. Sullivan*,[16] the Supreme Court held the common law of libel could not

7. Miskovsky v. Oklahoma Publishing Co., 654 P.2d 587 (Okla. 1982); Marchiondo v. Brown, 649 P.2d 462 (N.M. 1982); Leob v. Globe Newspaper Co., 489 F. Supp. 481 (D.Mass. 1980); National Rifle Association v. Dayton Newspapers, Inc., 555 F. Supp. 1299 (S.D. Ohio 1983); Ferguson v. Dayton Newspapers, Inc., 7 MEDIA L. REP. (Ohio App. 1982).
8. Scott v. News-Herald, *supra* note 1; From v. Tallahassee Democrat, Inc., 7 MEDIA L. REP. 1811 (Fla. App. 1981); Lins v. Evening News Association, 9 MEDIA L. REP. 2380 (Mich. App. 1983); Spiegel v. Newsday, 7 MEDIA L. REP. 1750 (N.Y. Sup. Ct. 1981).
9. Keller v. Miami Herald Publishing Co., *supra* note 1.
10. Mr. Chow v. Ste. Jour Azur S.A., 759 F.2d 219 (2d Cir. 1985); Havalunch, Inc. v. Mazza, 294 S.E.2d 70 (W.Va. 1982); Mashburn v. Collin, 355 So.2d 879 (La. 1977); Greer v. Columbus Monthly Publishing Corp., 4 Ohio App. 3d 235 (1982).
11. Costello v. Capital Cities Communications, Inc., 111 Ill. App. 109, 445 N.E.2d 13 (1982); Anton v. St. Louis Suburban Newspapers, 598 S.W. 2d 493 (Mo. 1980); McHale v. Lake Charles American Press, 390 So.2d 556 (La. App. 1980).
12. *See* Note, *The Fact-Opinion Distinction in First Amendment Libel Law: The Need for A Bright-Line Rule,* 72 GEO. L.J. 1817 (1984).
13. Ollman v. Evans, 750 F.2d 970 (D.C. Cir. 1984) *(en banc), cert. den.,* 105 S.Ct. 2662 (1985), *reversing* 713 F.2d 838 (1983). The district court's decision granting summary judgment to defendants is found at 479 F. Supp. 838 (D.D.C. 1983).
14. *Id.* at 978–984, 994–1002.
15. 788 F.2d 1300 (8th Cir. 1986) *(en banc), reversing* 759 F.2d 664 (1985).
16. 376 U.S. 254 (1964).

pass muster under the first amendment. It ruled that public officials must prove actual malice to recover damages in libel suits. Actual malice was defined as publishing a defamatory falsehood "with knowledge that it was false or with reckless disregard of whether it was false or not."[17] Later decisions extended the actual malice rule to public figure plaintiffs[18] and defined reckless disregard as "the defendant in fact entertained serious doubts as to the truth of his publication."[19]

A plurality of the Court in 1971 extended the actual malice standard to speech about matters of public significance, but that holding was abandoned three years later. In *Gertz*, the Court refused to extend the actual malice rule to private-figure plaintiffs, even if the speech involved was about matters of public concern.[20] Provided they did not opt for liability without fault, the Court permitted states to set the standard of fault that private-figure plaintiffs must prove.[21] Most states have set a negligence standard.[22] However, by establishing the constitutional opinion privilege, the Court confined defamation recovery to false statements of fact.

After *Gertz*, the American Law Institute stated the opinion privilege as:

> A defamatory communication may consist of a statement in the form of an opinion, but a statement of this nature is actionable only if it implies the allegation of undisclosed defamatory facts as the basis for the opinion.[23]

Whether a statement is opinion or fact is a question of law to be decided by judges and not juries.[24] Generally, courts have accepted the Institute's formulation. However, it is now controlling law that charges of "criminal activity, even in the form of opinion, are not constitutionally protected."[25] Further, some courts have held that general allegations of depraved conduct are actionable.[26] But it is clear that such allegations must be specific, and "broad-stroke references to unethical conduct, even using terms normally understood to impute specific criminal acts, may be understood . . . as

17. *Id.* at 280.
18. Curtis Publishing Co. v. Butts, 388 U.S. 130 (1967).
19. St. Amant v. Thompson, 390 U.S. 727 (1968), 731.
20. Rosenbloom v. Metromedia, Inc., 403 U.S. 29 (1971).
21. *Gertz, supra* note 1 at 347.
22. Embers Supper Club, Inc. v. Scripps-Howard Broadcasting Co., 9 Ohio St.3d 22 (1984) and cases cited therein.
23. RESTATEMENT, *supra* note 2, at § 566.
24. Orr v. Argus-Press Co., *supra* note 1, at 1114; Rinsley v. Brandt, *supra* note 1, at 1309.
25. Rinaldi v. Holt, Rinehart & Winston, Inc., *supra* note 1, at 397. *See also* Gregory v. McDonnell Douglas, *supra* note 1 and Cianci v. New Times Publishing Co., *supra* note 1.
26. Rinaldi, *supra* note 1.

opinion."[27] The difficulty with the Institute's statement of the privilege is that it provides no guidance on how opinion can be distinguished from statements of fact.

In two decisions, the Supreme Court has ruled that alleged libels cannot be analyzed in isolation from the contexts in which they are published. The decisions came in *Greenbelt Cooperative Publishing Company v. Bresler*[28] and *Old Dominion Branch No. 496, National Association of Letter Carriers, AFL-CIO v. Austin*.[29] Therein the Court held that the context within which statements are made is crucial in determining their meaning. The decisions provide guideposts rather than tests.

In *Bresler*, the *Greenbelt News Review* published a report that citizens had called a developer's negotiating position in a zoning dispute "blackmail."[30] In *Old Dominion*, a union newsletter described three nonmembers as "scabs" and a scab as a "traitor to his God, his country, his family and his class."[31] The developer in *Bresler* and the three nonmembers in *Old Dominion* won libel suits in state courts. The Supreme Court reversed both verdicts. The Court said the context of the stories left no doubt that the developer was not accused of the crime of extortion and the three nonmembers were not charged with treason.[32]

Given that context must be considered in determining whether a statement is one of fact or opinion, courts have been wrestling with what framework must be used to make the determination. One approach is to make it a judgment call.[33] Other courts have suggested that the test be whether the audience would understand the alleged libel as opinion or a statement of fact.[34] This was the approach in *Pring v. Penthouse International Ltd.*, a suit stemming from an article in which a thinly disguised Miss Wyoming was described as performing bizarre sex acts. The court said the ordinary reader would have found the acts so impossible to perform that the article was "pure fantasy and nothing else."[35] As one commentator has said, the difficulty with the test is that it only restates the problem.[36] No standards are provided for determining what audience perceptions would be.

The Second Circuit Court of Appeals developed a test in *Buckley v. Littell*[37] based on whether the alleged libel could be proven true or false. The suit

---

27. Lauderback v. ABC, *supra* note 1, 197. *Accord*: Lewis v. Time, Inc., *supra* note 1.
28. 398 U.S. 6 (1970).
29. 418 U.S. 264 (1974).
30. Greenbelt, *supra* note 28, at 7.
31. Old Dominion, *supra* note 29, at 268.
32. Greenbelt, *supra* note 28, at 14; Old Dominion, *supra* note 29, at 286.
33. Shiver v. Appalachian Publishing Co., 425 So.2d 1173 (Fla. App. 1983).
34. Mashburn v. Collin, *supra* note 10; Pring v. Penthouse International, Ltd., 695 F.2d 438 (10th Cir. 1982), *cert. den.*, 462 U.S. 1132 (1983).
35. *Pring, id.* at 443.
36. *Supra* note 3, at 105.
37. 539 F.2d 882 (2d Cir. 1976), *cert. den.*, 429 U.S. 1062 (1977).

arose from a book in which Franklin H. Littell, a theologian and professor, wrote that William F. Buckley, Jr., the conservative columnist, was a dangerous political extremist. Among Littell's charges was one that Buckley was a "fellow traveler" of "fascism."[38] The court held the words to be "concepts whose contents is so debatable, loose and varying, that they are insusceptible to proof of truth or falsity" and therefore must be considered opinion.[39] Another accusation stood on a different footing:

> Like Westbrook Pegler, who lied day after day in his column about Quentin Reynolds and goaded him into a lawsuit, Buckley could be taken to court by any one of several who had enough money to hire competent legal counsel and nothing else to do.[40]

The court ruled the accusation was one of fact. Since Pegler had lost a libel verdict to Reynolds, the court reasoned that the statement charged "Buckley was engaging in libelous journalism" by equating him with a proven libeler.[41] Therefore, the court said, the charge was a "factual assertion relating to Buckley's journalistic integrity" that could be proven true or false by such evidence as whether Buckley has lost any libel suits.[42]

A broader, three-prong test to determine whether a statement is one of fact or opinion was developed by the Ninth Circuit Court of Appeals in *Information Control Corporation v. Genesis One Computer Corporation*.[43] The three prongs are:

1. Consideration should be given to the meaning of "all words used, not merely a particular phrase or sentence."
2. Weight should be given to "cautionary terms used by the person publishing the statement."
3. Consideration should be given to the social/political context in which the alleged libels were made, including the "medium by which the statement is disseminated and the audience to which it is intended."[44]

Information Control was an outgrowth of a statement to an industry trade journal by Genesis about a breach of contract suit filed against it by Informa-

---

38. *Id.* at 887.
39. *Id.* at 894.
40. *Id.* at 895.
41. *Id.* at 896.
42. *Id.* at 895–896.
43. 611 F. 2d 781 (9th Cir. 1980).
44. *Id.* at 784.

tion Control. Information Control asserted the statement was defamatory and added a libel suit to the dispute between the companies. The statement read:

> In the opinion of Genesis' management, the action by ICC is intended as a device by ICC to avoid payment of its obligations to Genesis as a result of the sale of over two million dollars worth of ICC equipment, and in the opinion of general counsel to Genesis, Genesis has substantial defenses to the ICC action.[45]

The court noted the cautionary "in the opinion of" language of the statement and that the audience members were readers of a business publication who would anticipate hyperbole.[46] Further, the court found "(b)usiness litigants frequently disparage an opponent's suit as a meritless tactical device. Such charges may not be commendable, but they are highly unlikely to be understood by their audience as statements of fact rather than the predictable opinion of management."[47] The court ruled the statement was opinion which "(a)t least when made in the brief and conclusory language used here...may not be a predicate for a defamation action."[48]

The *Information Control* court was the first to develop a test that included language of apparency and the broad social and political context in which a statement was made. The court drew on California law, which has stressed that language in labor[49] and political[50] disputes is likely to be laden with hyperbole and therefore be understood as opinion. An important aspect of the decision is its inclusion of business as an arena where language can be as hyperbolic as political and labor disputes. Many of the decisions that are significant to the everyday lives of people are made in the private sector. The flow of information and ideas to citizens will suffer unless the private sector is open to vigorous journalistic examination. The major shortcoming of *Information Control* is its brevity. There is little examination of and elaboration on the prongs of the test.

One state court decision has made a major contribution to the effort toward finding a better test for determining the difference between opinion and fact. *Myers v. Boston Magazine Company, Inc.*[51] arose from a "Best and Worst" issue of *Boston* magazine in which James D. Myers, Jr. was described as the "worst" sportscaster in Boston and the "only newscaster in town who is

---

45. *Id.* at 783.
46. *Id.* at 784.
47. *Id.*
48. *Id.*
49. *Gregory, supra* note 1.
50. Scott v. McDonnell Douglas Corporation, 37 Cal. App. 3d 277, 112 Cal. Rptr. 609 (1974).
51. 403 N.E.2d 376 (Mass. 1980).

enrolled in a course for remedial speaking." The description appeared on a page that included similar "best and worst" designations, including one for "sexy athlete." While conceding the description of Myers as enrolled in a remedial speaking course was literally false, the publication context made the statement "no less figurative than a vague epithet or a soaring metaphor. And it deserves the same protection under the First Amendment."[52]

The significance of *Myer* is that the location within a publication where an alleged libel appears is important in judging whether it is opinion or a false statement of fact. If an article appears on the editorial or op-ed page, under a columnist heading, as a fine or popular arts review, or with a logo identifying it as analysis, it is a signal to the reader that it is opinion. It means that a story in a news section is more likely—but not conclusively—to be perceived by readers as fact rather than opinion.

II. TESTS IN *OLLMAN*

Bertell Ollman's suit was decided in favor of Evans and Novak by a 6-to-5 vote after an *en banc* hearing of the District of Columbia Court of Appeals against a background of a decade of development of the law on distinguishing between opinion and fact. As stated by Judge Robert Bork, it also was decided in the context of a rising tide of libel suits against the news media.

> Ollman wants a jury to award him $1,000,000 in compensatory damages and an additional $5,000,000 in punitive damages. In the field of journalism, these are enormous sums. They are quite capable of silencing political commentators forever. Unless the defamation was heinous and devastating, the amounts sought are entirely disproportionate. No one would think it appropriate for a state to levy such amounts as fines upon writers for statements of the sort made here. But, under current doctrine, lower courts have no way of saying such sums may not be sought in libel actions...or, indeed, of saying that damages may not be awarded as punishment or that such components of compensation as psychological anguish are inconsistent with the first amendment when the libel occurs in a public, political dispute.[53]
>
> The evidence is mounting that juries do not give adequate attention to limits imposed by the first amendment and are much more likely than judges to find for the plaintiff in a

52. *Id.* at 381.
53. *Ollman, supra* note 13, at 995. In July 1987, Judge Bork was nominated to fill a Supreme Court vacancy.

defamation case. It is appropriate, therefore, to take cases from juries when they are convinced that a statement ought to be protected because, among other reasons, the issue it presents is inherently unsusceptible to accurate resolution by a jury.[54]

In March of 1978, Ollman was nominated by a faculty committee to head the University of Maryland political science department. The nomination triggered opposition, including that of the acting governor of Maryland and two university trustees, because of Ollman's Marxism. The American Association of University Professors and a *Washington Post* columnist urged the university administration and trustees to make their selection based on academic qualifications and not Ollman's political ideology. Ollman fueled the controversy by announcing he would market a game whose outcome would be the nonviolent overthrow of capitalist society. In May of 1978, the Evans and Novak column was published on the *Post's* op-ed page and in other newspapers. Ultimately, the university president decided not to recommend Ollman's appointment. There is no evidence the Evans and Novak column influenced his decision.

Evans and Novak contended the issue of Ollman's appointment was not one of academic freedom, but whether he was an activist who would use the classroom to advance political goals. They cited writings—out of context, Ollman claimed—in which Ollman said most students come out of his courses with a "Marxist outlook."[55] They noted he had twice unsuccessfully sought election to the governing council of the American Political Science Association and had promised if elected to "use every means at my disposal to promote the study of Marxism and Marxist approaches to politics throughout the profession."[56] After reviewing a book that was described as Ollman's principal scholarly work, the columnists penned what was to be the crux of the libel dispute.

> Such pamphleteering is hooted at by one political scientist in a major eastern university, whose scholarship and reputation as a liberal are well known. "Ollman has no status within the profession, but is a pure and simple activist," he said. Would he say that publicly? "Not a chance of it. Our academic culture does not permit the raising of such questions."[57]

Ollman contended that the column as a whole, as well as portions of it, was false and libelous. A federal district court ruled the column was opinion

54. *Id.* at 1006.
55. *Id.* at 993.
56. *Id.* at 972.
57. *Id.* at 973.

and dismissed the suit. A three-judge panel of the appellate court reversed. The court agreed to reconsider the decision *en banc.* The 6-to-5 decision produced one opinion of the court, two concurring opinions and four dissenting opinions.[58] It is clear from the opinions that the split was generated by the quotation from an unnamed professor that Ollman had no status within the profession. Two tests for determining the difference between fact and opinion emerged. A four-part test was developed in Judge Kenneth Starr's opinion of the court.[59] In concurrence, Robert Bork used a "totality of the circumstances" test.[60] Three judges joined Bork's concurrence, one dissenting judge explicitly endorsed the four-part test while differing on the result, and it was unclear whether other dissenters adhered to either of the tests. Thus, it is not clear which test the court favors.[61]

The parts of Starr's test are:

1. Whether the alleged libel "has a precise core of meaning for which a consensus of understanding exists or, conversely whether the statement is indefinite and ambiguous."[62]
2. Whether the alleged libel is "capable of being objectively characterized as true or false.... Insofar as a statement lacks a plausible method of verification, a reasonable reader will not believe that the statement has factual content."[63]
3. Whether the linguistic context changes the literal meaning; that is, "the full context of the statement—the entire article or column, for example—inasmuch as other, unchallenged language surrounding the allegedly defamatory statment will influence the average reader's readiness to infer that a particular statement has factual content."[64]
4. Whether the broader context—writing conventions and social/political arenas—will "signal to the reader the likelihood of a statement's being either fact or opinion."[65]

An accusation of criminal activity, even if couched in the form of an opinion, was cited as an example of words that have a "precise core of meaning."[66] Situations where public offfials are called incompetent or it is

---

58. *Id.* at 971. One of the dissenting judges was Antonin Scalia, who has been elevated to the Supreme Court.
59. *Id.* at 978–984.
60. *Id.* at 998–1002.
61. Judge Patricia Wald, dissenting, said, "I basically agree with the majority's outline of the appropriate strategy for identifying absolutely privileged opinion.... *Id.* at 1034. Since a majority failed to agree on a test, her remark is puzzling.
62. *Id.* at 979.
63. *Id.*
64. *Id.*
65. *Id.*
66. *Id.* at 980.

charged that "academic ennui pervades the institution" were described as instances of "indefinite and ambiguous" statements.[67] The labeling of an associate of author Ernest Hemingway as a "toady" and "exploiter" of Hemingway's reputation was given as an illustration of statements that cannot be objectively proven true or false.[68] It is obvious that the test of whether a statement has a precise core of meaning and whether it is verifiable are closely related. Calling a newspaper columnist a fascist is both imprecise and unverifiable.

The linguistic context guidepost includes three situations. One is the *Bresler* type, where the context within a story changes a word or phrase to a figurative meaning. Usually "blackmail" is understood as a crime. When used in connection with a developer's zoning strategy, it is simply descriptive of a tough negotiating position. Crucial to the *Bresler* type is disclosure of facts upon which an opinion is based.[69] A second stems from *Myer* and considers placement of an article within a publication as the context. When an article appears on the editorial page or on a humorous "Best and Worst" page, it is a signal that it is opinion.[70] The third is language of apparency and found its origin in *Information Control*. While not determinative, particularly where there is an accusation of criminal activity, words such as "in the opinion of" or "this assessment" are useful indications of opinion.[71]

The fourth test looks to social and political context and to writing conventions. Strong and hyperbolic language are part of the tradition of political and labor disputes and "signal to readers or listeners that what is being read or heard is likely to be opinion, not fact. It is one thing to be assailed as a corrupt public official by a soapbox orator and quite another to be labelled corrupt in a research monograph detailing the causes and cures of corruption in public service."[72] Here the court recognized that seemingly defamatory language often lacks opprobrium in the political arena of *Bresler,* the labor arena of *Old Dominion*, and the business arena of *Information Control*. Further, certain forms of writings, such as satire, are indicative of opinion.[73]

The four-part test significantly enlarges the rule of the *Restatement (Second) of Torts*.[74] The *Restatement* holds that a defamatory opinion is actionable if the significant facts upon which it is based are not disclosed. Starr's opinion concludes that linguistic or social/political context can override

---

67. *Id.* at 981. The situations came from *Rinaldi, supra* note 1, and Avins v. White, *supra* note 1.
68. *Id.* The epithets came from Hotchner v. Castillo-Puche, 551 F.2d 910 (2d Cir.), *cert. den. sub. nom.* Hotchner v. Doubleday & Co., 434 U.S. 834 (1977).
69. *Id.* at 982.
70. *Id.*
71. *Id.* at 982–983.
72. *Id.* at 983.
73. *Id.* at 984.
74. RESTATEMENT, *supra* note 2, at § 566.

a failure to disclose significant facts. It is stated that disclosure is likely to be most significant "in the context of a front page news story or magazine article."[75] The opinion said that "in other contexts...factors besides disclosure are relevant in determining whether a statement implies factual allegations."[76] The test takes into account the *Restatement* "while not rejecting the other factors that may signal that a statement is to be read as opinion."[77]

Applying the test to the statement that Ollman lacked status within the political science profession, Starr said the statement viewed in context is one of opinion, noting that Evans and Novak are "well known, nationally syndicated columnists (appearing) on the Op-Ed page of a newspaper, the well recognized home of opinion and comment."[78] Further, since the columnist had used questions such as "What is the true measure of Ollman's scholarship?", language of apparency sent an opinion signal to readers.[79]

The judge conceded there was not full disclosure of the facts upon which the statement about Ollman's status as a political scientist—the crux of Ollman's case—was based, but the context suggests "the statement would be understood as opinion by the reasonable reader—even in the absence of full disclosure of facts signalling to the reader that the allegedly defamatory statement was a characterization."[80] While arguably he also could have applied a standard of broader political context because the columnists were commenting on an ongoing public controversy, the judge chose not to do so. As a result, linguistic context is the basis of Starr's opinion.

In a concurring opinion, Bork advanced a "totality of the circumstances" test.[81] Bork differed from the Starr opinion in objecting to what he claimed would be freezing judicial determination of the difference between fact and opinion into a rigid framework. A totality of the circumstances test would permit the boundaries of what constitutes opinion to be developed on a case-by-case basis.[82] Bork's test would take into account "the extent to which making (a statement) actionable would burden freedom of speech or press."[83] Unlike Starr, Bork made little reference to linguistic context. He stressed the political nature of the controversy surrounding Ollman and the professor's contributions to it.

75. Ollman, *supra* note 13, at 985.
76. *Id.*
77. *Id.*
78. *Id.* at 990.
79. *Id.* at 987.
80. *Id.* at 985.
81. *Id.* at 1002.
82. *Id.* at 994.
83. *Id.* at 997.

(I)n order to protect a vigorous marketplace in political ideas
and contentions, we ought to accept the proposition that those
who place themselves in the political arena must accept a
degree of derogation that others need not.[84]

If the statement about Ollman's status were judged standing alone and
only common usage of words were considered, Bork said, the passage would
be a libelous assertion of fact.[85] However, Bork noted that Ollman had engaged in more than teaching and scholarship. He had written an article on
spreading Marxism in the classroom and had run for office in the American
Political Science Association on a platform pledging to promote the study
of Marxism throughout the profession. He had marketed a game whose outcome was the nonviolent overthrow of capitalism.

The important point about all of this is that Ollman was not
simply a scholar who was suddenly singled out by the press
or Evans and Novak. Whatever the merits of his scholarship,
he was also a political man who publicly tried to forward his
political goals. ... That being so, he must accept the banging
and jostling of political debate, in ways that a private person
need not, in order to keep the political arena free and vital.[86]

Clearly, Bork believes that maximum latitude must be given to political
speech.

Generally, the dissenting judges relied on the *Restatement* rule and held
the statement about Ollman's professional status was one of fact because there
was no disclosure of the facts upon which the assertion was based. Without
full disclosure, such statements can "wreak considerable damage to reputation."[87] The position required a narrow reading of the statement. While there
was no background on the professor who was quoted regarding Ollman's status
and his reasons for the statement, it could reasonably be asserted that the
extensive background supplied by Evans and Novak satisfied the *Restatement*
rule. The dissenters defined the social context as an academic selection process.[88] This permitted them to ignore the developing body of law on the
significance of political context. They contended that whether Ollman had
scholarly status in the profession was capable of proof through testimony of
other political scientists or by a poll of members of the profession.[89]

84. *Id.* at 1002.
85. *Id.* at 994.
86. *Id.* at 1004.
87. *Id.* at 1023.
88. See particularly Judge Wald's dissent, *id.* at 1034–1037.
89. *Id.*

ROBERT L. SPELLMAN

III. ANALYSIS OF THE TESTS

Starr's test in *Ollman* provides a sophisticated framework for distinguishing between opinion and fact. It preserves and perhaps expands the *Restatement* rule for news stories. By stressing linguistic and social/political context, it significantly expands the protection for traditional journalistic opinion, such as editorials, opinion columns, and fine and popular arts reviews. Where context sends strong signals that statements are opinion, it is unnecessary to rely on the *Restatement* rule that all significant facts underlying an opinion be disclosed. Unlike the "totality of the circumstances" test of Bork, the four-part framework offers more certainty. Journalists know the standards by which their stories will be judged.

The major weakness is a lack of guidance in applying the test. This is illustrated by the agreement of some dissenters in *Ollman* with the test. They applied the four-part test and reached a different result. This suggests difficulties for journalists when it is asserted that conclusory statements often found in investigative stories or ambiguous quotes of sources in news stories are statements of opinion. The weakness could be overcome by adding a presumption based on the first amendment in favor of an opinion outcome. This would assist in remedying what Bork saw as the danger to journalistic enterprise of too many libel suits asking for too much money. It would be a safeguard against courts taking a narrow interpretation of ambiguous statements and reading them as libelous assertions of fact.

The strength of the Bork test is his use of the first amendment promise of vigor in the political arena as its lode star. It also is the test's major weakness. At least in *Ollman,* Bork speaks only of the political arena. There are other arenas where journalistic probing and oversight are important. Often what happens in business and labor arenas has more impact on people's lives than do political events. The test also lacks certainty. There is a vagueness to "totality of the circumstances." It fails to give the guidance that journalists need in crafting either news stories or traditional opinion.

IV. JANKLOW AND *NEWSWEEK*

In February of 1983, *Newsweek* printed an article in its national affairs section about the efforts of Governor William Janklow to have Dennis Banks, the American Indian activist, returned to South Dakota, where he had been convicted of rioting. The extradition effort was only the latest chapter in a long confrontation between Janklow and Banks. Janklow had prosecuted Banks in the mid-1970s, first as a special prosecutor and then as state attorney general. Janklow sued *Newsweek* for libel. The suit centered on the following paragraph.

> Along the way, Banks made a dangerous enemy—William Janklow. Their feud started in 1974, when Banks brought charges

against Janklow in a tribal court for assault. A 15-year-old Indian girl who baby-sat for Janklow's children had claimed he raped her in 1969. Federal officials found insufficient evidence to prosecute, but Banks persuaded the Rosebud Sioux chiefs to reopen the case under tribal law. Janklow, who was running for election as state attorney general at the time, refused to appear for the trial. But the tribal court found "probable cause" to believe the charges and barred Janklow from practicing law on the reservation. Eight months later Janklow—who had won his election despite the messy publicity—was prosecuting Banks. And his case—based upon the 1973 Custer riot—was successful. Found guilty of riot and assault without intent to kill, Banks jumped bail before sentencing.[90]

Janklow maintained the article libeled him by implying he had prosecuted Banks out of revenge. He noted that he started his prosecution of Banks while serving as special prosecutor prior to Banks accusing him of rape. He continued the prosecution after being elected attorney general. The Eighth Circuit Court of Appeals found the *Newsweek* story "would have been fairer to Janklow and more informative to the reader if the chronology of the rape charge against Janklow and the riot prosecution against Banks had been more fully explained."[91] Nevertheless, the court held the article "to be opinion, absolutely protected by the First Amendment."[92] The court based its decision on *Ollman* and said it chose "to adopt the four factors suggested in Judge Starr's scholarly opinion, and to expand them...to include elements of the concurrence by Judge Bork."[93]

In applying the four-part test, the court first found the article was not precise. It said the sentence about Janklow prosecuting Banks eight months after Banks had accused him of rape was true, and any "imputation of improper motive must be drawn from this sentence...by implication. The sentence is not nearly so precise as a direct accusation of improper motive."[94] The court rejected an assertion by Janklow that the statement was actionable because *Newsweek* could have written a clearer sentence.

> We believe the First Amendment cautions courts against intruding too closely into questions of editorial judgment, such as the choice of specific words.... Editors' grilling of reporters

---

90. *Janklow, supra* note 15, at 1303.
91. *Id.* at 1306.
92. *Id.* at 1301.
93. *Id.* at 1302.
94. *Id.* at 1304.

on word choice is a necessary aggravation. But when courts
do it, there is a chilling effect on the exercise of First Amendment rights.[95]

The court agreed it could be verified that Janklow's continued prosecution of Banks, which started before Banks accused him of rape, was not
triggered by the rape accusation. But it refused to accept Janklow's interpretation as the only possible reading of the article. Another plausible reading,
according to the court, would be that Janklow's personal handling of the
prosecution when he was attorney general could have been motivated by
revenge and "this implication would be difficult to prove."[96] The court warned
that "the singling out of impermissible motive is a subtle and slippery enterprise, particularly when the activities of public officials are involved."[97]

In looking at the literary context of the article, the court said opinion
is not confined to editorial or op-ed pages or to clearly labeled fine or popular
arts reviews. The court asserted it "would be a mistake rigidly to denominate
some publications or pages as those dealing only with opinion."[98] In particular,
as to national news magazines, the court stated:

> The magazines have a tradition of more colorful and feisty
> language, than do dailies; they are also required to condense
> to a few paragraphs those issues to which local papers devote
> days of coverage and thousands of inches of space.... Here,
> the magazine's generally freer style of personal expression and
> the article's transparently anti-Banks posture would signal the
> reader to expect a fair amount of opinion.[99]

The court, in assessing the broader social and political context of the
article, said speech about how well government and its officers carry out their
duties "lies at the very core of the First Amendment."[100] It maintained that
it is vital for the press to be able to "impugn the motives of public officials."[101]
The *Newsweek* story involved criticism of the conduct of a high public official
on "an issue of national importance, the treatment of Indian people" and few
discussions "could make a greater claim for First Amendment protection."[102]
Here the court was relying on the analysis by Bork in *Ollman* that political

95. *Id.*
96. *Id.*
97. *Id.*
98. *Id.*
99. *Id.*
100. *Id.*
101. *Id.* at 1305.
102. *Id.*

speech is a core value protected by the first amendment and the often rough language of political speech must be viewed with judicial tolerance.[103]

Finally, the court said a news story "reflects choices of what to leave out, as well as what to include."[104] Further, some omissions can be serious enough "to take what is ostensibly an opinion and convert it into a fact for legal purposes."[105] But, the court asserted, the judiciary "must be slow to intrude into the area of editorial judgment" and "under the First Amendment the decision of what to select must almost always be left to writers and editors. It is not the business of government."[106]

V. CONCLUSION

Taken together, *Ollman* and *Janklow* forge significant protection for vigorous investigative and interpretative journalism.[107] Of particular significance is the developing tolerance of the news media reporting on people and events in public arenas. The tolerance is not limited to the political arena, although that is where Bork would require the greatest tolerance. It also includes such areas as business,[108] labor,[109] and the arts.[110] In a capitalist society, much—some might say most—of that which determines how people live their lives is a result of actions taken in the private sector. The flow of information and debate on private sector actions that have public impact deserves the same level of protection as traditional political speech.

The broad interpretation of the opinion privilege in *Ollman* and *Janklow* takes on added significance from the core holding of *Gertz*. That holding refused to extend to private figure plaintiffs the requirement imposed on public figure plaintiffs in libel cases that they prove actual malice.[111] Many important public events or issues involve private figures. The holding of *Gertz* has a potential chilling effect on reporting of these events and issues. *Ollman* and *Janklow* help overcome that effect.

Events of the past two decades demonstrate that the public welfare is endangered by secrecy in both the public and private sectors. A broad judicial interpretation of the constitutional opinion privilege is useful in encouraging journalists to probe the institutions of modern society.

---

103. *Ollman, supra* note 13, at 996.
104. *Janklow, supra* note 15, at 1306.
105. *Id.*
106. *Id.*
107. *Ollman* has been followed in Scott v. News-Herald, *supra* note 1, (reconciliation of two tests), and Henry v. Halliburton, *supra* note 1 (totality of the circumstances), and relied upon in Mr. Chow v. Ste. Jour Azur, S. A., *supra* note 10 (RESTATEMENT test on disclosure of facts retained).
108. *Information Control, supra* note 43.
109. *Old Dominion, supra* note 29.
110. *Mr. Chow, supra* note 10.
111. *Gertz, supra* note 1, at 347.

DON SNEED
WHITNEY S. MANDEL
HARRY W. STONECIPHER

Constitution Provides Limited Libel Protection to Broadcast Commentators

Don Sneed is an associate professor of journalism at San Diego State University; Whitney S. Mandel is an assistant professor of broadcast journalism at San Diego State University; and Harry W. Stonecipher is Professor Emeritus of the school of journalism at Southern Illinois University.

According to recent court rulings, broadcast commentary, although often pejorative, ordinarily does not generate successful libel actions. Because the focus of libel litigation has shifted from its common-law origins to first amendment considerations, the broadcast commentator is afforded constitutional protection for most opinionated statements.[1] Protection is traceable to the common-law privilege of fair comment which protected the right of every citizen critic, including the media opinion writer, to fairly express opinions and to comment upon all matters of public interest and general concern.[2] Such comment had to be free of malice under the common law to be fair and reasonable; for example, it must not be made solely for the purpose of causing harm to the person about whom the comment was made, and it must be a statement of opinion and not a misstatement of fact.[3]

---

1. New York Times Co. v. Sullivan, 376 U.S. 254, 279–80 (1964). For further discussion of the "actual malice" rule as it applies to the protection of opinion, see text accompanying *infra* notes 13–23.
2. M. NEWELL, THE LAW OF DEFAMATION, LIBEL AND SLANDER 1 (1890). *See also,* Note, *The Fact-Opinion Distinction in First Amendment Libel Law: The Need for a Bright-Line Rule,* 72 GEORGETOWN L.J. 1817, 1819 (August 1984).
3. RESTATEMENT (SECOND) OF TORTS 566, Comment a (1977), hereinafter cited as RESTATEMENT.

The common-law privilege protecting opinionated statements was largely constitutionalized by the *Sullivan* "actual malice" rule in 1964,[4] but the real impetus for the shift away from the fair-comment privilege came ten years later when the Supreme Court in *Gertz v. Robert Welch, Inc.*[5] said in a statement not necessary to the decision:

> Under the First Amendment there is no such thing as a false idea. However pernicious an opinion may seem, we depend for its correction not on the conscience of judges and juries but on the competition of other ideas. But there is no constitutional value in false statements of fact.[6]

This declaration, while removing the qualifications and/or conditions of the common-law privilege, appears to raise the problematic fact-opinion distinction to the level of constitutionality without affording an analytical approach for the lower courts to follow.[7]

In a landmark 1984 case, *Ollman v. Evans,*[8] the U.S. Court of Appeals (District of Columbia Circuit) attempted to provide a set of guidelines by creating "four factors" to be used in assessing whether the average reader would view a publication as a statement of fact or an expression of opinion. Because states declare broadcast defamation as libel or so liberalize the slander suit requirements that there is little difference between libel and slander,[9] the *Ollman* case also has application to broadcast commentary.

This study will present a brief overview of both the common law and constitutional privileges protecting the expression of opinion. The various modes of analysis used in making the distinction between statements of fact and expression of opinion, including the D.C Circuit's *Ollman* approach, also will be examined. Recent cases from 1984 forward will be reviewed to indicate problems inherent in making the fact-opinion distinction for broadcast commentators. The goal is to clarify for the radio/television commentator the scope of the privilege and protection afforded to comments about public issues and other matters of public concern.

I. THE COMMON-LAW PRIVILEGE

Underlying the fair-comment privilege was the assumption that the public was entitled to unrestrained and widely disseminated criticism, no matter how

---

4. 376 U.S. at 279–280.
5. 418 U.S. 323 (1974).
6. *Id.* at 339–340. *See also,* RESTATEMENT 566, Comment c.
7. *See, e.g., The Fact-Opinion Distinction, supra* note 2.
8. 750 F.2d 970, 11 MEDIA L. REP. 1433 (D.C Cir. 1984).
9. W. OVERBECK & R. PULLEN, MAJOR PRINCIPLES OF MEDIA LAW (1985).

absurd.[10] There are two types of expression of opinion generally recognized by the courts. The first type is the so-called "pure type," which occurs when the broadcast commentator states the facts on which opinions are based. The pure type also occurs when both parties to the communication know the facts or assume their existence and the comment is clearly based on those assumed facts. The second type is called the "mixed type" of expression in that it is apparently based on facts that have not been stated or cannot be assumed to exist by the parties to the communication. Common-law privilege of fair comment has been held to apply only to the pure type of expression of opinion.[11]

The fair comment privilege requires that the courts make a distinction, therefore, between statements of opinion and statements of fact—whether directly stated or assumed.[12] Courts and commentators, however, have not always agreed upon how such distinctions should be made.[13]

II. THE CONSTITUTIONAL PRIVILEGE

The Supreme Court in *Sullivan* and its progeny generally have broadened protection afforded to the broadcast commentator under the "actual malice" rule, but the Court has failed to provide the lower court adequate guidance in regard to the fact-opinion distinction. Although disagreement exists, the general view is that the constitutional protection afforded expression of opinion under the *Sullivan* rule has extended the old common-law doctrine of fair comment[14] and incorporated it into the constitutional privilege,[15] or at least left unsettled the question of whether the constitutional rule wholly supplanted the common-law privilege.[16]

It was the Supreme Court's dictum in *Gertz* that has had the greatest impact upon the fact-opinion distinction. The *Restatement (Second) of Torts* notes that the Supreme Court's statement in *Gertz*, "under the First Amendment, there is no such thing as a false idea," indicates an expression of opinion cannot be the basis of a libel action involving public communication on a matter of public concern.[17]

---

10. RESTATEMENT OF TORTS 606, Comment c and d (2938).
11. RESTATEMENT 566, Comment b.
12. Veeder, *Freedom of Public Discussion*, HARV. L. REV. 413, 419 (1910). *See also, The Fact-Opinion Distinction, supra* note 2, at 1819–20.
13. *See generally,* Titus, *Statement of Fact Versus Statements of Opinion—A Spurious Dispute in Fair Comment,* 15 VAND. L. REV. 1203, 1221 (1962). *See also,* W. PROSSER, HANDBOOK OF THE LAW OF TORTS 820 (4th ed. 1971).
14. *See, e.g., The Fact-Opinion Distinction, supra* note 2, at 1821.
15. D. GILLMOR & J. BARRON, MASS COMMUNICATION LAW 166 (4th ed. 1984).
16. R. SACK, LIBEL, SLANDER, AND RELATED PROBLEMS 154 (1980).
17. RESTATEMENT 566, Comment c.

Although private communications on private matters would fall beyond-the constitutional privilege,[18] the logic of the constitutional principle would appear to apply to all expression of opinion based on either disclosed or assumed facts.[19]

After articulating the fact-opinion distinction, however, the *Gertz* Court made no effort to apply the distinction before deciding the case on other grounds.[20] The Supreme Court has been "virtually silent" concerning the fact-opinion distinction, leaving the lower courts to devise their own approaches.[21] The Court addressed the characterization of statements as fact or opinion in only two cases,[22] but both cases were decided upon other grounds. Thus, despite the fact that the *Gertz* statement is clearly *dicta,* a majority of the federal circuit courts have accepted the statement as controlling law.[23] Some thirty-two states, in addition to the District of Columbia and Guam, also have recognized a constitutional privilege protecting expression of opinion.[24]

III. THE OLLMAN FACT-OPINION FACTORS

Noting that the Supreme Court's "implicit command" in *Gertz* imposed upon both state and federal courts the duty of distinguishing fact from opinion in order "to provide opinions with the requisite, absolute First Amendment protection,"[25] the *Ollman* court, in one of the most comprehensive decisions to date involving the fact-opinion distinction, set out a four-step approach to making such a distinction.

The case is based on a syndicated column written by Rowland Evans and Robert Novak concerning the appointment of Marxist professor Bertell Ollman to head the Department of Government at the University of Maryland. The Court of Appeals for the District of Columbia Circuit, sitting *en banc,* reversed the decision of a three-judge panel, holding that the column was entitled to absolute first amendment protection as expression of opinion, based upon a

---

18. Dun & Bradstreet, Inc. v. Greenmoss Builders, Inc., 53 U.S.L.W. 4866 (June 16, 1985).
19. RESTATEMENT 566, Comment c.
20. *The Fact-Opinion Distinction, supra* note 2, at 1822.
21. *Id.* at 1824, *citing* Ollman v. Evans, 713 F. 2d at 844 (Robinson, C.J. concurring).
22. Greenbelt Cooperative Publishing Ass'n. v. Bresler, 398 U.S. 6 (1970); Old Dominion Branch No. 496, National Ass'n. of Letter Carriers v. Austin, 418 U.S. 264 (1974).
23. Eight of the twelve circuits had accepted the *Gertz* statement as controlling in reported cases through December 6, 1984. *See* Ollman v. Evans, 750 F.2d at 974 n.6
24. The fourth annual fifty-state survey of libel and privacy law, which covered all developments through 1984, reported new cases in nine jurisdictions in 1984 alone. The survey also indicated that twelve other states continue to utilize the common-law doctrine under the rubric of either "fair comment" or "public interest involving public figures." That number had dropped from fifteen reported in the 1983 survey. See, *Issue Status Summary,* LDRC 50-STATE SURVEY 767-770 (Libel Defense Resource Center, New York, 1984).
25. 750 F.2d 975.

four-part test for determining whether a statement is one of fact or opinion[26] and finally the U.S. Supreme Court in May 1985 denied a petititon for *writ of certiorari* to review the *en banc* decision.[27]

Two aspects of the 1984 case which make it especially pertinent are the nature of the Evans and Novak column which resulted in the libel action and the four factors set out by the court and how they were applied in determining the fact-opinion distinction.

The column at issue was published under the headline "The Marxist Professor's Intentions," and began with this statement:

> What is in danger of becoming a frivolous debate over the appointment of a Marxist to head the University of Maryland's department of politics and government has so far ignored this unspoken concern within the academic community: the avowed desire of many political activists to use higher education for indoctrination.[28]

The columnists also quoted an unnamed source as saying: "Ollman has no status within the profession, but is a pure and simple activist."[29]

Ollman alleged that the column was "totally false and defamatory" and that it denied his reputation as a scholar and portrayed him as a "political activist" who sought to use his classroom for ulterior purposes. Acknowledging that because of the "richness and diversity of language" it was difficult, even impossible, to lay down a "bright-line" rule to distinguish between assertions of fact and expressions of opinion,[30] the court's majority set out a four-part test to be used in assessing whether the average reader would view such statements as fact or opinion.

First, the *Ollman* court said, the "common usage or meaning of the specific language of the challenged statement" should be analyzed to determine whether "the statement has a precise core of meaning for which a consensus of understanding exists, or conversely, whether the statement is indefinite and ambiguous."[31]

Second, courts "should consider the degree to which the statements are verifiable—is the statement objectively capable of proof or disproof?"[32] The court noted that the reason for such an inquiry is simple: "a reader cannot rationally view an unverifiable statement as conveying actual facts."[33]

26. *Id.* at 970.
27. 105 S. Ct. 2662.
28. 750 F.2d at 972.
29. *Id.* at 972.
30. *Id.* at 977–978.
31. *Id.* at 979.
32. *Id.*
33. *Id.* at 981.

Third, courts must examine the context in which the statement is made. The statement must be taken as part of a whole, including tone and the use of cautionary language. The court explained that the full context of the statement—the entire column or broadcast—must be considered "inasmuch as other, unchallenged language surrounding the allegedly defamatory statement will influence the average reader's readiness to infer that the particular statement has factual content."[34]

A fourth factor, the court said is consideration of "the broader context in which the statement appears." Different types of writing or commentary have "widely varying social conventions which signal to the reader the likelihood of a statement's being either fact or opinion."[35]

This four-factor analysis, the *Ollman* court noted, should not be followed "in rigid lock-step fashion." A logical starting point in applying the fact-opinion analysis might be the broad social context or setting within the statement appears (the fourth step) and the language surrounding the challenged statements (the third factor).[36]

The court's majority decided that a "reasonable reader" who read the Evans and Novak column on the editorial page or op-ed page should be fully aware that the statements found there are not "hard" news and would be predisposed to regard what is found there to be opinion.[37] In analyzing specific allegations in the column, the court noted that the statement concerning Ollman's "status within the profession" was the "most troublesome" of all those alleged by Ollman to be defamatory. Still, the court found that a "confluence of factors" led to the conclusion that even those statements were protected opinion.[38]

Although all the statements in the column were found to be protected opinion, the court cautioned: "Of course, we do not hold that any statement on an editorial or Op-Ed page is constitutionally privileged opinion."[39]

IV. BROADCAST NEWS AND COMMENTARY

A considerable degree of protection has been granted by recent court rulings to opinions emanating from television and radio broadcasts, with ten of twelve decisions favorable to the news media.

In *Lauderback v. ABC*,[40] the court ruled as protected expression of opinion statements from a "20/20" television program which suggested that an

---

34. *Id.* at 979.
35. *Id.*
36. *Id.* at 980.
37. *Id.* at 987–989.
38. *Id.* at 989–990.
39. *Id.* at 987.
40. Lauderback v. ABC, 10 Media L. Rep. 2241 (8th Cir. 1984).

investigation of fraudulent sales of insurance policies amounted to unethical behavior. During the broadcast, such epithets as "rotten," "unethical," and "sometimes illegal" were used to describe the practices of agents who allegedly sold worthless policies. Agents other than the plaintiff, who are shown as defendants in criminal court proceedings, are referred to as "crooks" and "liars."[41]

The *Lauderback* court, in viewing the broadcast as a whole and relying on *Gertz dicta,* said that "while allegations of specific criminal conduct generally cannot be protected as opinion, broad brush-stroked references to unethical conduct, even using terms normally understood to impute specific criminal acts, may be understood by the reasonable viewer as opinion."[42] Furthermore, the court said there was full disclosure of the facts supporting accusations made during the broadcast.

Another ruling extending first amendment protection for opinion was issued in *Spelson v. CBS*[43] a case involving a broadcast which alleged that a chiropractor practiced "cancer quackery." The broadcast referred to "untrained, unqualified and unscrupulous health practitioners" who exploit desperate patients by using "phony medical machines . . . to defraud patients."[44] An editorial comment referred to "con-artist," "cancer quacks," and said the broadcast has shown "unscrupulous charlatans victimizing cancer patients" with "phony cures."[45] Citing *Gertz dicta,* the court ruled the broadcasts were statements of opinion protected by the first amendment.[46]

Constitutionally protected opinion also was granted to statements at issue in *Redco Corp. v. CBS, Inc.,*[47] a case involving comments aired on a "60 Minutes" television segment which implied, based upon disclosed truthful facts, that multipiece tire rims are dangerous, and which reported opinions, also based on disclosed true facts, that tire rim manufacturers were concerned more with profits than with safety. In the broadcast of a segment entitled "Killer Wheels," the court reviewed statements in the total context of the broadcast and cited as controlling *Gertz dicta* and *Restatement (Second) of Torts.*

In six other recent cases, radio and television stations have won rulings when statements were contested as libelous. In *Hallmark Builders v. Gaylord Broadcasting,*[48] comments on a television broadcast about problems in the

---

41. *Id.* at 2241.
42. *Id.* at 2245.
43. Spelson v. CBS, Inc., 10 MEDIA L. REP. 1608 (D.C. Ill. 1984); 11 MEDIA L. REP. 1900 (7th Cir. 1985), *aff'd.*
44. *Id.* at 1610.
45. *Id.*
46. *Id.* at 1613.
47. Redco Corp. v. CBS, Inc., 10 MEDIA L. REP. 1536 (D.C. Pa. 1984); 11 MEDIA L. REP. 1861 (3rd Cir. 1985), *aff'd; cert. denied,* 54 U.S.L.W. 3208 (1985).
48. Hallmark Builders v. Gaylord Broadcasting, 10 MEDIA L. REP. 1981 (11th Cir. 1984).

homebuilding industry that "home owners cry foul" and that "these were expensive homes with expensive problems" were ruled protected expression of opinion. In *Leader v. WSM, Inc.*,[49] a public official's statements were ruled as protected opinion; these statements asserted during a television broadcast that "most criminals are repentant after they're caught," that "later on they seem to return to the mold a lot of times," and that plaintiff's conduct is such that I don't think he is going to change." In *Motsinger v. Kelly*,[50] remarks by the host of a radio call-in show that the caller was the "ugliest man in Danville" were ruled as protected expressions of opinion incapable of being proved false. In *New Deal Restaurant v. WPIX*,[51] comments were ruled as protected expression of opinion; they were made by a television announcer who said, following a report on a restaurant which served hippopotamus, lion, and other exotic game, that "I take serious objection to serving up hippopotamuses and lions; I mean there must be enough food in the world, we don't have to eat them." In *Underwood v. CBS, Inc.*[52] statements broadcast on a "60 Minutes" television segment recounting an anecdote concerning an alleged hoax accomplished by a reputed gangster were ruled as protected expression of opinion. In *Pesta v. CBS*,[53] regarding another "60 Minutes" segment entitled "Tragic Assumptions," the words, "critical mistake" used to describe a doctor's failed attempt to save a teenage patient, were ruled as protected expression of opinion. The court also ruled in *Kurz v. Evening News Ass'n.*[54] that failure to properly investigate does not constitute actual malice. Finally, in *Action Repair, Inc. v. American Broadcasting Co.*[55] constitutional protection was afforded to a television reporter's statements that viewers should heed the caution "Buyer Beware" when considering dealing with the appliance repair company identified during the broadcast, and that people were choosing the wrong repair company when they chose this company.

On the other hand, two recent rulings have found that statements claimed as opinionated statements were factual and that a claim for libel was actionable. In one of those cases, *Hellman v. McCarthy*,[56] writer Mary McCarthy was interviewed on the "Dick Cavett Show" and was asked by Cavett: "Who are some authors who are overrated, and we could do without...?" McCarthy replied, "Lillian Hellman, who I think is tremendously overrated, a bad writer, and dishonest writer." Cavett also asked: "What is dishonest about her?" McCarthy answered: "Everything. But I said once in some interview that every

49. Leader v. WSM, Inc., 10 MEDIA L. REP. 1343 (Tenn. Cir. Ct. 1984).
50. Motsinger v. Kelly, 11 MEDIA L. REP. 2459 (Va. Cir. Ct. 1985).
51. New Deal Restaurant v. WPIX, 11 MEDIA L. REP. 1965 (N.Y. Sup. Ct. 1984).
52. Underwood v. CBS, Inc. 10 MEDIA L. REP. 1246 (Cal. App. 1984).
53. Pesta v. CBS, 13 MEDIA L. REP. 1828 (1986).
54. Kurz v. Evening News Ass'n., 144 Mich. App. at 212.
55. Action Repair, Inc. v. American Broadcasting Co., 776 F.2d 143 (7th Cir. 1985).
56. Hellman v. McCarthy, 10 MEDIA L. REP. 1789 (N.Y.S. Ct. 1984).

word she writes is a lie, including 'and' and 'the.' " In deciding the case against the news media, the court said "one must first determine whether the language complained of is susceptible of the particular defamatory meaning ascribed to it...." In this case, the court ruled that "the libel here labeling the plaintiff as a 'dishonest writer,' 'every word she writes is a lie' crosses the boundary between opinion and fact."

In a second case, *Westmoreland v. CBS*,[57] the court ruled that statements in a television broadcast which asserted that General William Westmoreland, serving as Army commander in Vietnam, prevailed upon his officers to draw dishonest conclusions and give false reports evaluating intelligence data, do not constitute protected statements of opinion. Despite the court's ruling, Westmoreland abandoned the action before the case went to the jury.

It is important to note that none of the broadcast cases utilized the four-factor test to distinguish between fact and opinion enunciated in *Ollman*. The chief reason that the test has not been used in broadcast commentary cases is that few have been decided since the *Ollman* case outlined the four factors in 1984. However, broadcast commentators should expect the *Ollman* four-factor test to play a key role in future cases involving broadcast commentary where allegedly libelous statements are disputed, especially since *Ollman* has been used in several recent cases involving disputed statements in magazines and newspapers.[58]

V. CONCLUSIONS AND RECOMMENDATIONS

An examination of recent broadcast cases indicates that in the absence of guidelines set out by *Ollman's* four-factor test, lower courts have devised a variety of ways to distinguish between fact and opinion. In the majority of recent cases, the courts have relied heavily on *dicta* in *Gertz* which states that under the first amendment, there is no such thing as a false idea, thus extending protected expression of opinion to statements involving private individuals so long as matters of public interest are involved and the assertions are deemed expressions of opinion and not misstatements of fact.

In other cases, additional levels of analysis have been introduced to distinguish fact from opinion. Most often, this additional level introduces language from the *Restatement (Second) of Torts*, with the courts examining statements to determine whether they constitute pure opinion which is protected by the first amendment, or mixed opinion, which is not. In still other cases, and evaluation of the meaning of the language used and a study of the context in which the statements appear is undertaken.

---

57. Westmoreland v. CBS, Inc., 10 MEDIA L. REP. 2417 (D.C. N.Y. 1984).
58. *See,* for example, Scott v. News-Herald, 13 MEDIA L. REP. 1241 (Ohio Sup. Ct. 1986); Janklow v. Newsweek, 12 MEDIA L. REP. 1961 (8th Cir. 1986); El Paso Times v. Kerr, 13 MEDIA L. REP. 1040 (Texas Ct. App. 1986).

In the absence of a controlling Supreme Court decision, *Ollman's* four-factor test appears to contain a summary of the most-often used guidelines now employed by lower courts. Although *Ollman* consolidates factors to be used in making the fact-opinion distinction, the courts frequently draw upon some, but not all, of the factors. What results is often a less-than-comprehensive test and a less-than-searching analysis of the fact-opinion distinction. With the fact-opinion distinction left to the vagaries of lower courts, broadcast commentators comment at some degree of risk, although recent decisions have been decided heavily in favor of the news media, suggesting that broadcast commentary is a relatively safe haven from libel verdicts. Still, there is reason for caution, since one decision, for example, suggests that precautionary terms are helpful aids to the broadcast commentator, while another decision notes that a precautionary term such as "I think" is inadequate to afford the broadcast commentator constitutionally protected expression of opinion.

Furthermore, one law review article suggests that the approaches courts have taken in making the fact-opinion distinction vary greatly, ranging from judgment calls to careful examination of the "totality of the circumstances" surrounding the publication. Noting that no "bright-line rule" has been formulated, the writer suggests that "it is possible that no such rule will ever exist, if for no other reason than simply because of the diverse usage of words and language."[59]

A second law review article critical of the *Ollman* four-factor test asserts that "factors like those used by the court in *Ollman* usurp much of traditional common law defamation by elevating those principles to constitutional standards."[60] Thus, with the smorgasboard of tests available for courts to use in making the fact-opinion distinction, it is possible that broadcast commentators and newscasters, faced with such uncertainty, may engage in self-censorship where there seems to be "close calls" in making the fact-opinion distinction.

What is known and helpful to broadcast commentators from recent cases is that the greatest degree of constitutional protection has gone to those whose program formats deal largely with opinion and investigative reporting. Recent decisions suggest, however, that in the absence of guidance from the Supreme Court, there is no guarantee an analysis that finds an allegedly libelous statement non-actionable in one jurisdiction would warrant the same disposition in another jurisdiction. Regardless, broadcast commentators and newscasters may take some small comfort in knowing that in recent cases involving libel claims in which the fact-opinion distinction was at issue, news media defendants have won favorable decisions approximately 82 percent of the time.

---

59. Moll, *Defamation—Actionable Statement of Fact Versus Privileged Opinion: Ollman v. Evans*, 34 KAN L. REV. 367, 377 (1985).
60. Becker, *Structuring Defamation Law to Eliminate the Fact-Opinion Determination: A Critique of Ollman v. Evans*, 71 IOWA L. REV. 913 (1986).

Still, broadcast commentators and newscasters would be well advised to apply the *Ollman* four-factor test before they make statements they believe to be constitutionally protected expressions of opinion.

The National Association of Broadcasters' (NAB) guidelines[61] to distinguish fact from opinion go a long way toward protecting broadcast commentary from libel verdicts. NAB recommends carefully examining the meaning of expressions of opinion used and the context of the language surrounding those expressions of opinion. Commentaries and editorials should be promoted as special segments of the news, put in a regular time slot, and clearly identified as opinion on the television screen and in the script.

Statements should be verified before commentaries of stories are aired, since case law proves that one cannot be successfully sued for opinion broadcasting unless the facts of a story are wrong. In addition, facts upon which opinion are based should come before the expressed opinion in the script. Using cautionary language such as "I think" and "This reporter's opinion" helps identify statements as opinion.

Although broadcasters would be wise to restrain from using derogatory words such as "jerk" and "degenerate," such words are usually considered expressions of opinion, and the courts have said there is no such thing as false opinion. Legal problems arise, however, when a word is not clearly identifiable as fact or opinion, such as "incompetent" or "alcoholic." If facts are first given describing, for example, the subject's drinking habits and alcoholism treatment, using the term "alcoholic" to express opinion would be based on fact. Words that imply criminal activity, such as "fraud," "cheat," and "crook" should be avoided. When covering legal stories, the accurate legal terminology should be used; words such as arraignment," "accused," and "convicted" have different legal meanings and could result in law suits if applied incorrectly.

When quoting others, first verify the accuracy of the statements and then use source attribution, such as "she said," "in his words," or "we quote." If the words are part of a public record, attribute them to the source.

Talent should be especially guarded with "happy talk," spontaneous comments, and humor, all of which may relay false facts. If reporters and anchors "thrust themselves" into a sensitive story with such comments as "keep after them," "well done," or "nice job," they are more likely to be sued with the station. The talent should refrain from giving personal opinions, such as "he should have to do time for that" or "the police shouldn't let her get away with that." If such comments are made, the statements may be neutralized by other talent saying "that's your opinion" or "he has never been found guilty of that in a court of law" to limit potential for damage. On sensitive and "live" stories, it is best to know in advance what the questions and answers will

61. National Association of Broadcasters, *Staying Out of the Libel Stew* (1986).

be. Although courts have never addressed the issues of "tone of voice," editorial meaning can be conveyed through delivery, so care must be taken to sound objective.

Most libel suits result from carelessness, such as incorrect synchronization of video and audio which may depict an individual in false circumstances. Careful examination of audio and video should be made so that impressions are accurate. Because careless use of generic or file footage also can create a false impression, this tape should always be used with caution and identified as such when it is used.

In a court of law, it helps to show that extra precautions were taken to be fair. Such preventive measures could go a long way toward making the broadcast commentary safe from libel verdicts.

Readings from COMMUNICATIONS AND THE LAW, 1

The articles collected in *Defamation: Libel and Slander* were published in the following issues of COMMUNICATIONS AND THE LAW.

"Herbert v. Lando: No Cause for Alarm," by Howard E. Goldfluss, originally appeared in vol. 1, no. 3, pp. 61-68, © 1979.

"Herbert v. Lando: Threat to the Press, Or Boomerang for Public Officials?" by Andre E. Briod, originally appeared in vol. 2, no. 2, pp. 59-92, © 1980.

"Fashioning a New Libel Defense: The Advent of Neutral Reportage," by Donna Lee Dickerson, originally appeared in vol. 3, no. 3, pp. 77-86, © 1981.

"The Future of Strict Liability in Libel," by F. Dennis Hale, originally appeared in vol. 5, no 2, pp. 23-37, © 1983.

"Protecting Confidential Sources in Libel Litigation," by Anthony Green, originally appeared in vol. 6, no. 3, pp. 39-51, © 1984.

"Retraction's Role Under the Actual Malice Rule," by Donna Lee Dickerson, originally appeared in vol. 6, no. 4, pp. 39-51, © 1984.

"Libel and the Long Reach of Out-of-State Courts," by Donna Lee Dickerson, originally appeared in vol. 7, no. 4, pp. 27-43, © 1985.

"Problems in Libel Litigation," by Erik L. Collins, Jay B. Wright and Charles W. Peterson, originally appeared in vol. 7, no. 5, pp. 41-57, © 1985.

"Avoiding the Chilling Effect: News Media Tort and First Amendment Insurance," by Robert L. Spellman, originally appeared in vol. 7, no. 6, pp. 13-27, © 1985.

"'Innocent Construction' Rule Survives Challenge," by Kyu Ho Youm and Harry W. Stonecipher, originally appeared in vol. 7, no. 6, pp. 43-60, © 1985.

"'Single Instance' Rule as a Libel Defense," by Kyu Ho Youm, originally appeared in vol. 9, no. 4, pp. 49-65, © 1987.

"Libel as Communication Phenomena," by Jeremy Cohen and Albert C. Gunther, originally appeared in vol. 9, no. 5, pp. 9-30, © 1987.

"Fact or Opinion: Where to Draw the Line," by Robert L. Spellman, originally appeared in vol. 9, no. 6, pp. 45-61, © 1987.

"Constitution Provides Limited Libel Protection to Broadcast Commentators," by Don Sneed, Whitney S. Mandel, and Harry W. Stonecipher, originally appeared in vol. 10, no. 2, pp. 19 30, © 1988.

Readings from COMMUNICATIONS AND THE LAW, 2

The articles collected in *Privacy and Publicity* were published in the following issues of COMMUNICATIONS AND THE LAW.

"The Public and the Fair Credit Reporting Act," by Blair C. Fensterstock, originally appeared in vol. 2, no. 1, pp. 31-43, © 1980.

"Resolving the Press-Privacy Conflict: Approaches to the Newsworthiness Defense," by Theodore L. Glasser, originally appeared in vol. 4, no. 2, pp. 23-42, © 1982.

"Motor Vehicle Records: Balancing Individual Privacy and the Public's Legitimate Need to Know," by Leslie G. Foschio, originally appeared in vol. 6, no. 1, pp. 15-20, © 1984.

"The Television Docudrama and the Right of Publicity," by Deborah Manson, originally appeared in vol. 7, no. 1, pp. 41-61, © 1985.

"The Big Dan's Rape Trial: An Embarrassment for First Amendment Advocates and the Courts," by Susanna R. Barber, originally appeared in vol. 7, no. 2, pp. 3-21, © 1985.

"The Freedom of Information Act Privacy Exemption: Who Does It Really Protect?," by Kimiera Maxwell and Roger Reinsch, originally appeared in vol. 7, no. 2, pp. 45-59, © 1985.

"Privacy Invasion Tort: Straddling the Fence," by Deckle McLean, originally appeared in vol. 7, no. 3, pp. 5-30, © 1985.

"Unauthorized Use of Deceased's Persona: Current Theories and the Need for Uniform Legislative Treatment," by Valerie B. Donovan, originally appeared in vol. 7, no. 3, pp. 31-63, © 1985.

"Press and Privacy Rights Could Be Compatible," by Deckle McLean, originally appeared in vol. 8, no. 2, pp. 13-25, © 1986.

"Photojournalism and the Infliction of Emotional Distress," by Michael D. Sherer, originally appeared in vol. 8, no. 2, pp. 27-37, © 1986.

"Recognizing the Reporter's Right to Trespass," by Deckle McLean, originally appeared in vol. 9, no. 5, pp. 31-42, © 1987.

"The 1978 Right to Financial Privacy Act and U.S. Banking Law," by Roy L. Moore, originally appeared in vol. 9, no. 6, pp. 23-44, © 1987.

"Unconscionability in Public Disclosure Privacy Cases," by Deckle McLean , originally appeared in vol. 10, no. 2, pp. 31-44, © 1988.

"Docudramas and False-Light Invasion of Privacy," by Tim A. Pilgrim originally appeared in vol. 10. no. 3, pp. 3-37, © 1988.

Readings from COMMUNICATIONS AND THE LAW, 3

The articles collected in *Censorship, Secrecy, Access, and Obscenity* were published in the following issues of COMMUNICATIONS AND THE LAW.

"Open Justice: The Threat of *Gannett*," by James C. Goodale, originally appeared in vol. 1, no. 1, pp. 3-13, © 1979.

"Introduction: The *Snepp* Case—Government Censorship Through The 'Back Door,'" by Henry R. Kaufman, originally appeared in vol. 1, no. 2, pp. 1-27, © 1979.

"First Ammendment Implications For Secondary Information Services," by Paul G. Zurkowski, originally appeared in vol. 1, no. 2, pp. 49-64, © 1979.

"Obscene/Indecent Programming: The FCC and WBAI," by Stanley D. Tickton, originally appeared in vol. 1, no. 3, pp. 15-27, © 1979.

"Heightened Judicial Scrutiny: A Test for the First Ammendment Rights of Children," by Denise M. Trauth and John L. Huffman, originally appeared in vol. 2, no. 2, pp. 39-58, © 1980.

"Obscenity and the Supreme Court: A Communication Approach to a Persistent Judicial Problem," by John Kamp, originally appeared in vol. 2, no. 3, pp. 1-42, © 1980.

"Shield Laws and the Separation of Powers Doctrine," by Louis A. Day, originally appeared in vol. 2, no. 4, pp. 1-15, © 1980.

"Attitudes of Media Attorneys Concerning Closed Criminal Proceedings," by F. Dennis Hale, originally appeared in vol. 3, no. 1, pp. 3-10. © 1981.

"TV in the Courtroom: Right of Access?," by Mary Kay Platte, originally appeared in vol. 3, no, 1, pp. 11-29, © 1981.

"The Trials and Tribulations of Courtroom Secrecy and Judicial Craftsmanship: Reflections on Gannett and Richmond Newspapers," by David M. O'Brien, originally appeared in vol. 3, no. 2, pp. 3-33, © 1981.

"The Right to Know: Whose Right and Whose Duty?," by Eugenia Zerbinos, originally appeared in vol. 4, no. 1, pp. 33-49, © 1982.

"Government Lawyers and the Press," by Anthony Green, originally appeared in vol. 5, no. 3, pp. 3-23, © 1983.

"'Consistent with Security' . . . A History of American Military Press Censorship," by Jack A. Gottschalk, originally appeared in vol. 5, no. 3, pp. 35-53, © 1983.

"Abating Obscenity As a Nuisance: An Easy Procedural Road for Prior Restraints," by Robert L. Hughes, originally appeared in vol. 5, no. 4, pp. 39-50, © 1983.

Readings from COMMUNICATIONS AND THE LAW, 4

The articles collected in *Advertising and Commercial Speech* were published in the following issues of COMMUNICATIONS AND THE LAW.

"The First Amendment Protection of Advertising in the Mass Media," by Bradford W. Scharlott, originally appeared in vol. 2, no. 3, pp. 43-58, © 1980.

"Comparative Advertising Law and a Recent Case Thereon," by Patricia Hatry and Jeffrey C. Katz, originally appeared in vol. 3, no. 2, pp. 35-47. © 1981.

"Implications of First Amendment Doctrine on Prohibition of Truthful Price Advertising Concerning Alcoholic Beverages," by Gary B. Wilcox, originally appeared in vol. 3, no. 2, pp. 49-66, © 1981.

"False and Comparative Advertising Under Section 43(a) of the Lanham Trademark Act," by A. Andrew Gallo, originally appeared in vol.. 8, no. 1, pp. 3-29, © 1986.

"Alcoholic Beverage Advertising and the Electronic Media," by Gary B. Wilcox, Dorothy Shea and Roxanne Hovland, originally appeared in vol. 8, no. 1, pp. 31-41, © 1986.

"The Future of Alcoholic Beverage Advertising," by Roxanne Hovland and Gary B. Wilcox, originally appeared in vol. 9, no. 2, pp. 5-14, © 1987.

"The Commercial Speech Doctrine: *Posadas* Revisionism," by Denise M. Trauth and John L. Huffman, originally appeared in vol. 10, no. 1, pp. 43-56, © 1988.

"The First Amendment Defense to Negligent Misstatement," by Robert L. Spellman, originally appeared in vol. 10, no. 3, pp. 59-72, © 1988.

"The Tobacco Advertising Debate: A First Amendment Perspective," by David D. Vestal, originally appeared in vol. 11, no. 1, pp. 53-67, © 1989.